FROM **BIBLICAL BOOK**
TO **MUSICAL MEGAHIT**

From Biblical Book to Musical Megahit

William B. Bradbury's *Esther, the Beautiful Queen*

Juanita Karpf

University Press of Mississippi / Jackson

The University Press of Mississippi is the scholarly publishing agency of
the Mississippi Institutions of Higher Learning: Alcorn State University,
Delta State University, Jackson State University, Mississippi State University,
Mississippi University for Women, Mississippi Valley State University,
University of Mississippi, and University of Southern Mississippi.

www.upress.state.ms.us

The University Press of Mississippi is a member
of the Association of University Presses.

Copyright © 2023 by University Press of Mississippi
All rights reserved

∞

Library of Congress Cataloging-in-Publication Data

Names: Karpf, Juanita, 1951– author.
Title: From biblical book to musical megahit : William B. Bradbury's
Esther, the beautiful queen / Juanita Karpf.
Description: Jackson : University Press of Mississippi, 2023. | Includes
bibliographical references and index.
Identifiers: LCCN 2023035018 (print) | LCCN 2023035019 (ebook) | ISBN
9781496845740 (hardback) | ISBN 9781496845757 (trade paperback) | ISBN
9781496848918 (epub) | ISBN 9781496848925 (epub) | ISBN 9781496848932
(pdf) | ISBN 9781496848949 (pdf)
Subjects: LCSH: Bradbury, William B. (William Batchelder), 1816–1868.
Esther, the beautiful queen. | Bradbury, William B. (William
Batchelder), 1816–1868—Performances. | Esther, Queen of Persia—Songs
and music—History and criticism.
Classification: LCC ML410.B26619 K37 2023 (print) | LCC ML410.B26619
(ebook) | DDC 782.1/17—dc23/eng/20230804
LC record available at https://lccn.loc.gov/2023035018
LC ebook record available at https://lccn.loc.gov/2023035019

British Library Cataloging-in-Publication Data available

In memory of Esther, my very own queen.
Run free, my beauty.

We closed our two conventions last night with a concert at which we gave Mr. Bradbury's oratorio of Esther, to a crowded house. This cantata takes with the music-loving people . . . and in it we think Mr. B made a decided hit.
—*New York Musical Review and Gazette*, 1858

I did n' think they would be so blasphemious as to write an opery about Scriptur'.
But they tell me it ain't an opery. It's a cantaty.
Tain't a hair's-breadth difference 'tween them. Both of 'em is caperin' roun' in false clothes.

As fur caperin' . . . I heard the perfessor say they jus' held up their hands now an' then, an' walked roun' singin' the very Bible words. 'Tisn't as if they throw'd themselves roun' in a furrin tongue sayin' nobody knows what at ye, like enough things you'd blush to hear, an' you innercent an' helpless-like sittin' there . . . . Well, it won't be so bad for them that's pertendin' to be Esther and her uncle. Maybe it might be a means of grace to some. But I wouldn't be in that old Haman's or his wife's shoes.
—Mary Gay Humphreys, *Jack Racer*, 1901

Years have passed since a good man died—a man whose name was Bradbury. He was a musical genius and composed many music books, of which over half a million were sold. When I was a boy his song books were in universal use. His cantata of Esther still lives, and will live always I hope, for it is a wonderful work, and has given exquisite pleasure to millions.
—Bill Arp, 1890

CONTENTS

xi	Acknowledgments
3	Introduction
7	**CHAPTER ONE:** Prelude: Bradbury, Musician and Entrepreneur
33	**CHAPTER TWO:** *Esther*: The Early Years
55	**CHAPTER THREE:** *Esther*, Revised
73	**CHAPTER FOUR:** Genre Intrigue
99	**CHAPTER FIVE:** Religious Controversy
127	**CHAPTER SIX:** Interlude: *Esther* Images
169	**CHAPTER SEVEN:** *Esther* and Minorities
199	**CHAPTER EIGHT:** An International Megahit
227	Epilogue
231	Appendix
233	Notes
263	Bibliography
277	Index

ACKNOWLEDGMENTS

Expressing appreciation to all those who have assisted me requires that I dig deep as work on this book has occupied me, on and off, for what seems like an eternity. Without the patience and guidance of innumerable people, this book project would not have been completed.

Years ago, I gave a conference paper in which I quoted a newspaper review of a piece referred to only as "the cantata of Esther." Fortuitously, Wayne Shirley (Library of Congress, now Emeritus), was in the audience. Wayne graciously informed me that the "cantata of Esther" of which I spoke was none other than William B. Bradbury's choral work, *Esther, the Beautiful Queen*. In the discussion that ensued, his contagious enthusiasm for *Esther* affected me profoundly. I have Wayne to thank for introducing me to a fascinating piece of Americana and for encouraging me to pursue the research that eventually led to this book.

Numerous other attendees at conferences and symposia where I gave papers about *Esther* have graciously shared with me innumerable supportive comments and sage advice about my work. Although, unfortunately, I cannot recall the names of all these individuals, a few come to mind: William Banfield, Michelle Boyd, Michael Broyles, Charles Carson, Christina Gier, John Graziano, Tammy Kernodle, Kendra Leonard, Felicia Miyakawa, Kay Norton, Katherine Preston, Thomas Riis, Lawrence Schenbeck, Douglas Shadle, Jean Snyder, Judith Ann Still, Jacklin Bolton Stopp, and Judith Tick.

I would not have been able to complete this project without the many kind and knowledgeable people working at libraries, archives, and historical societies. To all of you, I send heartfelt appreciation for your assistance and expertise.

Kathy Abromeit, Oberlin College Conservatory Library
Charles Allen, Hampton University Museum and Archives, Hampton, VA
Wes Anderson, Barnes County Historical Society, Valley City, ND
Jenny Barry, Cook County Library, Libertyville, IL

Mariah Berlanga-Shevchuk, Five Oaks Museum, Portland, OR
Chelsi Cannon, Loma Linda University Library, Loma Linda, CA
Elaine Carr, Uintah County Regional History Center, Vernal, UT
Kellen Cutsforth, Denver Public Library, Denver, CO
John R. Davis, Special Collections, University of Maryland Library, College Park, MD
Sara Caroline Davis, J. Willard Marriott Library, University of Utah, Salt Lake City, UT
Rebecca Chasse, University of New Hampshire Library, Durham, NH
Virginia Feher, University of Georgia Library, Athens, GA
James Ford, Adventist Heritage Center, Andrews University, Berrien Springs, MI
Andrew Foster, Virginia Museum of History and Culture, Richmond, VA
Michelle Fuller, Uintah County Regional History Center, Vernal, UT
Allison Gallagher, Oberlin College Library, Oberlin, OH
Erin Greeno, United Church of Canada Archives, Toronto, Ontario, Canada
DeLisa M. Harris, Special Collections, Fisk University Library, Nashville, TN
Dana Hicks, La Jolla Historical Society, La Jolla, CA
Louisa Hoffman, Oberlin College Archives, Oberlin, OH
Linda Housman, Oakham Historical Society, Oakham, MA
Menna James, Rhondda Cynon Taf Library, Wales, UK
Norman J. Jones, Oakwood University, Huntsville, AL
Mary Kearns, Castleton Free Library, Castleton, VT
Tawnya Keller, J. Willard Marriott Library, University of Utah, Salt Lake City, UT
Lorna K. Kirwan, Bancroft Library, University of California, Berkeley, CA
Daryl Leach, Rhondda Cynon Taf Library, Wales, UK
Diane Lee, Oberlin College Library, Oberlin, OH
Donzella Maupin, Hampton University Archives, Hampton, VA
Tomeka Meon Myers, Library of Congress, Washington, DC
Joanne Mok, SPH Media Limited, Singapore
Michael Olivarez, Loma Linda University Library, Loma Linda, CA
Kelvin E. Ong, Micrographics Data, Singapore
Serene Ong, Micrographics Data, Singapore
Anne Oyerly, Andrews University Library, Berrien Springs, MI

Lisa Palella, San Francisco History Center, San Francisco, CA
Jeffrey Quick, Kulas Music Library, Case Western Reserve University, Cleveland, OH
Chamisa Redmond, Library of Congress, Washington, DC
Jacquelyn D. Reese, University of Oklahoma Library, Norman, OK
Matthew Rowe, Yale University Beinecke Library, New Haven, CT
Dean Smith, Bancroft Library, University of California, Berkeley, CA
Robert Spinelli, Fisk University Library Archives, Nashville, TN
Barbara Stovall, Oakwood University, Huntsville, AL
Vanessa Thaxton-Ward, Hampton University Museum and Archives, Hampton, VA
Heather Thomas, Library of Congress, Washington, DC
Joshua A. Williams, Fisk University Library Archives, Nashville, TN
Morgan Wilson, University of New Hampshire Library, Durham, NH
Amanda Zalken, United Church of Canada Archives, Toronto, Canada
Kenneth Zech, Reedley Historical Society, Reedley, CA

For advice and assistance with some of the images that appear in this book, I thank Chris Wideawake (Phototec, Rutland, VT), an expert in historic photographs, who kindly gave of his time and expertise.

I also graciously acknowledge the assistance of those who responded to email inquiries about numerous topics related to my research, including Paul Cort, David D. Grafton, J. Randolph Grymes III, Jennifer D. Lee, Hollis Thoms, and Alan Burl Wingard.

Lewis Nielson, my husband, has been a stalwart ally and a constant supporter of my work. The music examples in this book benefited enormously from his expertise with notation software. I owe him immeasurable gratitude.

I also appreciate the efficiency of the editorial staff at University Press of Mississippi. The suggestions for revisions from external reviewers proved to be most helpful. My work is much better as a result of their careful reading. Any errors in, or limitations of, this book are solely mine.

To those who provided assistance and advice but whose names I have not mentioned above, I apologize for my oversight. You should know that your support helped make this book possible.

FROM **BIBLICAL BOOK**
TO **MUSICAL MEGAHIT**

INTRODUCTION

In October 1856, American composer William B. Bradbury conducted the premiere of his choral work, *Esther, the Beautiful Queen*. Almost immediately and quite unexpectedly, the piece soared in popularity. Eventually, *Esther* fever spread coast to coast, and by the early twentieth century, countless US residents could claim some sort of association with the work.[1] That is, with the exception of author and humorist Eugene Wood, who quipped, "I suppose I am the only man in the United States of America . . . who not only has never taken part in *Esther, the Beautiful Queen*, but who has never even witnessed a performance of that great work . . . . I ought to feel proud of the distinction, but I'm not. It makes me feel lonesome. You saw it, and I didn't. You were in it, and I wasn't."[2] The innumerable references to *Esther* in historic newspapers and periodicals lent credence to Wood's sentiments as the piece had already been performed hundreds of times when he penned his comment.

Even now, communities reminisce about *Esther* productions in bygone days that elicited glowing reviews and generated considerable local pride. Iowa newspaper columnist Lynn Zerschling recently wrote about just such an event that took place over 125 years ago: "Few musical or dramatic performances ever given in Sioux City have met with greater success than the presentation of the cantata 'Queen Esther' at the Peavey Grand Opera House by some of the city's best vocalists. They were accompanied by a full orchestra and a chorus of 100 voices."[3] Similar recollections of *Esther* performances appear among the multitudes of blogs and genealogy posts on the web. Moreover, countless historical societies preserve the artifacts of these performances in the form of clippings, printed programs, posters, and photographs. So, too, elderly family members may still recall an *Esther* performance they participated in or attended. As I began work on this book many years ago, my mother recalled how much she enjoyed singing in one of *Esther*'s choruses as a young girl. In another nostalgic moment, Iowa teacher and missionary

Drusilla Stoddard remembered *Esther* with this succinct comment: "Can I ever forget the happiness I found in the cantata 'Queen Esther'?"[4] Respected music critic Frederic S. Law shared this fond memory of *Esther*: "I remember the singing of . . . 'Esther, the Beautiful Queen' in which my mother sang the part of Esther . . . . I have heard operas in all the principal cities of Europe . . . but I may safely say that none other made a deeper impression upon me. I remember vividly running to the rose bush in our garden and selecting a white rose for my mother to wear in her hair—with great care, too, for was she not to sing the role of the 'beautiful queen'?"[5]

As the title *Esther, the Beautiful Queen* suggests, Bradbury wrote this piece as a musical setting of the biblical Book of Esther narrative. He intended his music to be regarded as religious, sung without any staging, acting, or costumes. Most of the earliest performances of *Esther* took place at "musical conventions"—events convened throughout the eastern states by Bradbury along with a few of his contemporaries. These gatherings attracted multitudes of aspiring vocalists intent on improving their musicianship. Bradbury often selected the *Esther* score as a piece with which to teach music reading and the fundamentals of singing. Students could look forward to performing portions or all of *Esther* as a fitting and welcome culmination to a series of convention classes. However, even as Bradbury insisted on his original sacred and instructional purposes for *Esther*, the work eventually transitioned into a staged extravaganza. Although many such performances fueled controversy about theatrical interpretations of biblical narratives, the work was, nonetheless, performed in more places than any similar American composition of its era. In short, by the dawn of the twentieth century, *Esther* had become a musical theater megahit.

Yet how could a work, written as an unstaged sacred and instructional piece, achieve and sustain the level of widespread appeal associated with musical theater? First, consider the music itself: Bradbury created an accessible score with uncomplicated melodies and harmonies. Many of the melodies in *Esther* resemble Bradbury's hymn tunes or popular songs familiar to a vast majority of the works' mostly Protestant performers and audiences. For, as confirmed by politician and newspaper columnist Bill Arp, *Esther*'s eminently memorable and singable tunes lingered in the minds of innumerable community residents: "Everywhere you go the sweet strains of this cantata are heard. The children chant it on the way to school; the mothers at the fireside; the lawyers at their desks."[6] And with the exception of a few numbers, the music in *Esther* could be readily learned and sung by novices. Of course, the *Esther* vogue received a substantial boost owing to the piece's utility as a fundraising vehicle as proceeds from many performances supported local charitable causes such as those associated with churches, schools, hospitals, and libraries. Furthermore, because Bradbury wrote most of his score for amateur musicians, all communities found the work to be quite approachable by church choirs and local talent. With its solos, small ensembles, and large chorus numbers for adults and children, *Esther* provided singers of varying ages and abilities with performance opportunities.

After Bradbury published his score in 1856, an unprecedented and unique social and reception history of over one hundred year's duration unfolded in *Esther*'s wake. This storied history includes debates about sensitive issues, especially matters concerned with questions of morality engendered by theatrical performances of biblical narratives. Yet by the 1870s, the addition of dramatic action and costumes rapidly established the gold standard for *Esther* productions and Bradbury's unstaged, pious, and instructional intentions for the work slipped from prominence. Moreover, the piece came to exemplify the musical self-determination of communities because performers and audiences, rather than Bradbury himself, facilitated its widespread dissemination and amazing stylistic transformation. Not only did audiences eventually come to enjoy *Esther* as pure stage entertainment, but communities experienced a renewed sense of solidarity and purpose as they recruited singers, rehearsed, made costumes, and built sets and props. Still, no matter how lavishly staged, most audiences and performers continued to find in *Esther* moral, instructional, and spiritual benefits as the work's songs, choral scenes, and attendant pageantry conveyed messages of reassurance, empowerment, and optimism.

A fascination with all things Oriental also influenced the reputation and reception history of *Esther*. For the purposes of this book, I use the term "Orientalism" to refer to a nexus of benign cultural reactions to life in the ancient Holy Land, as was prevalent in the United States during the nineteenth and early twentieth centuries. Orientalist expressions had long enjoyed considerable popularity in home décor, jewelry, architecture, and the visual arts, to name but a few of these stylistic appropriations. Not surprisingly, Orientalist imagery also found its way into productions of *Esther*, particularly noticeable in costumes and staging. Participants in *Esther* performances often made their own stage attire and found, in illustrated bibles and other sources, inspiration for designing and assembling Orientalist costumes. Critics frequently commented on the "Oriental" appearance of this homemade stage attire and how seemingly accurate the players portrayed their exotic characters and situations.

Minorities, especially Black people, Chinese Americans, and Asian immigrants, also contributed, substantially, to the richness of *Esther*'s reception history. Through productions of *Esther*, minorities engaged in successful fundraising initiatives for their own unique cultural, religious and educational institutions, especially those beyond the purview of whites. Minorities also found, in *Esther*'s text, unique socio-political messages of hope and resilience that helped sustain them amid the dailiness of racial discrimination. With these performances, persons of color also sought to mediate tensions between whites and various diasporic populations.

Ultimately, *Esther* came to be known internationally as, by the 1870s, US newspaper readers learned of productions in many overseas locations, including performances in Africa, Asia, Australia, Canada, Great Britain, and New Zealand. Not only did Bradbury's piece travel to distant countries, but *Esther*'s extraordinary popularity endured well over a century, with documentation of performances appearing in newspapers and in other sources as recently as the 1990s. This extraordinary level of acclaim, however unintended by Bradbury himself, belatedly affords him a deserved position of significance in the historiography of American musical theater.

My goal with this book is to present an account of *Esther*'s meteoric rise from its rather humble beginnings to become a beloved piece of religious musical theater. As with any such effort, there undoubtedly remains much that could be added to this history or alternative ways to interpret the rich trail of evidence that documents *Esther*'s reception. In fact, I invite, and look forward to, future analyses of *Esther* with varying accounts of the work's significance, especially if more historic documents are identified and become available. I have intentionally written this book with a broad and varied readership in mind. Although the ability to read music notation would be an added asset while reading, this journey through history can be appreciated by most anyone, including those with little musical experience. Furthermore, I have only sparingly used specialized vocabulary or technical terms. As Bradbury intended his music to be accessible to all singers and audiences, I hope this book will prove engaging and enjoyable for any reader.

CHAPTER ONE

PRELUDE
Bradbury, Musician and Entrepreneur

Reflecting on Bradbury's fame as a composer, a Chicago newspaper confidently stated: "There are few of our readers who have not heard of William B. Bradbury, whose melodies have brightened the homes and gladdened the hearts of Americans."[1] Indeed, during his lifetime, he enjoyed a widespread reputation as a composer of popular songs, and several of his hymns remain perennial favorites.[2] Songwriting comprises only part of his legacy, however, as he was also an innovative teacher, journalist, editor, and publisher, and a highly successful manufacturer of pianos.

Born on October 6, 1816, in the coastal village of York, Maine, Bradbury spent most of his formative years working on a farm maintained by his parents, David Bradbury (1785–1838) and Sophia Chase Bradbury (1788–1867).[3] An enduring appreciation for his bucolic upbringing sustained him throughout his career. As the *New York Tribune* recalled: "His fondness for rural life was a beautiful thing in his character. He looked upon Nature with the eyes of a poet, and was never more happy than in the midst of her bountiful scenes.... He was accustomed to speak of the pleasures he enjoyed in taking an old worn-out piece of land, and by deep plowing and rich cultivation, make it look up and 'laugh.'"[4] Music also played a central role in family life during Bradbury's youth. His parents were respected amateur singers in the York region, and family members devoted considerable time to social and church singing. A young Bradbury showed unusual aptitude, at an early age, for teaching himself the intricacies of music reading, and he strove to develop at least some proficiency on every instrument he encountered.[5] Bradbury's devout faith also owes much to his upbringing as his family worshiped at a local Protestant church and sang in the choir.

Early Music Training and Teaching

In 1830, Bradbury traveled to Boston, Massachusetts. Shortly after arriving in the city, he obtained a piano through the efforts of Calvin Allen (1806–1887), a member of the managerial staff at the Chickering Piano factory. Bradbury pursued his first formal music lessons when he began to study harmony, piano, and organ with respected teacher and publisher Sumner Hill (1799–1883). Inspired by his lessons with Hill, he decided to devote his life to music, especially teaching. His determination to pursue a career in music and the teaching profession met with criticism, however, as acquaintances and relatives warned him of the challenges musicians encountered not only to earn a livable wage, but also to achieve and sustain a respectable reputation. In contrast to this advice, Bradbury received unswerving support for his aspirations from Calvin Allen.[6]

To acquire knowledge of teaching methods and pedagogical literature, Bradbury enrolled at the recently established Boston Academy of Music, founded by Lowell Mason (1792–1872). He also sought out performance opportunities and successfully auditioned to sing in Mason's celebrated Bowdoin Street Church choir. Shortly thereafter, church officials appointed him organist. This assignment presented unanticipated difficulties, however, as the church's antiquated instrument was barely playable, its unresponsive manual in dire need of repair. A frustrated Bradbury lasted only three months in this post. By way of explanation for his hasty departure, he informed Mason that the organ's sticking keys required twice the usual effort—depressing and lifting—and thus, he quipped, he merited double pay.[7]

In 1836, Mason recommended Bradbury for a full-time assignment in the coastal town of Machias, Maine. The appointment included teaching singing and music-reading skills to large classes and private students. Bradbury accepted the position after successfully negotiating his terms with local officials. For unknown reasons, he vacated this appointment after only about a year and a half. He returned to Boston briefly in 1838, and on August 28 of that year, married Adra Esther Fessenden (1818–1892) with whom he had enjoyed a lengthy friendship.[8] The newlyweds moved to the seaport city of Saint John, New Brunswick, Canada, where Bradbury secured a teaching assignment. He achieved remarkable success in this position, but health problems forced him to abandon, temporarily, his teaching activities. The birth of the Bradburys' first child, in 1839, added to the couple's financial and emotional stress. Within months, the Bradburys left Saint John and returned to Boston. Upon encountering the family, Bradbury's friend, Simeon Pease Cheney, a noted composer and singer, described them as "in an almost destitute condition."[9]

An opening for a singing teacher at Boston's famed Marlborough Chapel happily coincided with Bradbury's recovery from illness. Those familiar with his teaching in Machias, Maine, recommended him for this assignment, which he succeeded in obtaining. Shortly thereafter, the position of organist at the Chapel also became available. After reviewing many applicants, church officials decided to audition two finalists: Bradbury and his friend, composer and teacher George Frederick Root (1820–1895). Each of the finalists took charge of services one Sunday, and based on their performances, the Chapel's administration selected Bradbury for the job. For unknown reasons, Bradbury left this position around a year later to accept a teaching assignment in Dover, New Hampshire. However, circumstances in Dover did not altogether satisfy Bradbury and he again sought yet another appointment. With the assistance of Lowell Mason, he soon obtained employment at the First Baptist Church of Brooklyn, New York.[10]

Singing Classes for Children

In 1841, the restless Bradbury left his Brooklyn position and began teaching at the Broadway Tabernacle in New York City. He held this appointment for much of his career and his major responsibilities entailed working with children. Then the largest performance and meeting space in the region, the cavernous Tabernacle could accommodate large choruses and audiences of over two thousand (figure 1.1).[11]

Bradbury's classes at the Tabernacle offered the first free music instruction for children in greater New York. Many teachers and superintendents visited his classes to observe his methods. As a result of what they heard and saw, other churches and institutions sought his services and advice. In particular, Washington King (1815–1861) and Charles W. Feeks (1812–1887), founders of New York's prestigious Classical and English School, invited Bradbury to provide music instruction for their students. Beyond teaching at the Classical and English School and the Broadway Tabernacle, Bradbury introduced music instruction to New York's public schools.[12]

Figure 1.1. Broadway Tabernacle. The Miriam and Ira D. Wallach Division of Art, Prints and Photographs, New York Public Library Digital Collections.

In consultation with the Broadway Tabernacle's administration, Bradbury formulated a plan whereby the church set aside a sum of money to be used to offset the cost of providing free singing classes for children. He also offered to organize large concerts to be given by all the children at the close of each term. By charging admission to these events, the money received could be used to repay the sum advanced by the church. The first such performance attracted a huge crowd and the money it raised far exceeded expectations. A review of this event typified public acclaim for Bradbury's "juvenile" concerts:

> Mr. Bradbury gave a concert at the Tabernacle on Monday evening last [November 22, 1841], of one of his Juvenile Schools, numbering about two hundred [singers]. A large audience were greeted and delighted with some specimens of singing, which were exquisitely tasteful and beautiful, and which evinced the practicability and use of imparting correct musical instruction at an early age. Great praise is due to Mr. Bradbury for his persevering and successful efforts to awaken the public interest in the too neglected subject of juvenile singing.[13]

Another review noted, of one of Bradbury's subsequent Tabernacle concerts, "a more beautiful sight was seldom seen than the 700 children . . . [whose] sweet and well-trained voices filled the vast house with melody. It is astonishing that children can so early be brought to such a degree of proficiency in music."[14] Celebrated writer and poet Walt Whitman frequented the children's concerts conducted by Bradbury and published several reviews of them. Whitman's boundless enthusiasm for these events permeated the essays he wrote about them, as evident in the following passage:

> If any person among the three thousand present on Wednesday evening last [February 18, 1846], at the Children's concert, at the New York [Broadway] Tabernacle, had previously entertained doubts of the capacity of all boys and girls to learn to sing, we think he must have had them thoroughly dissipated by what he heard there on that occasion. For our own part, we never witnessed a more agreeable spectacle, or listened to harmony which, taking all things into consideration, was more creditable to the performers or their leader . . . . At Mr. Bradbury's concert on Wednesday evening, there were four hundred neatly dressed, fresh looking boys, and the same number of sweet, pleasant-faced girls—a sight to make a man's better nature swell within him, and banish the bad utterly away . . . . It was indeed a holy sight! . . . All of the songs were distinctly enunciated, and the time [rhythmic accuracy] would have done credit to an opera chorus . . . . We are strongly in favor of these children's concerts, and hope they will continue to be given frequently. The universal diffusion of music among the young, who are to form the future men and women of America, will do incalculable good in the way of refinement and manners.[15]

As children's concerts at the Tabernacle continued to draw sizable crowds, Bradbury sensed a need for new choral music appropriate for use in teaching young singers. Accordingly, he began to arrange and compose specialized repertoire for children and became a pioneer in music of this style and purpose. In 1847, Bradbury published a revision of *Flora's Festival*, a choral work for children based on music written mostly by John Hill Hewitt (1801–1890) along with a few numbers attributed to other composers.[16] Works of this type and configuration became known by the subgenre designation of "musical recreation" or "juvenile oratorio."[17] A complimentary press notice confirmed the immediate success of *Flora's Festival*:

> This is, indeed, a novelty in the department of juvenile music, being entirely different in its character from anything ever before attempted, representing in song, a fairy feast of flowers. It is divided into three parts ["Morning," "Noon," and "Night"], and consists of choruses, semi-choruses, duetts [sic], quartetts [sic], solos, recitatives, etc., etc., in all, about twenty-seven different pieces, selected chiefly from the finest authors, arranged for and adapted [by Bradbury] to the voices of youthful singers.[18]

In his preface to *Flora's Festival*, Bradbury stipulated that the score could be performed by "any number of singers, from twenty-five to a thousand. Three or four hundred well-trained voices would perhaps be the most effective in a large house." He also recommended that the children "be uniformly dressed" for performances of the piece. To enhance the celebratory nature of the score's text, he provided details about decorating the hall in a festive and colorful manner using evergreens and flowers.[19] Decades later, a former student of Bradbury recalled his teacher's famous singing classes for children and their concerts at the Broadway Tabernacle:

> Bradbury's class of five hundred children, the girls all in white, and the boys in their best suits, was a thing to be enjoyed, and to be remembered at this day with infinite pleasure by men now middle-aged. Music was not at that day taught in the city public schools and Mr. Bradbury conceived the idea of teaching the city's children [at the Broadway Tabernacle] gratuitously . . . . [E]very parent and relative of every child in his chorus was sure to be a purchaser of a ticket, and [consequently] . . . the Tabernacle, which could hold about four thousand people, was always crowded.[20]

Tunebooks

In the early 1840s, Bradbury began compiling tunebooks, a popular format that had been in vogue in the United States since the eighteenth century. With some fifty-nine such publications to his credit, Bradbury was one of the most prolific anthologists of his era. In fact, the American public became acquainted with his prodigious output of hymns and religious songs largely through his tunebooks. During the nineteenth century, the US publishing industry flooded the market with hundreds of these inexpensive collections.[21]

A letter published in a Pennsylvania newspaper noted, of tunebook content, that numerous composers were turning out "piles of music" in an astonishingly short amount of time. The writer singled out Bradbury, in particular, "whose floods of lighter musical literature of the day has well-nigh deluged the land."[22] In complete agreement with this statement, Boston author and businessman James M. Hewins (1817–1891) observed, of the proliferation of song anthologies: "We have tune-books without number." Owing to the "rage for novelty which everywhere prevails," Hewins continued, "[A] new tunebook is wanted every year just as the makers of them intend."[23] The preference for this profit-driven format came about, in part, because American musicians did not import the system of aristocratic and royal patronage that supported many European composers, performers, teachers, and publishing ventures. Instead, tunebooks both generated and responded to market demands, especially those associated with the emergence of music education and musical consumerism in general.[24]

To maintain a competitive edge, tunebook printers used inexpensive materials for production, such as newsprint and lightweight cardboard, rather than more substantial paper, bound with leather or cloth. Other recognizable features, such as dimensions characteristic of an octavo, also helped sell tunebooks. According to clergyman and musician Christopher W. Knauff (1838–1911), "[T]unebooks of the age were shaped oblong—very long sidewise. When one held in his hands the open volume, he felt as if he had to manipulate the top part of a mercantile ledger cut short."[25] Consumers came to expect the oblong shape of tunebooks—usually around eight inches in width and six inches in height—and the resultant sobriquets of "longboy" and "open ender" helped sustain this popular visual image. To further induce singers to purchase the latest music compilations, some printers commissioned eye-catching illustrations for tunebook covers (figure 1.2).

Beyond their recognizable exterior appearance, tunebooks offered a variety of song literature in familiar and appealing genres and styles, including accessible arrangements of well-known European opera and oratorio arias, folk melodies, parlor songs, and religious works. Tunebook compilers, arrangers, and composers enthusiastically partnered with publishers in the competition for sales. Together, they issued new volumes of music as often as possible, and in advertisements for them, promised the latest songs and hymns, usually combined with a preface that offered the most innovative and helpful instructional methods. To bolster sales and

Figure 1.2. Cover, William B. Bradbury, *Golden Censer* (New York: William B. Bradbury, 1864), engraved by J[ohn] W[illiam] Orr (1815–1887), a prominent New York illustrator. In this engraving, some of the tunebook's song titles appear on an oversized censer, held aloft by cherubs; titles also intermingle with the smoke rising from the censer.

profits, Bradbury and his publishers regularly advertised his tunebooks in leading periodicals.

Bradbury compiled his first tunebook for children, *The Young Choir*, in 1841, with the assistance of elementary school teacher and textbook author Charles W. Sanders (1805–1889).[26] A favorable review of this first collaborative effort, offered after "careful examination," appeared in the *New York Evangelist*:

> The elementary lessons are . . . very clear and simple and admirably adapted . . . . The music of this collection is made of original and selected pieces, generally of a light and flowing and easy style . . . well calculated to interest the juvenile mind, and impress it with some good moral lesson. The new music in the work, while it possesses no striking marks of originality, is well arranged

and certainly well adapted for the use of juvenile singing *schools*. It gives evidence of having been composed by those accustomed to juvenile instruction, and such, too, as understand their business [italics original].[27]

The Young Choir soared in popularity, with some 50,000 copies sold within a short time period. Buoyed by their success, Bradbury and Sanders teamed up a year later to compile their second anthology, *The School Singer*.[28] Bradbury used this publication for the inaugural concert of his "United Juvenile Choir" of children from the New York City region. The *Evening Post* printed this enthusiastic announcement:

> Mr. W. B. Bradbury would respectfully announce that his first Juvenile Musical Festival will be given in the Broadway Tabernacle on Wednesday evening, April 19, 1843, by his United Juvenile Choir, numbering upwards of four hundred young singers from various schools in different parts of the city . . . . The music will be mostly new and of a highly interesting character, consisting chiefly of popular airs . . . being selections from a new singing book for the young entitled the "School Singer."[29]

Bradbury's publications for adults commenced with two instructional tunebooks issued in 1844: *The Social Singing Book* and *Bradbury's Singing School for Ladies and Gentlemen*.[30] Clearly, Bradbury had come to realize the benefits of teaching the parents of the children who sang in his "juvenile" choirs. Such instruction would not only encourage families to sing together in their homes, but also contribute enormously to the spread of popular music, and of course, to the sales of his tunebooks. Along with Lowell Mason, George F. Root, and other contemporaries, Bradbury believed in music education as a way to improve congregational singing during church services. His pedagogical goals did not encompass the creation of artistic singers nor did he promote the cultivation of musical erudition or an appreciation of European-based concert music. Rather, he sought to inculcate virtue, morality, and happiness and to encourage the acquisition of what he considered to be useful and essential musical knowledge and singing skills.

In addition to his work with Sanders, Bradbury collaborated with composer and compiler Thomas Hastings. Hastings also enjoyed an esteemed association with the Broadway Tabernacle as the director of the church's adult singers. Bradbury and Hastings issued their first publication, *The Psalmodist*, in 1844, and followed this popular book with *The New York Choralist* in 1847, *Congregational Harmony* in 1849, *The Mendelssohn Collection*, also issued in 1849, and *Psalmista*, in 1851.[31] In the preface to *The New York Choralist*, they reiterated the competitive nature of tunebook publication: "The time has gone by, we suppose, when any apology can be expected for the presentation of a new [tune]book. The great mass of singers who can read music, are ever anxious to have something new for perusal and practice before them; and those of us who would continue to benefit them by [our] labor must endeavor to meet this demand."[32]

European Sojourn

By the mid-1840s, Bradbury had decided to pursue additional music studies in Europe. Writing in his journal, he noted, "[I]n July 1847, I sailed with my wife and one daughter (Emily Maria) . . . . Starting for Europe [on July 2, we] arrived at Portsmouth [England] in just four weeks from day of sailing."[33] Of the trip, he commented, "Our long voyage was pleasant, (if such a journey can be called pleasant at all) . . . and we enjoyed a remarkable succession of fine weather and favoring breezes."[34] Various US newspapers published the letters Bradbury wrote during this excursion. In them, he described his tour of the Alps and elucidated the state of European music performance and music education he encountered. Bradbury's letters demonstrate his ability to ably engage readers with charming and informative prose.[35]

After his arrival in England, Bradbury visited several schools in London and met with the country's most respected music educators. He found the methods and philosophies of the many pedagogues whose classes he observed to be commendably progressive and innovative. One teacher he met, John Pyke Hullah (1812–1884), enjoyed a laudable reputation comparable to that of Lowell Mason, often referred to as "the father of music education" in the United States. Hullah, famous as "the most popular class[room music] teacher in England," advocated "universal musical cultivation . . . among the masses." Bradbury expressed considerable enthusiasm for Hullah's philosophy and methods:

> Upon my introduction to him, he [Hullah] cordially invited me to attend a rehearsal of one of his best classes . . . . They were engaged in rehearsing the

Oratorio of "Judas Maccabaeus" [by George Frideric Handel] . . . . I could not help but observe with pleasure that not only were the young and gay indulging in an exercise at once rational, instructive and healthy, but the more aged also . . . . I verily believe some [of Hullah's students] were old enough to have been the Professor's grandparents.[36]

Here and elsewhere during his European sojourn, Bradbury witnessed singing by mixed ensembles with singers of varying ages rather than choruses populated solely with children or only of adults. The realization that singers of all ages and abilities could be combined to create meaningful and fulfilling musical and educational experiences would later influence him when he composed *Esther*.

Several weeks later, Bradbury traveled to the continent and toured the Swiss, German, and Tyrolean Alps. He transcribed songs performed by indigenous peoples he met en route, and this music provided material for subsequent publications. The success of the tunebooks in which these pieces ultimately appeared established Bradbury as one of the most important collectors and arrangers of the popular mountain song genre in the United States during the nineteenth century.[37]

Bradbury and his family subsequently made their way to Leipzig. He had "for many years looked forward to [visiting Leipzig] with hope and expectation and . . . also, with no little anxiety." In his description of music education in Germany, he once again made reference to the importance of music-making in schools and homes:

> That Germany has the most thorough system of [music] education needs not to be here repeated. That vocal music is here cherished, cultivated and adopted into the school and into the family, both on account of its influence upon the mind and the affections, is also known . . . . It is here no uncertain experiment . . . . I came to Germany as to the fountain head of music. My expectations were high. They have not been disappointed. On the contrary, they have been met, doubly met.[38]

While in Leipzig, the Bradburys occupied an apartment three doors away from the family of Felix Mendelssohn. Toward the end of October 1848, Mendelssohn's health rapidly declined. Bradbury recalled the concern of city officials for Mendelssohn's comfort, and accordingly, workers covered the street in front of the composer's residence with sawdust to subdue the noise made by horses' hooves on the cobblestone pavement. On November 4, 1848, some four weeks after Bradbury's arrival, Mendelssohn died—an event, Bradbury stated, that "filled all Germany with mourning." As he poignantly recalled of Mendelssohn's funeral: "I saw his lifeless corpse which, as all remarked, retained, to an uncommon degree its natural and life-like appearance. I shall never forget the sweet expression of his countenance. His death was as peaceful as his life was pure."[39]

For a period of some eighteen months, Bradbury took lessons with some of the most respected teachers at Leipzig Conservatory. He studied singing with Ferdinand Böhme (1815–1883), harmony with Moritz Hauptmann (1792–1868), composition with Ignaz Moscheles (1794–1870) and piano with Ernst Ferdinand Wenzel (1808–1880). Unfortunately, Bradbury published relatively few comments about his studies. He described Moscheles as "kind and courteous" and his lessons with him as full of "golden apothegms of art, always to be remembered." Moscheles, by this time a renowned concert pianist, imparted valuable information about the state of the development of the piano and ways he believed the instrument could be improved. These technical discussions, while a digression from Bradbury's composition lessons, proved useful to him when he later entered the piano manufacturing business.[40]

During his absence from the United States, Bradbury continued to collaborate with Thomas Hastings on tunebook projects. Together, they worked on a new compilation, *The Mendelssohn Collection*, to commemorate Felix Mendelssohn's life and music. Advertisements for this collection coincided with the book's release in 1849, shortly before Bradbury's return to the United States.[41] These notices indicated that the compilers chose "original and selected matter from the best sources, much of which was composed, arranged, or selected by Mr. Bradbury during his late residence in Germany."[42] Hastings enthusiastically recorded the book's success, writing, "[T]he 'Mendelssohn' [*Collection*] goes [sells] well—better even than its predecessors."[43] At this point in their careers, the collaborative team of Bradbury and Hastings competed, openly and unabashedly, with Mason and his followers for tunebook sales. Hastings boasted that books he compiled with Bradbury sold briskly even "among the Masonites," thus confirming the financial rewards of this partnership. He further added,

> [T]he *Mendelssohn Collection* sells far ahead of its preceptors in the same line, and is also ahead of Mason's latest book. The publishers have sold since the middle of August [1849] ... near 28,000 copies. The *Choralist*, too, continues in favor. Our books now go [sell] freely down East, even in Boston. A multitude of Mason's old adherents have become our patrons. This no doubt galls him, but we cannot help it. If his next publication is no better than the two preceding ones, he will, I should think, about use himself up.[44]

Return from Europe

The *New York Observer* enthusiastically welcomed Bradbury's return to the United States:

> W. B. Bradbury, Esq., so long and so favorably known in this city as a teacher and composer of vocal music, has just returned to this city after an absence of two years, which time he spent chiefly in Germany and Switzerland, under the most favorable advantages for improvement in the profession to which he is devoted. He will be heartily welcomed by his former pupils, and many parents and others will be pleased to enjoy for their children the benefit of his instructions, enhanced in value, as they must be, by the opportunities he has had abroad of study under the best of masters.[45]

Bradbury's observations of European music education impressed upon him the need to increase his teaching of children. Accordingly, he commented,

> [A]s a nation we have neglected entirely this subject in our early education, and the natural result is that the large proportion of our adult population cannot sing .... Could our school committees, trustees and parents be prevailed upon to take this matter in hand and be in earnest about it—if they would have it properly and on a permanent basis introduced into the schools as a branch of study, not of recreation merely—an incalculable amount of good would follow. The next generation ... would feel its revivifying influences, in their social and home circles.[46]

Bradbury resumed his former position at the Broadway Tabernacle, conducting choruses and working with children. To "induce whole families to join," the Tabernacle charged reduced tuition rates for women who desired to take his classes. He also organized mammoth performances, including a revival of *Flora's Festival* and other choral extravaganzas.[47]

Beyond teaching at the Tabernacle, Bradbury also began to tour to distant locations as a director of musical conventions and as an instructor at "normal" institutes dedicated to teacher training. His conventions, with lessons scheduled over a period of a few days, usually attracted over one hundred aspiring singers. Advertisements for these gatherings provided details about his plans to teach both adults and children along with offering instruction in social and family singing and church music.[48] His conventions often culminated in a concert of his new compositions, such as *Esther*.

Bradbury also became active in the Normal Musical Institute movement. In contrast to musical conventions, institutes lasted several weeks and offered instruction in teaching methods for music teachers and for classroom teachers who desired to learn more about how to teach music in a general classroom setting. As one advertisement indicated, institutes served "primarily to impart through instruction to such ladies and gentlemen as may wish to qualify themselves for teachers of music . . . choristers or conductors, teachers of adult or juvenile classes, etc.; secondarily, to such as desire to make higher attainments in the art of music generally, for their own private or individual benefit."[49] For his first institute, organized in New York City, Bradbury collaborated with Mason and Root (figure 1.3).

Subsequent institutes occurred in many locations throughout the East and Midwest. Bradbury used his latest tunebooks at institutes and conventions and hence discovered the enormous potential for their sales at these gatherings. He often announced the titles of his most recent publications ahead of time for those participants who wanted to purchase copies in advance.

During the early and mid-1850s, circumstances precipitated major changes in Bradbury's life and career. By 1853, the Broadway Tabernacle, a substantial source of income for the Bradbury family, had begun to consider relocating to a smaller building. The future of his Tabernacle appointment now appeared somewhat uncertain for Bradbury, and he increased his touring activities and traveled to more distant destinations. As the bustle of business and industry escalated in the vicinity of Bradbury's New York residence, he sought other, more rural accommodations outside the city limits.[50]

Figure 1.3. Left to right: George F. Root, Lowell Mason, and Bradbury, ca. 1853, taken at a Normal Musical Institute, photographer unknown. Autographs appear below image. Sesquicentennial of School Music in American Public Education (SESSMUS) Collection, Special Collections in Performing Arts, University of Maryland Libraries.

Fortuitously, a property in Bloomfield, New Jersey, of considerable interest to Bradbury, had become available. The small-town environment and rural setting of Bloomfield must have appealed to Bradbury as it undoubtedly reminded him of his youth in York, Maine. The family left New York sometime in late 1855 or early 1856.

After relocating to Bloomfield, Bradbury's income continued to increase from his frequent publication of best-selling tunebooks and his engagements as a teacher at musical conventions and institutes. The appearance of *Esther* in 1856 and the extraordinary sales of its score also bolstered his financial standing. Within a short time of his move to Bloomfield, Bradbury had attained the status of a country gentleman who could afford not only the upkeep of a sizeable residence, but also the maintenance of quarters for three live-in servants: a housekeeper, a coachman, and a groundskeeper.[51] (For a likeness of Bradbury in his middle years, see figure 1.4.)

Figure 1.4. Autographed engraving of Bradbury, origin and date unknown. Image courtesy of the Library of Congress.

Piano Manufacturing

Bradbury's entrée into the realm of piano manufacturing not only rapidly earned him a place among New York's business elite, but also augmented his income. In partnership with his brother, Edward G. Bradbury, he purchased a sizable interest in the piano firm of Lighte and Newton in 1854. The company, originally established in 1849 by Henry J. Newton (1823–1895) and German-born craftsman Ferdinand C. Lighte (1816–1872), enjoyed a regional reputation for its innovations in piano construction.[52] Bradbury informed his private journal that his brother would run the daily operations of their piano factory while he "should be left at liberty to follow my profession of teacher and composer . . . . [W]e agreed to share the profits alike—thus far it has proved a profitable business."[53] Press items confirm that Bradbury continued to travel frequently throughout the northeastern United States while his brother supervised their piano establishment. New Yorkers welcomed the Bradbury brothers into the world of piano manufacturing and confirmed that "the name and style of the new firm will be Lighte, Newton &

Bradburys."⁵⁴ The *New York Evangelist* printed the following announcement regarding this business venture:

> [William Bradbury] would respectfully give notice to his musical friends everywhere, that after a familiar acquaintance with the pianos made by Lighte & Newton, he has become fully satisfied of their superiority, and he can with the utmost confidence invite all in search of an excellent piano to call and judge for themselves. He would further state, that while all the attention necessary will be given to the further improvement and general interests of the Piano-forte business, these duties will not at all interfere with his professional engagements as Author and Lecturer.⁵⁵

Bradbury also listed various establishments where his pianos could be purchased, including retailers in Boston, Buffalo, Cincinnati, Columbus (GA), Louisville, Memphis, Nashville, Pittsburgh, St. Louis, and in Montreal and Toronto, Canada. In a newspaper notice, E. G. Bradbury wrote, "We cordially invite our friends and patrons, and all wishing a superior instrument to call and examine our stock and elegant wareroom. We feel confident that our facilities for manufacturing are now such that we shall be able, more readily than heretofore, to supply the increasing demand for our unrivaled instruments. We are now manufacturing twenty pianofortes per week which is more than any other firm is doing in this city."⁵⁶ He provided this description of the promised and most recent technical improvements and innovative features of the firm's pianos:

> Lighte and Bradbury's Patent Insulated Full Iron Frame New Scale Grand and Square Piano-Fortes. The Insulators between the iron frame and wooden portions of the instrument, prevent the tinny, or metallic tone, so justly complained of in the ordinary use of the Iron Frame, and give freedom to the vibrating portions of the instrument; thereby insuring a durability hitherto unattained, while the singing quality, power, and richness of tone, are greatly enhanced; thus entitling the Insulated Iron Frame to the *first position* in modern improvements to the Piano-forte [italics original].⁵⁷

By the end of the first year of the Bradburys' partnership, the firm had doubled its profits. At the close of its third year, the business had expanded over two hundred percent and employed around 165 people.⁵⁸

Yet in spite of the Bradbury brothers' optimism, diligence, and financial success, problems soon plagued their piano business. Budgetary and legal disagreements arose between E. G. Bradbury and Lighte along with concerns about the manner in which the latter had allowed the factory to become "very much run down through neglect."[59] The economic Panic of 1857 imposed additional burdens, and in December 1859, fire destroyed a sizeable portion of the factory building. Insufficient insurance benefits failed to compensate the Bradburys adequately for the extensive damage. To see the firm through these crises, William Bradbury invested considerable personal savings in the firm and also borrowed money from Lowell Mason and others.[60]

In 1861, the Bradbury brothers decided to withdraw from the firm and completed the legal arrangements to do so two years later. William Bradbury purchased all interests from his brother, Newton, and Lighte. He formed his own company in partnership with piano craftsman Freeborn Garrettson Smith (1828–1911). As historian George W. Howard (1833–1895) recalled, "Mr. Smith was the master mechanic, the presiding genius who supervised the construction of every instrument manufactured by . . . Mr. Bradbury."[61] The firm, now called Bradbury Pianos, relocated to larger quarters, and at Smith's recommendation, Bradbury inaugurated his own fashionable showroom. In less than four years, Bradbury claimed to have sold some 18,000 pianos—reputedly more than any other US manufacturer.[62]

Even as his piano business expanded and he traveled frequently to conduct music conventions, Bradbury continued to publish about two tunebooks a year. He also established his own publishing company and became prominent as an editor and journalist. From 1854 until 1862, he served as contributing editor of the *Choral Advocate and Singing Class Journal*. In March 1859, he entered into legal agreement with New York publisher Francis J. Huntington (1803–1878) to purchase half-ownership of the *New York Musical Pioneer and Choristers' Budget*, then published solely by Huntington. After finalizing the purchase, Bradbury assumed the editorship of the periodical. However, owing to financial problems and disagreements over the material to be published in this periodical, Bradbury eventually withdrew from the editorship and sold his interest back to Huntington.[63]

The End of the Civil War

As a well-connected businessman and a member of a coterie "representing the best intelligence, culture, and respectability," Bradbury was invited in 1865 to join some 180 New Yorkers on a lengthy boat excursion. The organizers of the trip chartered the famous steamship *Oceanus* for a voyage from New York Harbor to Charleston, South Carolina—a distance of nearly 800 miles.[64] Once at their destination, the passengers attended the ceremonial raising of the American flag at Charleston's beleaguered Fort Sumter—a commemoration of considerable national significance and appeal. Participants in this excursion included prominent leaders of the abolition and temperance and suffrage movements, most notably Rev. Henry Ward Beecher, William Lloyd Garrison, and Oliver Otis Howard.[65] Bradbury, in his official appointment as "Director-General of Music" for the voyage, conducted onboard singing as the ship headed south. During the excursion, he taught passengers his newest patriotic song, "Victory at Last," eventually published in the popular sheet music format.[66] As recalled by Justus C. French and Edward Cary, *Oceanus* passengers sang this latest composition of Bradbury's "with a vociferous effect, which might almost have been heard on shore. This song became one of the indispensable spiceries" of the voyage.[67]

To accommodate spectators at the Fort Sumter event, the US government provided seating for some 3,000 guests.[68] Bradbury led a military band and conducted the huge throng in the singing of patriotic tunes, including his enormously popular song "Rally Around the Flag."[69] An officially appointed photographer captured the scene as the American flag rose slowly on its halyard (figure 1.5).

As the *Oceanus* made her way from Charleston back to New York, passengers received tragic news "from a signal message given us by a southbound steamer, of the assassination of President Lincoln!"[70] The assassination occurred during the evening of April 14, 1865, hours after the flag ceremony at Fort Sumter.

Final Years

The excursion to Charleston proved inordinately taxing for Bradbury. Beginning in late 1865, his health declined, and doctors soon determined

Figure 1.5. Flag-raising ceremony, Fort Sumter, Charleston, South Carolina, from a stereograph, April 14, 1865. Bradbury is most likely the tall figure in the center of the image, dressed in light-colored attire, his back to the photographer as he stands on a podium and conducts. Civil War photographs, 1861–1865, Library of Congress, Prints and Photographs Division.

he was suffering from tuberculosis. His illness forced him to greatly reduce touring and spend increasing amounts of time resting at his Bloomfield, New Jersey, estate rather than attending to business affairs in New York or touring frequently.[71] Journalists initially painted a grim picture of his prognosis: "[S]ome of the papers have been mentioning that our esteemed friend, William B. Bradbury . . . who has for some time past been lying ill at his residence . . . is about to die."[72] A determined Bradbury responded to this remark with what one paper referred to as a "characteristic note": "I am not going to die, yet; but live, get well and work." The press added, of Bradbury's retort: "That sounds just like him!"[73]

Bradbury sought medical care and rest in neighboring Montclair, New Jersey, at the town's Mountain House. A fashionable, if small, resort residence, the Mountain House location was famous for its "health and salubrity of atmosphere and beauty of mountain scenery [that] is not surpassed by any in the country."[74] Bradbury's frail health became particularly noticeable at a commemorative event given at the Mountain House in his honor:

> On a beautiful Sabbath in June [June 16, 1866], at nine o'clock in the morning, the [students and faculty of Montclair's Caldwell Presbyterian Church Sunday] school assembled at the church, and, after forming in line, headed by the superintendent [Bradbury's friend Philip Henry Doremus], marched in procession to the Mountain House, where Mr. Bradbury was then boarding. He was seated in an invalid [wheel]chair in one end of the large parlor. The school formed in a circle about him and sang several choice selections from his collection of Sunday-school hymns. The children then passed in single file as they left the room, each one presenting him with a bouquet with their best wishes. It was a touching scene, which left its impress on the hearts of the children while . . . [Bradbury] shed tears of joy and gladness.[75]

The *Newark Daily Advertiser* remarked on Bradbury's weakened condition at this event and added, "[H]e attempted to speak but was overcome with emotion, and his voice was too feeble for utterance."[76]

Not surprisingly, given Bradbury's precarious health, residency at the Mountain House failed to offer substantial improvement. In pursuit of respite from illness, he left the damp climate of New Jersey in the fall of 1866 and sought out the purported benefits of less humid weather in a more northern location. He traveled to Minnesota, a state that, at the time, attracted those suffering from tuberculosis owing to the region's cool, dry air, profusion of mineral water springs, and abundance of therapeutic sulfur mud baths. The Minnesota press boasted, "As a resort for invalids, particularly the consumptive [tuberculosis patients], the clear dry days, with the pure air and water of this State, have made it a famous resort for the searcher after health."[77] According to another newspaper, "[E]ven a Minnesota winter is beneficial to consumptives."[78]

A journalist for the *St. Paul Daily Press* welcomed Bradbury: "I learn with pleasure that Mr. Wm. B. Bradbury has taken up his abode with one of our citizens, and will remain till next spring. It is the earnest wish of all that he may find in our restoring climate a new and healthful vitality."[79] His energy already sapped by the ravages of illness, Bradbury seldom made public appearances while in Minnesota. Nonetheless, he agreed to perform at a couple of events, including one in November 1866 at which he sang a selection of his most recent compositions.[80] The press cautioned that his plans to teach a children's singing class, culminating in a Christmas day concert, would take place only "if his health will permit."[81] Apparently, Bradbury's rapidly weakening condition prevented him from conducting these holiday festivities as no press account of such an event has been located. Rather than remaining in Minnesota until spring of 1867, as originally planned, he returned to New Jersey toward the end of December 1866.

Not unexpectedly, Bradbury's visit to Minnesota failed to produce a lasting remission from tuberculosis. After his return to New Jersey, he decided to withdraw from his business activities in New York. F. C. Smith bought out Bradbury's portion of his piano firm in 1867, but per legal agreement, retained the Bradbury name. The New York *Independent* expressed cautious optimism about this decision, hoping that "once relieved of the pressing cares of [his piano] business," Bradbury would be able to repel, at least for a time, "the inroads of disease."[82]

With the arrival of spring in 1867, Bradbury's health apparently improved for a short time.[83] However, this temporary respite gave way to a rapid decline in his condition. Nonetheless, he managed to complete one final tunebook, *Fresh Laurels*, issued in August 1867. He worked at a rapid pace, an effort a Minnesota newspaper claimed "aggravated the pulmonary disease under which he was laboring."[84] Shortly after the book's appearance, another journalist reported, "Of his latest work, *Fresh Laurels* . . . it is remarked that the state of his health during its compilation must have influenced the sentiment of many of the pieces in it. It exhibits evidence of the conviction that [he knew] it would be his last work."[85] Some singers found the content of *Fresh Laurels* to be more challenging to learn than the music of his previous tunebooks. Bradbury offered this reassurance to amateur singers regarding the accessibility of these latest pieces: "Is the music too difficult? We assure you it is not. There is such a variety of pieces so easy and simple . . . that no fault will be found on this score; while, at the same time, we have inserted a number of [selections of] a higher musical order."[86] The publishing firm of Biglow & Main eventually claimed sales of an astounding 1,300,000 copies of *Fresh Laurels*.[87]

Bradbury's friend T. F. Seward recalled a typical day in the final weeks of his life: "Having partaken of a light lunch, if the weather was at all favorable,

Figure 1.6. William B. Bradbury, ca. 1866. Library Company of Philadelphia.

he very frequently ordered his carriage for a long ride." As Seward further elaborated, "[H]ere is an illustration of his peculiar constitution and temperament. There were many times for months before he died when any casual observer, seeing his great exhaustion and complete prostration after slight effort, would suppose it impossible that he could survive a day, yet the power of endurance behind that excessive weakness was something marvelous."[88] Seward admired Bradbury's determination to prevail even when doing so imposed considerable stress and eventual exhaustion: "There was rarely, if, indeed, there has ever been a time in his life when he was not habitually overtaxing his powers."[89] (For a likeness of Bradbury created toward the end of his life, see figure 1.6).

Bradbury died peacefully on January 7, 1868, at his New Jersey estate, surrounded by family and friends. Notices of his death appeared in newspapers throughout the country.[90]

Reminiscences of Bradbury

Few descriptions from friends and associates of Bradbury's personality and physical appearance survive. A writer for the *Musical Visitor* offered this description of Bradbury's physique and demeanor: "He was nearly six feet in height, and his unusually red hair and blue spectacles always made him a conspicuous figure.... He was of an unusually pleasant disposition, [and] the idol of his child pupils."[91] Simeon Pease Cheney recalled of his friend:

> [H]e was an active, ardent, sensitive man, of rather slim form, common height and sandy complexion.... Mr. Bradbury was a self-reliant and determined man. He was ambitious to the last degree, a brave, heroic worker, and of unsurpassed industry and endurance. Being a nervous man, he was, of course at times, irritable; but he was really kind and tender-hearted. A few weeks before his death he said to a friend [T. F. Seward], "I long to be free from this evil body which does so much to drag me down. This busy brain and hasty nature lead me oftentimes to things that are contrary to the real feelings of my heart."[92]

A correspondent for the Cincinnati *Commercial* described Bradbury as,

> like a true Yankee, rather slim; a large mouth, in opening he displays a fine assortment of pearly teeth; sharp eyes, which look through gold-mounted spectacles; hair and whiskers fiery red—the former erect "like quills," &c., the latter being rationally permitted to extend to the natural limit—a fancy the Professor no doubt contracted while a musical student in Germany. Another Teutonic feature is the long-stemmed meerschaum, which is always near at hand.[93]

Thomas Hastings remembered Bradbury as "full of vitality," adding, "he struggled grandly to master his spirit and keep control" whenever he "exhibited impatience."[94]

Closing Thoughts

Bradbury's accomplishments bore the stamp of Yankee ingenuity associated with the resourcefulness and ambition of his New England forebears and contemporaries. As a businessman, Bradbury seized opportunities and circumstances and plied them into considerable financial reward. What music journalist and critic John S. Dwight belittled as his accumulation of "a mass amount of hay while the sun shines" actually served as a model for eclectic and enterprising musical entrepreneurship.[95] Bradbury responded astutely to the sentiments and tastes of his time and his publications outsold those of most of his competitors. I devote the next chapter to the composition and early performances of what became his most celebrated piece, *Esther, the Beautiful Queen*.

CHAPTER TWO

ESTHER
The Early Years

Bradbury composed *Esther, the Beautiful Queen* in 1856. He set a text based on the biblical Book of Esther, assembled by his friend Chauncey Marvin Cady (1824–1889).[1] The two men met in 1852 and enjoyed a close association, as fondly recalled by Cady:

> Though totally unlike him in many respects and often differing with him in business matters, we were drawn together by a sort of boon companionship—half work, half play—that made us intimate till his death. When I was in New York, he was always inventing excuses to get me over to his country residence in Bloomfield, N.J., and I was as fertile in inventing excuses to go. He had always new manuscripts to show me, plans for new [tune]books to talk about, a glee to which he wished me to help him adapt words, a cantata to block out, or some good German verses for me to turn into bad English. And I was always made to feel so thoroughly at home by his charming wife and children, and was always so sure of having a good time that I would rarely refuse to go, even when other duties called me elsewhere.[2]

Bradbury wrote hastily and completed nearly all of the *Esther* score in a mere five days. Cady offered this account of their collaboration:

> In the summer of 1856 he [Bradbury] wanted me to help him lay out the plot and adapt the words of a cantata [based] upon some Bible subject . . . . [The Book of] Esther, we agreed, was susceptible to some rare dramatic effects . . . . We had settled upon the general plan of the plot and the opening chorus was written, when, to escape all interruption, we . . . sought out a secluded boarding house . . . borrowed a portable melodeon [figure 2.1] . . . put it in our room and went to work. We rose at daylight each morning, and worked till breakfast, I upon the selection and arrangement of the words, and he com-

Figure 2.1. Portable Melodeon. The decorative horizontal brace at the bottom of the instrument was removable and the lyre-style legs and pedal mechanism folded under the keyboard cabinet for easy moving. *Mason and Hamlin's Cabinet Organs and Melodeons* (Boston, 1863), 23.

posing the music. After breakfast we worked on till dinner. Sometimes my words decided the rhythm of his music and sometimes he would get ahead of me, and block out an air [melody] or chorus to which I measured off and tried on the words again for about two hours . . . . After tea we resumed our work which we kept up till about eleven o'clock [p.m.]. This programme we followed from day to day till Saturday noon, when it was time for us to take the train back to New York and the "cantata of Esther, the Beautiful Queen" was finished, except the manual labor of writing out a chorus or two . . . . Those who know how long it takes to sing it [*Esther*] entirely [through] will realize something of the rapidity with which Mr. Bradbury had to work in order to compose all but the first chorus in four days.[3]

Like Bradbury, Cady composed hymns and parlor songs and also directed musical conventions. In addition, he contributed numerous articles to newspapers and music periodicals, and he served as editor of the journal *Musical Review and Choral Advocate*. Several prominent musicians contributed items to this periodical, especially members of Lowell Mason's circle. Cady also collaborated in the production of tunebooks and assembled lyrics for many vocal works. Shortly after the completion of *Esther*, he moved to Chicago and taught at the city's Normal Musical Institute, a school for teacher training. He and Ebenezer Towner Root (1822–1896), brother of George F. Root, founded the publishing firm of Root and Cady in December 1858. The firm soon became one of the leading music dealers and publishers in the United States, most notably during the Civil War era. In October 1871, the Great Chicago Fire destroyed most of the company's infrastructure and merchandise—a loss from which the firm never recovered.[4] Subsequently, Cady relocated to Ohio and studied at the Oberlin College School of Theology. He then joined the Oberlin Band, a group of Oberlin College affiliates who, as missionaries, taught in Asia. For most of his remaining years, he resided in China and Japan.[5]

Esther's Plot

Bradbury organized the *Esther* score as an oratorio-like composition with distinct sections labeled "Part I" and "Part II." The work features a substantial dramatis personae consisting of choruses, ensembles, and solo parts. Two large choruses, one representing the Jews in the Book of Esther, the other comprised of Persians and Medians, function as crowds that comment on or reinforce crucial events in the narrative. The score also calls for twelve soloists who depict characters in Cady's version of the biblical Esther narrative, as listed below.

Esther the Queen—soprano
Ahasuerus, King of Persia and Media—bass
Haman, Overseer of the Realm—baritone
Zeresh, Haman's Wife—alto
Mordecai—tenor
Queen's First Maid of Honor—soprano
Hegai—bass [eunuch who oversees the king's harem]
High Priest—baritone
Zeresh's Maid of Honor—alto
Harbonah—tenor or baritone [another of the king's eunuchs]
Messenger—reader
Prophet [or Prophetess]

Cady relied on the Book of Esther for most of his lyrics and supplemented these with a few of his own lines along with brief passages from Isaiah, Jeremiah, Lamentations, and the Psalms. Bradbury appended another well-known version of the Esther story to the published score—the essay "Concerning Esther, and Mordecai, and Haman," written by first-century historian Flavius Josephus.[6] Although nearly 6,700 words in length, this essay nonetheless sometimes appeared in printed programs distributed at performances of *Esther*. Bradbury did not set any of Josephus's prose to music, but he considered its inclusion in his score to be important enough to justify the considerable expense of additional paper and printing costs. For, as he wrote, "Josephus's account of Esther is so full and complete, that it will very much enhance the interest of the piece."[7]

Cady's version of the Esther narrative differs, at times, from the account in the Hebrew Testament. To begin with, Cady includes God in his text, whereas God is not mentioned in the Book of Esther. Additionally, Cady omitted the verses chronicling the unfortunate circumstances that befell Vashti and led to her disappearance. Instead, the Messenger opens Part I with passages read from the Book of Esther summarizing events that occur after Vashti's dismissal (Esther 2:16–18 and 3:1–2). These verses introduce Esther and establish Haman as a noble recently elevated in rank above all other court officials.[8] A chorus follows in which Persians and Medians honor Haman at Ahasuerus's command, with obsequious jubilation. This celebratory mood quickly gives way to a solo by Haman who draws attention to Mordecai's refusal to bow and obey the king. By way of explanation for this purported insolence, Haman reveals Mordecai's identity as that of a "despised" Jew. In a subsequent solo, Haman reminds Ahasuerus that Mordecai's behavior typifies that of all Jews, none of whom observes the laws of the kingdom. The Messenger then introduces Haman's proposed solution to the problem of supposed Jewish disobedience—the annihilation of all the Jews in the king's realm. After agreeing on their genocidal plan, Ahasuerus and Haman celebrate with a joyous duet punctuated by outbursts of laughter. A Jewish Prophet then sings a poignant solo, warning the Jews of the destructive plot hatched by Haman and the king. Mordecai, privy to the details of their plan, laments his fate and that of the Jews. He begs Queen Esther, his Jewish niece, to "go thou unto the king" and petition for the lives of their people to be spared. She agrees to do so, but with evident trepidation. At this point in the narrative, Ahasuerus remains unaware of Esther's relationship to Mordecai or her Jewish identity. Esther reminds Mordecai that anyone—even the queen—who dares approach the king unbidden faces certain death. Accordingly, she sings her famous words: "I'll go unto the King, tho' not according to the law! And if I perish, I perish" (Esther 4:15). Terrified of the potential outcome of her promise to confront Ahasuerus, Esther asks Mordecai to summon all the Jews and join with them in prayer and fasting. In compliance, Mordecai and the chorus of Jews reverently sing the words "to thee, O Lord, we raise our cries" (based on Psalm 28).

Bradbury did not provide music for the dramatic encounter of Esther and the king, and instead, the Messenger declaims verses from Esther 5:1–3, summarizing this event. When Esther meets with the king, she barely hints at the existence of a petition she would like to present to him and thus sidesteps the subject of the proposed massacre of the Jews. Instead, she invites the king to a banquet prepared expressly for him and Haman. The king and Esther conclude this exchange with a duet in which they bestow lavish praise upon one another. At the conclusion of the duet, a chorus of Persians and Medians lauds Haman and enthusiastically anticipates the queen's banquet. In a sudden change of mood, a disgruntled Haman complains that no edict has been issued ordering the annihilation of the Jews and thus Mordecai still lingers at court. Haman's wife, Zeresh, proposes that Mordecai be executed by hanging "on a gallows fifty cubits high," and she urges her husband to take this idea to the king. Her solo and subsequent chorus conclude Part I.

A chorus of Jews in prayer opens Part II with text taken from Psalm 46. As insomnia plagues the king that night, he orders a member of the palace entourage to pass the time by reading to him the court's "book of records" containing all royal edicts and events. These readings include a communication from Mordecai in which he accuses two court chamberlains of plotting to harm the king (Esther 6:1–2). The next morning, Ahasuerus asks of Haman, "What shall be done unto the man whom the king delighteth to honor?" Haman assumes the king intends to pay tribute to him. However, the choruses suggest Mordecai as the eventual recipient of the king's magnanimity owing to his warning about the chamberlains' traitorous plot. The matter remains unresolved, and text spoken by the Messenger (Esther 6:14 and 7:11) announces Esther's banquet. (Cady includes only one banquet in his text, whereas the Book of Esther contains several such celebrations.) In the duet and chorus that follow, the king and Haman join in their praise of Esther. At the conclusion of the banquet, the king asks Esther to state her petition. She reveals her Jewish identity and pleads for the lives of her people to be spared. The king grants her request and asks who had ordered the annihilation of the Jews. Esther identifies Haman as the person responsible for the proposed genocide. Harbonah draws the king's attention to a nearby gallows, erected by Haman for the purpose of executing Mordecai. The king gives orders to execute Haman instead on the same gallows. Ahasuerus then proclaims, "Mordecai the great . . . shall wear the seals of state" (Esther 7:2–7). A quartet follows ("Do I Wake or Am I Dreaming?"), sung by Hegai, the Queen's First Maid of Honor, Zeresh, and Mordecai. These characters reflect upon their fate: Zeresh expresses mournful resignation and defeat, while the other three contemplate the triumph of Esther and the Jews. At this point, Cady's text bypasses the biblical narrative as the conclusion of *Esther* does not include the vengeful slaughter of Persians and Medians by the Jews. Instead, the work ends in a spirited and reverent Finale celebrating the redemption of the Jews with all voices joining in a contrapuntal setting of Psalms 100 and 150.

The *Esther* Score

Bradbury published *Esther* simultaneously in New York with Mason Brothers and in Boston with Oliver Ditson.[9] As he announced, the first copies of his score became available in late summer of 1856: "I shall issue, early in September, a new cantata entitled 'Esther, the Beautiful Queen.'"[10] The bound score resembled a small tunebook with a soft cover and pages of inexpensive paper.[11] In keeping with the practices of many nineteenth-century tunebook compilers, Bradbury arranged most of the score in TASB order—tenor-alto-soprano-bass—rather than in the more familiar configuration of SATB. This arrangement of voices had been commonplace in the United States since the later eighteenth century.[12] In addition, nearly all of *Esther*'s choral numbers do not include accompaniments, although the work was seldom, if ever, performed a cappella. In fact, Bradbury provided only incomplete accompaniments or none at all in twenty of the piece's twenty-nine numbers. Unlike most European composers, especially those of the Baroque era, Bradbury did not incorporate figured bass symbols beneath the score as might ordinarily be expected by keyboardists who relied on such symbols as a guide for improvisation. Instead, keyboardists of Bradbury's era created accompaniments for many works scored in TASB configuration by using the adjacent soprano and bass voices as a guide for realization. He employed the same organization in many of his tunebooks and offered this explanation for its utility:

> For the convenience of pianists . . . we have arranged the parts so as to have the Soprano and Bass staves together. The Alto is next above the Soprano, and the Tenor is on the upper staff, as in church music [hymns and Psalm tunes]. This arrangement . . . is not according to the organization of the human voice, hence not philosophical, but custom and the convenience of many of our young pianists, have seemed, as in church music, to render it necessary. We adopt it as a matter of expediency.[13]

Even though Bradbury did not supply figured bass symbols in *Esther*, he expressed confidence that keyboardists and singers would consider music printed in TASB order to be quite approachable. *Esther*'s uncomplicated harmonies rendered the process of improvisation very accessible. He first employed this scoring arrangement during his association with Thomas Hastings and their collaboration on tunebook projects. According to Hastings, TASB scoring and its customarily diatonic harmonies—often primary chords in root position—obviated the need for figured bass symbols. He stated that the proximity of soprano and bass voices readily suggested "combinations and successions in harmony" of considerable aid to accompanists.[14] Lowell Mason further reinforced Bradbury's allegiance to TASB scoring and an absence of figured bass symbols with his insistence that keyboardists should "accustom themselves . . . to play from the four parts or vocal score; we can assure them that this manner of playing is the only true one."[15]

Beyond a lack of accompaniments in much of *Esther*, Bradbury also relied on other notational shortcuts to save paper and printing costs. In several places in the score, he omitted transitional passages. Such transitions, he presumed, could readily be extemporized by a competent keyboardist. For example, Part I, no. 5, and Part II, no. 14, contain incomplete measures as the last beat of one passage simultaneously functioned as an anacrusis to a subsequent section, notated in a different meter. The resultant incongruity and awkwardness of rhythm and meter could only be remedied with an improvised interlude. Another space-saving strategy involved the use of repeat signs without first and second endings. These notational omissions required a keyboard accompanist to improvise transitions between seemingly disjunct sections or to create first and second endings.

Musical Example 2.1. Bradbury, *Esther*, "Go Thou Merrily" (Part I, no. 14), final eight measures, showing accompaniment cues. In this excerpt, the choruses and Zeresh urge Haman to make "haste" and "go thou merrily unto the king" in order to expedite Mordecai's execution.

In a few numbers, Bradbury supplied prose directions as a substitute for written-out music, or he inserted cues. For example, in Part I, no. 2, his directions read: "[I]nstrument playing chorus [parts] for an accompaniment." In Part I, no. 8, he instructed the keyboardist to "play [the first] eight measures as a symphony," and thus an introduction to this number had to be created based on the subsequent choral parts. Additionally, he sometimes added notated cues to suggest an outline for improvisation. For example, the accompaniment cues might appear in the soprano and bass voices, as shown in musical example 2.1.

Or, in other instances, one of the voices, combined with prose instructions, could be used as a guide, as shown in musical example 2.2, where Bradbury provided a left-hand accompaniment and directed the keyboardist to "play also the Melody in Octaves" in the right hand.

Bradbury intended the numbers scored for solo voice or small ensembles to be performed by more experienced singers. These numbers included written-out accompaniments with relatively little duplication of vocal pitches as, presumably, more seasoned vocalists would not have needed an accompanist to double their notes. In contrast, he notated the numbers requiring improvised accompaniments such that considerable doubling of the voice parts could occur if needed, and this feature certainly benefited novice singers. Many reviews of performances of *Esther* document this sort of fluidity, variability, and improvisational nature of portions of the work. Bradbury did not specify what instrument(s) should be used for accompaniments and conductors often employed only a single keyboard instrument such as

Musical Example 2.2. Bradbury, *Esther*, opening measures, "A Song of Joy" (Part I, no. 5) showing cued accompaniment along with prose instructions that read: "Accompaniment—Play Also the Melody in Octaves."

a melodeon. For example, in performances in 1871 sung by the Fisk Jubilee Singers, accompanist Ella Shepard (1851–1914) "presided at the [small portable cabinet] organ, played with true artistic touch, showing consummate skill and taste, as well as a thorough knowledge of musical rules, as to [harmonic] progressions or modulations ... improvising [in a] correct and tasteful [manner]."[16] It seems fair to assume that the writer of this review was familiar with Bradbury's score and the need to extemporize most of the work's accompaniments. Yet rather than utilizing only a keyboard instrument, some conductors engaged a small ensemble of local musicians who managed to read from Bradbury's imprecisely notated score. Just such an ad hoc ensemble accompanied singers in a New Orleans performance in 1859, as noted by the local press: "[T]he accompaniments ... were given by a melodeon, a pianoforte and a stringed quartet."[17]

The more traditional formal scheme associated with oratorios and cantatas usually relied on recitatives to further plot development or to heighten a sense of drama. Yet Bradbury did not include recitatives in *Esther* and instead inserted solo chant or spoken passages as a means of clarifying the narrative. For *Esther*'s five chant numbers (Part I, nos. 3, 4, 11, and Part II, nos. 2, 12), he used sparse notation of mostly half and whole notes to be performed arhythmically with many words intoned on one pitch (musical example 2.3).

As mentioned above, excerpts from the Bible appear in several places in the score. Bradbury's instructions called for either "a clergyman" to recite

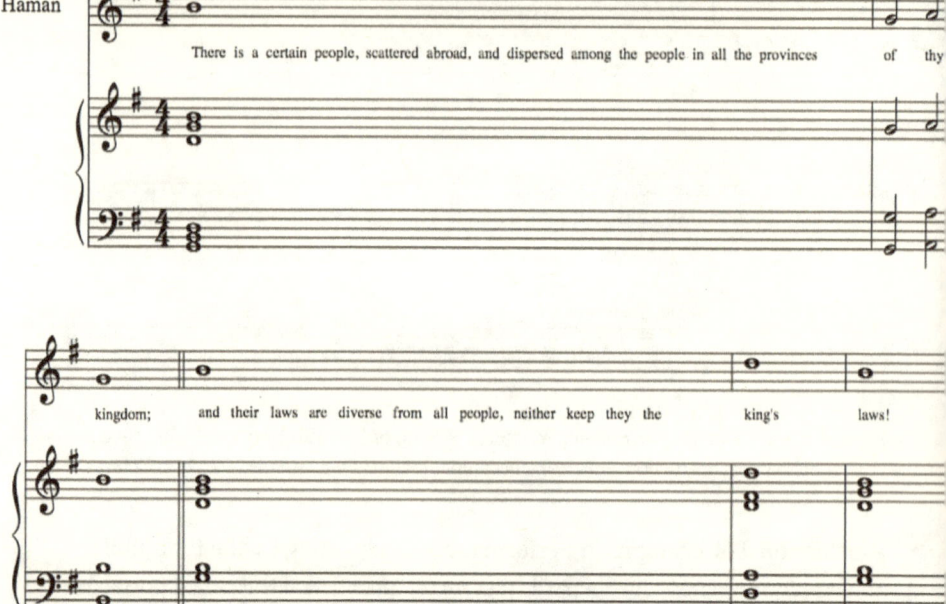

Musical Example 2.3. Bradbury, *Esther*, "There Is a Certain People" (Part I, no. 3), mm. 1–6. Transcribed from the original with Bradbury's notational scheme retained.

these passages "from the pulpit" or for the conductor to "select the best reader" available for this role, designated as the "Messenger." The verses selected by Cady for the Messenger to declaim operate similarly to traditional recitatives by summarizing plot events, furthering narrative development and establishing the status of principal characters. One of the earliest extended reviews of *Esther* offered astute observations about the work's lack of recitatives:

> The appropriate office of music is to express emotion; but in every musicodramatic work, narration is found necessary to connect the links of emotion and render the production complete and symmetrical. The problem is, in what form to give this narration. Generally, it has been the custom to employ recitative, a hybrid between melody and declamation. The objection to this is that recitative is dry, constrained and poky, even if sung well. When, therefore, we consider how really few good singers can render a recitative well, its use in a work of popular design is fraught with grave objections. In this work [*Esther*] the difficulty is avoided by having the narrative parts read by a

clergyman or some other person of elocutional culture. *Esther, the Beautiful Queen* has now been performed several times in different parts of the country, and it may console fossil critics to be informed that so far as we can learn, this feature promises to work well. Aside from this, the general features of this production do not differ from others of a similar design.[18]

ESTHER AND MUSIC EDUCATION

Esther initially became known to the US public as an instructional piece. As musicologist Richard Crawford observes, the rise of music education in the United States offers the most viable context with which to evaluate the style and purpose of music written and disseminated by many nineteenth-century American composers. Unlike their European counterparts, Bradbury and the Mason circle created much of their music expressly for pedagogical purposes, worship services, and for community participation and enjoyment. Bradbury became what Crawford describes as one in

> a roster of American musicians who charted their own path to musical achievement, not by following rules laid down by Europeans, but by ceaselessly, even heroically, exploring their own talents and gifts . . . . The musical value that seems to have concerned them most was how well their music fit the tastes of the people for whom it was written . . . . Their musical rhetoric was certainly not ours, and the music they composed may not please our tastes. But they had a hand in shaping our legacy, and some of their assumptions and goals survive.[19]

Bradbury announced his educational purpose for *Esther* in the score's subtitle: "designed for musical conventions, festivals and music societies." Thus, the earliest phase of *Esther*'s reception history should be viewed through the lens of the nascent music education movement, especially as Bradbury himself first conducted the work as the culmination of a series of singing classes he offered at innumerable communities. Under Bradbury's careful guidance, *Esther* presented students with opportunities to hone their skills in music reading, choral singing, and musical expressivity. Furthermore, the *Esther* score introduced singers to the intricacies and challenges associated with an extended multimovement work. Audiences at performances of *Esther*, particularly those in rural locales, were also exposed to this type of music, often for the first time. In keeping with his commitment to universal music teaching and learning, Bradbury wrote *Esther* for singers of varied ages and abilities. By including solos in his score, he accommodated more experienced singers while never compromising his belief that music instruction should embrace communal learning and group participation as much as possible.

Until the late 1830s, most US music teachers relied on rote learning, considerable repetition, and imitative methods to teach singing. The acquisition of an ability to read standard music notation was not necessarily considered an essential outcome of instruction during this era. Therefore, a sizeable percentage of US church attendees often found it prohibitively difficult to navigate their way through a hymn tune scored in standard notation. This situation did not go unnoticed by newspaper critics, one of whom grumbled that "half of our congregational singing is not worthy of the name.... As for congregational singing itself, it is feeble, faint and a good deal of it, the sing-by-proxy order."[20] To address this deficiency, Bradbury and many of his contemporaries sought ways to improve singing in churches. Through their efforts, music education and singing began to serve interconnected social, expressive, and religious functions. Bradbury's introduction to this innovative tripartite purpose for teaching and learning occurred during his student years at the Boston Academy of Music. *Esther* became the score Bradbury often relied upon to fulfill his instructional objectives.

Bradbury believed that music teaching and learning should be morally elevating and beneficial for all involved with an emphasis on "simplicity and progressiveness, but also pleasure."[21] He carefully crafted his classroom comments to convey a sense of optimism and confidence to his students, however mediocre their singing or infinitesimal their progress. Staunchly opposed to what he characterized as the "old fogey school" of education, Bradbury disparaged the continued presence of music teachers who ignored "modern innovations" and failed to impart thoroughly reasoned and "friendly criticism" to their students. Such teachers disregarded the ultimate humanistic, moral, and spiritual goals of teaching and perpetuated what he referred to as an "unpleasant state of feeling" in their classrooms.[22] Additionally, he developed an expedient and efficient teaching style and he asserted that "a good practical knowledge of the art of singing" should be attainable "in the shortest possible space of time."[23] Careful management of singing classes became a signature of his pedagogy, and he advised teachers to "lose no time in needless talk."[24] He confidently stated, "[I]n a lesson of one hour, the beginner is astonished and delighted to find how *easy it is to sing by note* [i.e., by reading standard music notation] [italics original]."[25] As one of his students recalled, "his power of drill was remarkable," and he could "prepare a thousand children for a concert in a few evenings. We have seen him enter a new adult class, hear them sing, pleasantly point out their errors, and in one hour seem to accomplish the work of a month of evenings. His manner on these occasions was singularly kind, persuasive, assuring."[26] Bradbury democratized instruction by prioritizing group learning, thereby encouraging a sense of belonging and collective responsibility and accomplishment among all those present. His teaching strategies must have remained fluid and subject to immediate alteration as he undoubtedly depended on his skill at error detection rather than doggedly adhering to a predetermined and inflexible sequence of lessons. He also relied on active learning as his students participated in the skills being taught and produced desired results themselves rather than remaining passive recipients of knowledge imparted by a teacher. Bradbury's oratorio for young singers, *Flora's Festival*, exemplified this philosophical principle. Not only did this work serve as a unique and innovative vehicle for teaching large groups of children, but it also engaged them in motion and gesture while singing.

In addition to teaching hymns and religious pieces, Bradbury found commensurate instructional opportunities in secular music such as parlor ballads, patriotic songs, and arrangements of opera and oratorio arias. He pioneered the use of mountain or Alpine songs and folk melodies as teaching repertoire, and attributes of these styles can be detected in his *Esther* score. As mentioned earlier, he introduced specialized teaching repertoire appropriate for children. In *Esther*, he occasionally called for "treble" or young voices and encouraged children to sing in the numbers written for mixed choruses.[27] He took advantage of the cross-disciplinary potential inherent in music teaching, and accordingly, set didactic lyrics for some of his children's songs. Many of his lyrics reinforced spelling skills, enhanced vocabulary building, and instilled the meaning of numbers and arithmetic functions along with words that valorized patriotism and nature's beauty. The text of *Esther* provided lessons in moral conduct of particular significance to Bradbury and his circle, namely, the offices of righteous conduct, the evils of despotism, and the virtue of courage and determination in the face of overwhelming adversity.

Bradbury employed a method of teaching notation using vocables or pitch names rather than the actual lyrics of a piece. The use of vocables also aided singers as they learned rhythmic configurations and the intricacies of meter.[28] Yet Bradbury and Cady did not employ vocables solely as isolated teaching devices, and in fact, they can be found in several places within the *Esther* score, most noticeably where choral voices themselves supply a vocal accompaniment for a solo passage by intoning pitches on the syllable "la" (in particular, Part I, no. 14). Thus, Bradbury's students came to appreciate singing with vocables not as a rather meaningless exercise, as they actually employed the same skill when performing certain passages in *Esther*. The use of vocables in *Esther* also served a very practical purpose. When singers, especially children, were occupied with vocables, they did not have to remain idle for long periods of time and therefore they could better attend to, and concentrate on, the ongoing music rehearsal or performance.

Bradbury also scored *Esther* in ways that enabled amateur singers to execute dynamics and other expressive elements. To ensure the clarity of choral portions of the work, he arranged the voices in mostly homophonic texture, often in syllabic settings, supported by accessible harmonies. He organized choral numbers such that no single group or section of a chorus could dominate at the expense of clear execution of melody or rhythm. In this way, the accurate enunciation of lyrics and performance of attendant dynamics became collective responsibilities as voice motion inevitably followed the rhythm of words.[29]

Bradbury conceived *Esther*'s notational scheme with music teaching and learning in the forefront of his mind. The TASB configuration found in most of *Esther*'s choral numbers provided keyboardists with opportunities to improve their skills as improvisers and to learn efficient and effective strategies for working with amateur singers. Yet as an experienced pianist and church organist, Bradbury also valued the assistance of a consummate keyboard accompanist when he taught, rehearsed, and performed *Esther*. Undoubtedly, he fulfilled this role himself on many occasions. Through his years of teaching, Bradbury came to realize the importance of skillfully improvised introductions to *Esther*'s choral sections as these extemporized passages allowed singers to recall, in their mind's ear, the pitches and rhythms of each number before singing them. Novices could rely on pitch doublings from an accompaniment as they strove to learn more challenging melodic intervals. Additionally, Bradbury's use of adjacent soprano and bass voices helped singers appreciate the harmonic foundation of music and its significance. He taught fundamental concepts of harmony in his classes, and he believed that familiarity with this dimension of music helped improve intonation and ensemble cohesion.[30]

Musical Conventions

Beginning in the early 1850s, Bradbury promoted his pedagogical methods and taught instructional pieces, especially *Esther*, at the innumerable musical conventions he organized. He rapidly earned a reputation as a competent, dedicated and charismatic convention director and his expertise was widely sought. A review of a convention in Ravenna, Ohio, documents Bradbury's extraordinary popularity among communities and convention attendees:

> Permit me to say that the Music Teachers, Ministers, Choristers and lovers of sacred song, who failed to attend the great Musical Convention, which just came off in this village, have suffered no small loss. For four successive days, the old Court House has resounded to graceful melodies and chaste harmonies. The master spirit of the occasion has been Prof. Wm. B. Bradbury, of New York. To those who have had the good fortune to meet him it is unnecessary to say that in addition to native genius and indefatigable industry and profound musical attainments, Prof. B. possesses in an eminent degree that peculiar tact and electrifying enthusiasm which are indispensable to success in teaching. The Convention has passed off most delightfully, and its influence cannot fail to prove most happy. Prof. B. may know that he has not only won many warm personal friends among us; but in the judgment of all has done much to awaken an interest, raise the standard of musical taste, and promote more correct musical execution.[31]

The musical ability of convention attendees varied widely and often presented challenges to teachers, even those of considerable skill and knowledge. By the time *Esther* was published, Bradbury had already taught for some fifteen years and had codified, in his tunebook prefaces, a method of teaching music, literacy, and singing to large groups. He dedicated the opening lessons of conventions to exercises in vocal technique, rhythm, meter, and diction, thereby reinforcing and further developing the musical abilities of his students. Yet even as he promoted his instructional purpose for *Esther*, the score did not include any prefatory lessons in music reading or singing techniques.[32] We can assume, therefore, that he improvised convention activities based substantially on exercises he created, spontaneously, from the music of *Esther* and other works. Announcements in newspapers and widely read music periodicals alerted readers to his intention to teach and conduct *Esther* at conventions. He set a most desirable and enticing outcome for prospective convention attendees as they could look forward to performing a large-scale work in its entirety before an audience. Quite often, Bradbury selected *Esther* for these closing programs.[33]

Bradbury's conventions earned him glowing reviews throughout the 1850s and early 1860s. An aspiring Long Island, New York, singer offered this assessment of his community classes: "We are trying to improve ourselves in music. And we had heard of such things as Musical Conventions, and that there was a man called Prof. Wm. B. Bradbury, and some folks said they'd seen him and said *he was a rouser* [italics original]."[34] Rural communities in the Midwest also expressed considerable enthusiasm for Bradbury's conventions, as confirmed in this review:

> Mr. B's invitations to [conduct conventions in] different sections of the West have become so numerous of late that he finds it impossible to accept more than one-half of them. On his way to this place [Chillicothe, Ohio] he stopped in Livingston [C]ounty, NY, and in Ashtabula [C]ounty, Ohio, at each of which places he met [taught] classes of two hundred members. He goes hence to Illinois, Wisconsin and Michigan. His terms are only fifty dollars a day.[35]

A couple of points made by the reviewer just quoted would benefit from contextualization. First, by the descriptive term "West," the writer referenced any location east of the Rocky Mountains. Second, Bradbury's "terms" of "only fifty dollars a day" actually represented a substantial sum in the 1850s.

Bradbury's ambitious traveling itineraries took him to numerous communities in the eastern half of the United States, and announcements for his proposed conventions appeared in countless newspapers and periodicals. For example, one such announcement indicated, "Mr. Bradbury will hold conventions as follows: at Garrettsville, NY, commencing Sept. 23; Montrose, PA, commencing Sept. 30; Greenport, LI [Long Island, New York], commencing Oct. 8; Burlington, IA, commencing Oct. 15; others will be duly announced." To this ambitious itinerary Bradbury added, "I intend to spend the month of October, and perhaps part of November, at the West, in the vicinity of Chicago, Ill.; [I] am already engaged in Beloit, Wis.; Janesville, Wis.; Burlington, Iowa; Peoria, Ill.; Princeton, Ill. And [I am] in correspondence with several other places.... I shall hold Conventions of three days each, (in some cases two days,) and must arrange them so as to spend the least time possible traveling from place to place."[36]

ESTHER'S EARLIEST PERFORMANCES

Bradbury conducted excerpts from *Esther* at musical conventions during the summer of 1856, just prior to the work's initial publication. As Cady reported in July of that year, the Suffolk County (New York) Harmonic Society hosted a musical convention at which Bradbury rehearsed one hundred and twenty singers in "a chorus with obbligato solos" from his "forthcoming cantata of *Esther, the Beautiful Queen.*" Cady confidently predicted of *Esther*, "[T]his cantata will prove to be one of the most useful as well as popular compositions of this kind ever issued in this country."[37] Almost immediately, his prediction became reality, and newspaper accounts confirmed innumerable performances of *Esther* throughout the East and Midwest during the later 1850s and beyond.

Bradbury premiered *Esther* in its entirety during a convention tour undertaken in the fall of 1856. He inaugurated this tour in New York State with convention performances on Long Island in October. Following a convention he conducted in Greenport, New York, a writer offered this glowing critique:

> We have just closed one of the most interesting musical festivals [conventions] we have yet enjoyed under the efficient conductorship of Prof. W. B. Bradbury.... The interest of the present session was greatly enhanced by the introduction of Prof. B's new and truly beautiful Oratorio of *Esther.* The largest church in Greenport was filled to overflowing to listen to the first performance of this new musical production; and if the uninterrupted interest manifested by one of the largest and most intelligent audiences ever assembled in Greenport, is any indication of success, we bespeak for the "Beautiful Queen" a most popular and brilliant reign.[38]

Following his decided success in New York, Bradbury made his way to Illinois. For a series of performances in Peoria from October 21 to 24 of that year, a reviewer complimented Bradbury and offered him "high praise as an able composer and conductor."[39] A local historian recalled these performances:

> A noted [singing] society was formed [in Peoria] in 1855, with the purpose in view of elevating the character of church music [singing] . . . . [T]hey invited Prof. William B. Bradbury, a noted composer of sacred music, to hold a musical convention at Peoria, which invitation was accepted [by him]. The convention . . . continued for about ten days and attracted a large attendance of amateur musicians from Peoria and the surrounding country. The drill consisted largely of mastering the Cantata of "Esther, the Beautiful Queen," a composition of Mr. Bradbury's, then entirely new and probably then produced in public for the first time.[40]

Performances of *Esther* in Decatur, some eighty miles from Peoria, sung by the community's Musical Union and directed by Bradbury, soon followed.[41]

Bradbury also conducted conventions in Iowa during the fall of 1856. A convention in Burlington, held from November 11 to 13 of that year, earned a lengthy supportive review. Occasionally, Bradbury also performed a solo part in *Esther*, and for the Burlington convention, he sang the role of King Ahasuerus.[42] As one convention participant commented:

> Notwithstanding this [convention] meeting was an experiment, it being the first of the kind held here, it was attended by singers of neighboring towns, as well as of Burlington. About one hundred availed themselves of this rare opportunity. . . . Instruction was given in nine lessons. . . . Especially were the remarks made by Mr. Bradbury . . . in respect to the spirit of the singers, and the social and moral effect of a proper cultivation of music, calculated to elevate the tone of feeling, and lead singers to sing not for themselves alone. The convention closed with a concert at which . . . Mr. Bradbury's new Oratorio, *Esther, the Beautiful Queen* was performed . . . . This piece is not difficult to perform, yet it is pleasing and, in many passages, we think, very beautiful. We think the result of this Convention has been good. The immediate effect was, that a hundred singers, who had never sung together before, formed into an effective chorus [and] . . . after a practice of but three days upon new music, performed in a concert, before an intelligent and discriminating audience

who . . . listened with scarcely a whisper or a footfall. In addition, greater interest than usual seems to be manifested in primary singing-schools [for children] . . . . We have heard Mr. Bradbury and this Convention mentioned only in terms of commendation . . . . Mr. Bradbury has our warmest thanks for his efforts and success in advancing the cause of music among us, we feel assured that we express the sentiments of this community and especially of those who became acquainted with him while here.[43]

Bradbury returned to the Midwest the following year to conduct *Esther* and teach at conventions. The *Musical Review and Gazette* elaborated on one of these gatherings:

Our Convention [in Canton, Ohio] was a grand affair, and gave general satisfaction to all who participated in it . . . . Our people are beginning . . . to understand the aim of such conventions . . . the great benefit to be derived from attending them . . . and that the good work will rapidly progress among us. A great interest has been awakened upon the subject of music and a decided improvement in choir and club-singing is perceptible since our Annual Conventions were commenced. Mr. Bradbury's friends here are legion; and during our last convention, he acquitted himself in such a manner as to render himself a still greater favorite than before. You may judge of his labors, when I inform you that though our convention lasted but four days, we gave two concerts, the music upon the second night being almost entirely different from that of the first, and a great deal of preparation being consequently required. On the second night we gave the first part of *Esther*, which was most favorably received by the audience, and was quite well rendered by the Convention singers.[44]

Bradbury thrilled audiences and participants at a subsequent convention organized expressly for the choir of the Chicago Musical Institute:

We have heard of Prof. Wm. B. Bradbury, of New York, have read of him, used to carry one of his [tune]books to singing school winter nights, and have been taught from them by a teacher with spectacles on, and a tuning fork in hand. Did not know then–did not dream of such a thing–that we should one day have the pleasure of an introduction to the author of those tunes . . . . But we have been [introduced to Bradbury], and added to that, we listened to the performance of his Cantata of "Esther, the Beautiful Queen," by the members of the Chicago Musical Institute, under the conductorship of Prof. B. personally. To say that we were interested and pleased would hardly express the measure of pleasure it afforded us. We cannot say the performance was faultless, but we are no professional critic and dare not risk our reputation in effort to point out errors. The Book of Esther has always been one of great interest to us, and especially did the triumph of justice over power, as revealed in the interesting history, make its impression in our school-boy days. No one who has read and re-read this interesting book can fail to have discovered a field for this very style of composition which Mr. Bradbury has occupied so creditably. If any of our readers have an opportunity to hear it [*Esther*] performed, they will thank us for this advice–go and listen.[45]

Bradbury also conducted an early performance of *Esther* in Franklin, Massachusetts, in 1858. The participants at this convention initially voiced some concern about their perception of the score's difficulty, but they were soon disabused of these sentiments and ultimately expressed satisfaction with their closing performance:

> We were doubtful, when we commenced, whether we should ever be able to perform it [*Esther*] in public . . . . [Yet] it was a decided success, and upon earnest solicitation, it was repeated; the result was happy; it has given the singers confidence in themselves, and our good people have learned that they can be pleased with our own home singing. And allow me to say, in closing, that the oratorio of *Esther* is one of the best compositions for practice in associations and choirs that I have ever seen.[46]

Other directors also featured *Esther* as a concluding performance for their conventions. A review of a performance in Ohio, sung at Oberlin College's spring commencement exercises of 1858, earned this enthusiastic notice:

> In the evening the Oberlin singers performed the magnificent Cantata of "Esther, the Beautiful Queen" in the local and cavernous Congregational Church. The seats were all packed full and many were unable to find even standing room. We understand that over three thousand tickets were sold. It was a great crowd. The cantata was finely performed . . . . The concert was a pleasant affair, creditable to all concerned in its management.[47]

Another particularly noteworthy performance of *Esther* took place in Peoria, Illinois, in 1862. Local music teacher and church choir director Seth Abbott (1817–1901) prepared a sizeable chorus and invited Bradbury to work with the musicians in a convention to take place over a period of three days. Upon his arrival, Bradbury drilled the singers, and during an afternoon of lessons, he began to take notice of a particular young singer's extraordinary voice. When Bradbury inquired as to the identity of the vocalist he admired, Seth Abbott informed him that the gifted singer was his daughter, Emma Abbott (1850–1891). Bradbury effusively responded, "That accounts for it. She sings as a lark does, because she can't help it, and she sings beautifully too. There isn't another voice in the room that compares with her in possibilities." Emma, cast as Queen Esther, was the youngest singer assigned to a principal part for this performance. Bradbury coached her for the role. After the performance, he invited her to sing pieces of her own choosing for him. Among her selections, she offered Bradbury interpretations of Stephen Foster's popular ballad, "Old Folks at Home," along with two opera arias, "I Dreamt that I Dwelt in Marble Halls" from Michael William Balfe's opera *Bohemian Girl* (1843) and "Hear Me, Norma" ("Mira, O Norma") from Vincenzo Bellini's *Norma* (1831). According to Emma's friend and biographer, Sadie E. Martin, Bradbury said to Emma, at the conclusion of her performance, "[M]y dear, fortune and fame are sure to be yours."[48] How prescient an observation as Emma Abbott would later become an internationally acclaimed soprano soloist and respected opera impresario.

Closing Thoughts

The earliest performances of *Esther* established the work as an eminently approachable piece aptly suited to the instructional goals of musical conventions. By the mid-1860s, Bradbury had successfully presided over the momentum of an *Esther* craze that rapidly spread throughout many eastern states and the Midwest. However, failing health forced him to abandon touring and promoting *Esther*. In the hands of numerous other music directors, *Esther* no longer served, exclusively, the objectives of the nascent American music education movement, especially the activities associated with musical conventions. In addition, many music directors added staging and costumes to their performances of *Esther*, and the piece soon acquired a reputation as community entertainment rather than a piece for instructional or religious use. The reception history of *Esther* entered a new era after Bradbury's death, when two US musicians published revisions of the work. Even as their versions of the score retained Bradbury's original music, they codified the addition of costumes and acting to performances of the work. I devote the next chapter to a discussion of these revisions.

CHAPTER THREE

ESTHER, REVISED

By the 1860s, performances of *Esther, the Beautiful Queen* often included costumes, acting, and stage sets.[1] In response to this decided alteration in purpose of his score, Bradbury vociferously reiterated his original intentions:

> The story of Esther is of course familiar to all, but though a very fine subject for dramatic study, it was never intended by me to be put upon the stage, or to be attended by any of the paraphernalia requisite to stage-effects, such, for instance, as dress, scenery, acting, etc. etc. . . . Among other questions asked, one, if we remember rightly, was "Whether, in the drinking song, so-called, between the King and Haman, we would allow a drinking-scene to be introduced with table, cups, and appearance of wine?" etc. Our answer would be, *No*, by no means. To our own mind, such an attempt would mar the effect, destroy the whole design, and convert the whole of that part into a mere burlesque . . . . We dare not forget that we are treating of a story from the sacred Scriptures, and if it is proper to introduce such playing or acting *here*, it is equally proper to introduce it in other parts. We have even heard of a *gallows* being erected, and an effigy of Haman hung thereon! Of course, the effect must be ludicrous in the extreme, and thus a subject from the Bible, a sacred story of thrilling interest, is made the theme, not only for amusement, but for merriment and ridicule! The object of the manager [i.e., director of a theatrical *Esther* production] may be good, but it should be remembered, that all such attempts [at staging] fall so far short of the [original] design as to amount to naught but a mere burlesque upon the things intended to be delineated. We therefore beg our friends who have become interested in this, our first entire cantata, not to do us the injustice to attempt its performance theatrically, tragically, or comedily, or *comically*, but merely and purely as a musical representation of a most interesting Scripture-scene [italics original].[2]

However strenuously Bradbury opposed the use of theatrical elements in performances of *Esther*, his objections went substantially unheeded. Two enterprising US musicians, R. W. Seager and Leon Keach, took sagacious advantage of the rise in popularity of staged presentations of the original score by publishing revised editions of the work. Their revisions offered recommendations for costuming, props, and acting. Seager's edition, in particular, set the dramaturgical gold standard for virtually all productions that took place during the mid-1870s and beyond.

First Revision

Richard Watson "R. W." Seager (1832–1913), born in Byron, New York, was, apparently, a music autodidact. For a time, he resided in Minnesota, conducted community choruses, and briefly served as principal of the newly established St. Paul Academy of Music.[3] He also performed as a baritone soloist and attracted regional press attention, one paper complimenting his "very sweet, clear voice" deemed especially "effective in ballads."[4] However, Seager's various attempts to establish himself as a sought-after singer and teacher eventually faltered, and he admitted, "the wreck of my business in St. Paul" imposed "great pecuniary distress."[5] Subsequently, he left the area and began to promote himself as an itinerant director of community choruses and musical entertainments. He soon earned a widespread reputation for staged productions of popular choral works, such as Bradbury's oratorio for children, *Flora's Festival*, George F. Root's costumed operatic cantata, *The Haymakers* (1857), and Root's dramatic cantata, *Belshazzar's Feast, or the Fall of Babylon* (1860).[6] Of one such event, Seager described, in glowing terms, a performance he directed in Oberlin, Ohio: "I have a class of between three and four hundred members, meeting every day in the College Chapel, and it is *splendid*. They know what music is here. It is decidedly the most musical town I have ever visited, and the children and young folks are full of it. We close with the splendid cantata, 'Flora's Festival,' on Wednesday evening August 3 [1866] [italics original]."[7]

During the mid-1860s, Seager began producing staged performances of *Esther*. A St. Paul, Minnesota, journalist recounted Seager's role in the transition of Bradbury's score from a two-part oratorio-like work to a "sacred opera":

Some ten years ago Professor Seager, who resided here [in St. Paul] at that time, and had a good deal of local fame as a director of music, conceived of the idea of transforming the cantata [*Esther*] into a sacred opera, and did so with decided success . . . . He . . . has devoted these intervening years to its elaborate presentation in the leading cities and music centers of the country. "Queen Esther," as now revised and dramatized, has attracted immense audiences for three to five nights in nearly all the large cities.[8]

In March 1874, Seager published his revision of the original *Esther* score.[9] Among the alterations he made, Seager appended descriptions to his list of principal roles, as follows:

King Ahasuerus—bass or baritone; of commanding presence; a good actor
Queen Esther—soprano; stately, graceful and dignified
Haman—baritone; distinct articulation; haughty in bearing; a good actor
Zeresh—alto; solo singer; proud; disdainful
Mordecai—tenor; earnest and dignified
Mordecai's sister—soprano; clear distinct voice and articulation
Prophetess—soprano; dark; black hair
Scribe—bass or baritone; a good reader
Harbonah and Chamberlain—tenor
Guards—bass
Queen Esther's Attendants—smaller than Queen
Hegai—bass
High Priest—bass or baritone
Queen's Pages
Semi-chorus of children
Chorus of Persians—youngest, shortest people; light hair
Chorus of Jews—tallest people; dark hair

Seager's list included a subtly ethnicized recommendation for the role of the Prophetess to be portrayed by a "dark" woman with "black hair." A mysterious figure, the Prophetess offers an exotic and pivotal presence in Cady's version of the Esther narrative. Additionally, Seager called for singers with "dark" hair for the chorus of Jews while the Persians were to have "light hair."

To confirm legal right to the work, Seager indicated, on the title page, that he had "revised and adapted for dramatic presentation" the entire piece. He claimed, "[N]o monument more lasting, nor a sweeter memory" than such a revision could appropriately memorialize Bradbury's legacy.[10] The Oliver Ditson publishing firm printed Seager's edition with Bradbury's original plates and retained all of the score's music, Josephus's essay, and nearly all of Cady's text. In his alteration of the original oratorio-like organizational scheme of two parts, Seager reconfigured the score into acts and scenes. Additionally, he inserted stage directions and deleted most of the quotations from the Book of Esther (to be read by the Messenger in Bradbury's version). He also appended two choruses to the end of the score: "To God on High" by Felix Mendelssohn and "Beautiful Are Thy Towers, O Zion" by US hymn composer Luther Orlando Emerson (1820–1915).[11] Neither of these choruses relates in any way to the Esther narrative or to Bradbury's score. Newspaper reviews and surviving programs seldom mentioned these choruses, and therefore it seems safe to assume they were rarely sung at performances of *Esther*. Seager's revision soared in popularity, so much so that some press accounts attributed the actual composition of the score to him while others attempted to correct this misconception. As one journalist summarized the situation: "Mr. Seager did not compose the original cantata of 'Esther'. . . . To William B. Bradbury, who died in the zenith of his glory and fame as a maker of charming melodies, is due the eternal honor of composing this simplest, most unpretentious, but most delightful and enduring of musical dramas. Mr. Seager simply dramatized it."[12]

Nonetheless, Seager promoted his relationship and identity with *Esther* so convincingly that many newspapers credited him, in obituaries, with the composition of the original score.[13]

Seager put forth considerable effort to justify the staging of *Esther*. As one journalist noted in a paraphrase of Seager's comments in this regard, "No epoch of history, ancient or modern, so abounds in thrilling events and incidents" as the biblical Book of Esther. "Every phase of human emotion—exultation, woe, ambition, joy, despair—is here depicted. Words, music and action seem so palpably essential, each to the other, that amateurs readily acquire artistic skill in their enunciation—audiences sit entranced, bewildered, scarcely realizing that it is their own sisters, brothers, sons, daughters, wives, sweethearts that are filling, so effectively, the roles of ancient 'Persians' and 'Jews.'"[14] Seager made lofty claims about the success of his staged musical entertainments and *Esther* especially. He informed an Atlanta reporter that, by 1894, 30,000 singers had participated in his productions in 210 cities. In addition, he boasted not only of having organized one hundred "vocal societies," but also that "a million people in nineteen states and [Canadian] provinces" had been "electrified" by his "superb and brilliant performances of *Esther, the Beautiful Queen*." He frequently included these credentials in newspaper announcements calling for singers to populate choruses of at least one hundred adults consisting of "fifty gentlemen, basses and tenors." Such announcements further stipulated, for example, "[R]ehearsals will be held two evenings each week for a period of six weeks, involving a course of vocal and physical training."[15]

In his essay "Directions for Organization, Costuming, and Etc." prefatory to the actual score, Seager confirmed practices already employed in most theatrical productions of *Esther* and expected by virtually all audiences. He offered lengthy recommendations to local participants for making costumes and scenery and outlined simple but effective suggestions for staging and action. For the set, he advised, "Properties: throne: a platform six feet by four, one or two steps high, handsomely covered. Two high back chairs, covered with [A]fghans or lap robes. Canopy if practicable. Note! throne may be set in rear center [stage] and remain there permanently. For guards' armor, four battle axes made of tin or wood, and mounted on staves 5 and ½ feet long. Flagon and goblets bronzed or gilt." To assemble costumes, Seager made these recommendations:

> Costumes for Jews, ladies: sash of black calico 3 ½ to 4 yards long, the ends torn into fringe 3 inches long. One side might be decorated with silver paper, stars and bars, or any devices. Turbans of same material with white and black streamers. Hair down, flowing.
>
> Persians: red, blue, pink, yellow, or any bright color for sash and turbans; gilt paper, beads, &c., for decoration. Hair down. Sashes to be worn over white skirt, plain or "filigreed," not lower than short walking dress—the shorter the prettier. No shoes or boots for men, women, or children. A bolt of braid, price 10 cents, color to match sash and turban, for each foot and ankle, to be crossed twice upon, and under the foot, and so up the ankle to the knee, fastened. Gentlemen and boys wear first a pair of socks, over which draw "two story" stockings, and put the braid as described, imitation of sandals, first rolling up the pants, or folding them in, and drawing the stockings over them. Gents wear

sash[es] similar to ladies, or a plain frock belted around the waist, and turbans .... The entire wardrobe for 60 singers may be gotten up neatly at an expense of $75, or solo costumes may be procured from a costumer, and sashes made at 50 cents each.... Robes and crowns for leading characters may be made of velvet, richly trimmed, of flannel, or cambric, and decorated with gilt paper.[16]

Seager also gave these instructions for stage blocking and action:

And now for the *action*: Scene 1st, Persians: When the curtain rises they [the chorus] may be discovered upon the stage, or come tripping in as Haman enters from left wing.... All sing to Haman, with appropriate gesture, as he passes back and forth, and all bowing at the words, "Bow down to Haman," he returning the salutation in part. Just at the close of chorus and while "Behold this Mordecai, &c.," is being played as prelude, Mordecai enters from left and walks across in front, looking scornfully at Haman, and is discovered by Haman and Persians, who at once become angry. Mordecai continues across to right, remaining in view of singers but back of wing, while solo and chorus "Behold, &c.," are sung [italics original].[17]

For the drinking scenes—so strongly objected to by Bradbury—Seager proposed this action:

"Act I, Scene 1. King's Pages, with goblets and flagons on stand at right .... Pages advance on either side with wine, keeping step to music.... Pages kneel and salute in front of King and Haman before handing [them] wine, then step back and salute, and return to place in the rear [of the stage] .... At the [lyrics] 'More wine, more wine' Pages refill goblets, and come forward again, [then] retire." Significantly, Seager added the lyrics "more wine, more wine" with accompanying stage action during the drinking and laughing duet sung by the king and Haman (Seager's Act I, Scene 1). For arguably the most dramatic scene in the work—the meeting of Esther and Ahasuerus—Seager recommended this action: "Act 3rd, King on throne. Scribe to the left, appears to be entertaining him from scroll. Guards in position. Enter Queen and Maids from right; her alarm; silent prayer; [Esther] advances and falls upon one knee, at foot of throne, as guards charge upon her. King discovers her, springs forward and raises her with right hand, holding out sceptre with left, which Queen touches with right hand while both walk forward."[18] For Act 5, Scene 2, Seager added dancing:

Queen's Pages advance to waltz step, with wine. King gives one goblet to Haman and offers the other to the Queen, who declines [to accept the wine]. King and Haman then drink while waltz is going on. A beautiful thing is this Page's waltz if two graceful little girls can be procured to do it. Don't try anyone who has not learned the "step".... [Pages dance the waltz] about twice across [the stage] and return to place. For encore, Pages dance the "Galop" once across.[19]

With the publication of Seager's edition, *Esther* productions rapidly became money-making endeavors. A shrewd entrepreneur, Seager quickly came to appreciate the potential profits he could realize by directing staged productions of *Esther*. To recruit, rehearse, and conduct singers, he drew up contracts with local officials stipulating his fees and those of his assistants, who were usually relatives. He sometimes assigned himself a singing role as Ahasuerus, Mordecai, or Haman and used this additional responsibility as justification for increased remuneration. He also required additional payment whenever one of his family members appeared on stage. Newspaper reviews confirm that his son, Frank Seager, sometimes played the role of the Herald under his father's direction, while his adopted daughter, Ella Knapp Seager, occasionally sang as Mordecai's sister, the Queen's Maid of Honor, or in the title role of Queen Esther.[20] Seager's services alone required a considerable outlay of money and he did not shy away from informing communities, "[M]y terms for producing 'Queen Esther'... are $500."[21] Typically, his agreements also indicated that any extra funds remaining after the meeting of production expenses could be presented to a local charity.

Although Seager provided instructions for making stage attire, he eventually purchased a set of costumes for use in *Esther* productions and rented these to community participants who preferred this option rather than creating theatrical attire themselves. As one journalist later recalled of Seager's costume collection, "[H]is room at the hotel [Atlanta's posh Kimball House], when the reporter called, seemed literally bedecked and bejeweled with costumes... piled upon tables, chairs and the floor."[22] His wife, Mary Frances W. Seager (1834–1892), curated his production wardrobe and collection of stage accessories, and charged substantial fees for her services. Seager included an assessment of "$75 per night... for the use of my wardrobe" and added, "whether or not the rent for $2000 worth of costumes and properties is excessive or not I do not know, but $75 is my price."[23] No matter how much

Seager claimed to have invested in his wardrobe collection, the quality and appearance of his costumes occasionally displeased audiences, critics, and players. The most publicized account of dissatisfaction with Seager's rented stage attire, and with his reputedly unpleasant interaction with community residents more generally, occurred in Denver in 1883. Regional newspapers singled out a few of his costumes as particularly egregious offenders of theatrical standards and taste. For instance, a journalist described one outfit as "a cheap red nightgown" accessorized with an unconvincing "tinsel crown." For the same series of performances, the High Priest wore an unappealing "cotton velvet robe" of disproportionate size that "swept about him like a fog around a liberty pole."[24] Another critic bluntly noted: "[T]the dreadful costumes of the chorus made the wearers look like so many jumping jacks plucked untimely from a comic Christmas tree. Every member wore long stockings, which were white once, and each stocking was twined about with narrow bands of many-colored tape, giving the legs of young men and women the semblance of so many sticks of cork-screw candy."[25]

Seager promoted his edition of *Esther* with lengthy tours during which he produced performances in communities from coast to coast. Most of his productions attracted considerable newspaper coverage, such as in Waterbury, Connecticut, in 1874. The advertising flyer for this performance promised "full Median, Persian and Jewish" costumes and a "semi-chorus and marching chorus of forty little people" (figure 3.1). Under Seager's direction, participants amazed audiences with their "picturesque" presentation and brilliantly colored robes, described as "rich and varied."[26]

In April 1877, Seager directed a well-received production in Newport, Rhode Island, earning this glowing review:

> And now, to sum up the result of it [Seager's production] . . . Two hundred people have had a capital good time rehearsing a book full of songs and choruses that people will sing, whistle, hum and enjoy for a long time to come. They have learned a good deal about dramatic movements and gestures that must surely add something to their ease, grace and confidence in themselves . . . . [I]t is expected that the affair has given an impetus to music, set people to considering how they may rationally enjoy and improve themselves, and has improved the social and church singing of the community. When every singer participating in these entertainments has been an absolute enthusiast over it from first to last—when the performance has to be presented a third

Figure 3.1. Flyer, production of *Esther*, Waterbury, CT, 1874, directed by R. W. Seager. Author's personal collection.

night to an overcrowded house, people offering to pay a dollar for standing room to witness it and hundreds turned away for want of room, it really looks as though there were merit in it.[27]

Seager then made his way to the West Coast and produced another lavish performance, also in 1877, at San Francisco's Grand Opera House. As a local newspaper commented, "The representation was a succession of scenes of great splendor, especially the opening, the banquet and the Finale. In the latter, an effective pageant or triumphal procession is introduced, and afterward, a chorus of forty misses and little girls in fantastic costumes, bearing flowers [stroll] to the throne. This scene is really brilliant and beautiful, and decidedly amusing."[28] Seager's opulent set and choral groupings for this production also created quite a stir. The crowd scenes, in particular, must have taken up all of the expansive opera house stage—85 by 106 feet—in order to accommodate 300 singers and breathtaking "scenic effects" featuring a "particularly beautiful and imposing . . . triumphal march, banquet scene and the execution of Haman."[29]

The diary of Trenton, New Jersey, resident Edmund C. Hill offers a firsthand account of an *Esther* production prepared by Seager. Hill, remembered as the "father of the Trenton park system," sang under Seager's direction in 1876, when he was approximately twenty years of age.[30] Hill enthusiastically announced to his diary, in mid-April of that year, "The cantata of *Esther* is to be rendered . . . . Prof. R. W. Seager is the director." At the first exploratory rehearsal, "about a hundred [singers] were present. The singing was spirited and good . . . . We are to practice every night for two weeks." Hill's diary entries indicate that Seager worked with singers daily and coached them on stage action early in the series of rehearsals: "Prof. Seager is a good trainer. He had us singing with the books [scores] and then without. He had us all marching tonight." On April 24, Hill confidently noted rehearsals were "getting along nicely." However, he expressed some concern over the inability or perceived reluctance of some participants to commit their music to memory: "The [choir and principal cast] members do not memorize as well as they ought to, but with the books they sing very well." By April 25, Hill had been assigned a principal role in the production: "Mr. Seager gave me the part of Herald of Chamberlain. My part that I sing is not very hard. I sing once or twice in the quartette [Act V, scene 3] and in all the Persian choruses." Seager had already earned a reputation as an astute predictor of singers' potential, and as Hill related, "[T]he cast of characters [selected by Seager] . . . is generally considered very good." As Hill recorded, stage action and a few costumes were used in rehearsal on April 27: "We had our first stage rehearsal. Some dresses [costumes were worn]. Everything went off nicely. We did not get off until eleven o'clock [p.m.]. I sang my part as 'Herald' and did ever so much better than I expected." The seemingly late dismissal time of eleven p.m. suggests that Seager must have sensed the need to extend the length of this particular rehearsal in order to bring the cast's singing and acting to what he considered a satisfactory level.

The first of three performances took place on May 1. As Hill informed his diary: "Esther was presented in a highly dramatic form with elegant costumes, lights, brass band, etc. . . . The first [performance] of our much talked of oratorio came off tonight; audience about 700 or 800. Certainly not [a] very flattering [turn out]. Everything went off splendidly. I sang my part tolerably well." Hill enthused over the performance of Seager's daughter and wrote, "Miss [Ella Knapp] Seager as Esther [was], of course, very good." The players in this production assembled their own stage attire to varying degrees of success. Hill complained about one of the soloist's lack of taste and skill as a costumer, resulting in attire that "looked like a fright." After the second performance he confided to his diary, "[T]he papers, today, rang with praises," but "the attendance at Esther was not so good as last night." A more robust crowd attended the third performance.[31]

Many communities were unwilling or unable to pay Seager rent for the use of his costumes and instead assembled their own. Writing for the *Ladies' Home Journal*, Margaret Gordon recalled working with neighbors to assemble costumes and procure stage accessories:

> The neighborhood had been ransacked for . . . brass, copper and iron vases and bowls to serve as stage fittings . . . . The platform [stage] was draped with curtains and rugs. The costumes were all home-made. Cheesecloth is an admirable material for a foundation garment, and old-fashioned broche and paisley shawls and silk and chiffon scarfs and sashes were used as drapery. Glass beads, spangles and fringes may be sewn on as trimmings. A cheesecloth gown may be decorated with flower figures cut from cretonne or calico. If these are basted on with coarse mercerized thread in large stitches they will look like rich embroidery.[32]

A review of a Hammonton, New Jersey, production in 1876 lauded the singer's stage attire, entirely of their own creation: "The costuming was grand, in drapery and effect, and great taste was manifest in the makeup and trimmings. And when we consider that the costumes were gotten up by the singers themselves, the work and skill displayed is simply wonderful. King Ahasuerus ... was ... arrayed in garments of purple and gold .... [Esther's] dress was exceedingly rich, and royal indeed. The supposed brilliants of her crown, and [those] upon her dress, shone with regal splendor."[33] Audiences at a production in 1880 in Mt. Sterling, Kentucky, eagerly anticipated *Esther*'s opening scene, the stage set according to Seager's directions. Singers and community members went to considerable effort to assemble their homemade and ornate regalia, as described in this review:

> The costumes of the ladies sparkled with gold and silver and rare gems and brilliant colors, while the gentlemen in an array of apparel of the gayest colors and most elaborate patterns made a scene long to be remembered .... The king's robes were made specially for this occasion and were handsome in the extreme. He wore a red tunic, trimmed with gold bullion and fringe, and over this an elegant purple velvet robe was thrown, trimmed with white ermine. The [king's] crown was a work of wondrous art, and the sandals rich in their heavy bands of gold .... [Esther] was clad in red velvet, trimmed in ermine and gold, and wore a gold crown that sparkled and glittered in a profusion of lovely gems .... [Haman] was arrayed in dark silk ... trimmed in green, red and gold, and surmounted by a golden crown and handsome feather .... Mordecai's robe, after his triumph, was of light blue, trimmed with gold, and was one of the most beautiful on the stage.[34]

Homemade costumes also amazed audiences in attendance at performances in Leadville, Colorado, in 1895. A local newspaper enthused over the stage attire, with special attention paid to the "cute and lovely ... queen's Pages in their white gauze, silver-braided dresses and tiny slippers."[35] The locally assembled costumes for an Oregon production "had been planned with special reference to that period of Jewish history to which the beautiful biblical story belongs, and some of them were exceedingly sumptuous—the dress of the High Priest, for example, which consisted of a rich red gown and cap, with vestments of light silk heavily embroidered in scarlet flowers."[36]

Second Revision

Composer, pianist, and conductor Leon Keach (1854–1896) published his revision of *Esther* in 1896 (figure 3.2). Little information about Keach survives. As a sought-after accompanist, he collaborated with some of the most celebrated soloists of the later nineteenth century, including violinist Maud Powell (1867–1920), tenor Italo Campanini (1845–1896), and sopranos Marie Selika (ca. 1849–1937), Emma Cecilia Thursby (1845–1931), and Lillian Nordica (1857–1914). Of Keach's skill as an accompanist, a reviewer lauded his "superior abilities as a musician" and noted, of one concert in particular, "[H]e performed exceedingly well and gave universal satisfaction."[37] A Vermont journalist added, "Keach's name is familiar to many musical people" and he "ranks among the best Boston pianists."[38] Keach also performed with the Highland Social Quintette Club, an esteemed chamber ensemble organized by him in 1869.[39] Among his best-known compositions were two comic operas, *The Corsair* (1887) and *The Mermaid, or the Curse of Cape Cod* (1888).[40] Keach conducted and directed many other operas, most notably during his affiliations with the Boston English Opera Company and the Lyceum Opera Company. A long-time resident of Boston, he served for twenty-seven years as music consultant and editor for the Oliver Ditson publishing firm.[41]

In the preface to his edition of *Esther*, Keach recapitulated many of Seager's ideas:

> The publishers of *Esther*, Bradbury's beautiful cantata, with a view of making it yet more worthy of its successful past, have issued this new edition, containing important additions to the music and text, opening a new field for its use—presentation in costume with appropriate dramatic action. They have considered especially the demand for an adaptation suitable to amateur stage performance, and believe that in its new form this demand has been effectively and successfully fulfilled. None of the original matter [written by Bradbury and Cady] has been omitted and many new choruses and solos have been added, greatly enhancing its value.[42]

In actuality, Keach inflated the number and types of alterations he made to *Esther*. Of course, his edition hardly presented a "new field" for theatrical performances of *Esther* as Seager had introduced nearly all of Keach's ideas more than twenty years earlier. Keach replicated Seager's operatic organizational

Figure 3.2. Cover, *Esther, the Beautiful Queen*, Leon Keach, ed. (Boston: Oliver Ditson, 1896).

scheme of five acts with divisions into scenes, but he eliminated the choruses by Mendelssohn and Emerson. He duplicated Seager's stage directions and supplemented these with a few of his own recommendations. Although Keach retained Bradbury's vocal music, he composed an overture to the work (musical example 3.1) and added piano accompaniments. In those places in

Musical Example 3.1. Leon Keach, ed., *Esther*, Overture, mm. 1–24.

need of connecting passages, he inserted introductions and interludes.[43] He also updated the score's notation by reconfiguring the vocal parts in SATB order. Keach's accompaniments in the choral numbers tend to double the voice parts in largely homophonic texture, thus replicating Bradbury's intentions. The resultant modernized score reflected Keach's skill as a pianist and composer and his extensive experience in the world of opera and dramaturgy.

Beyond the addition of piano accompaniments, interludes, and connective passages, Keach's score contains other departures from Bradbury's version. For example, he expanded the number of principal roles to include a Beggar (bass), a Median princess (alto), and a Persian Princess (soprano). None of these characters appears in the biblical Book of Esther or in Cady's text. Keach provided the following list of roles:

Esther, the Queen—soprano
Ahasuerus, the King—bass
Haman, the King's Counsellor and Overseer of the Realm—baritone
Mordecai, a Jew—tenor
Zeresh, Haman's wife—contralto
Mordecai's Sister—soprano
Prophetess—soprano
A Median Princess—alto
A Persian Princess—soprano
Scribe—bass
Beggar—bass
Hegai—bass
High Priest—bass
Herald—tenor
Harbonah—tenor
Guards—bass
Queen Esther's Attendants—smaller than Queen
Persians
Jews
Pages
Guards
Maids of Honor

Keach did not assign either of the princesses a solo, but the Beggar enters in the final act to sing a somber number prior to the celebratory banquet. To the performer of the "Song of the Beggar," Keach gave the enigmatic instruction to sing "briskly, almost savagely." An unobtrusive piano accompaniment effectively supports this mostly syllabic setting of Psalm 9:16 and Job 21:26 (musical example 3.2).

In another departure from Bradbury's score, Keach added the rather cryptic suggestion, prior to the Finale, that "the cantata is most effectively ended here." If directors decided, instead, to perform the remainder of the score,

Musical Example 3.2. Leon Keach, ed., *Esther*, "Song of the Beggar" (Act 5, scene 2), mm. 1–12.

Keach offered the option of replacing Bradbury's Finale ("Praise Ye the Lord," Part II, no. 15) with Mendelssohn's "To God on High." (As mentioned earlier, Keach did not provide notated music for the Mendelssohn work in his revision.) This substitution seems that much more puzzling when we remember that critics and audiences responded most favorably to Bradbury's closing chorus. As reviews seldom mentioned the absence of Bradbury's Finale, it seems likely that directors did not omit *Esther*'s original concluding number. Keach's score sold well, enabling the Oliver Ditson company to issue a reprint in 1924. Unfortunately, Keach died suddenly in 1896, the same year he published his edition of *Esther*. He never had an opportunity to conduct *Esther* or develop relationships with numerous communities, musicians, and audiences as did Bradbury and Seager.

Closing Thoughts

Seager's and Keach's revisions of *Esther* standardized staging practices that had evolved during Bradbury's later years. Theatrical renditions of *Esther* provided singers with opportunities to engage in dramaturgical self-determination and to develop poise and creative spontaneity while on stage. Equally important, as aspiring actors explored the contents of attic trunks and wardrobes for suitable costume materials, they drew upon latent imagination and resourcefulness to create stage attire. However, costuming designs and dramaturgical choices did not always meet with approval among conservative citizens and clergy. Furthermore, questions arose as to the actual genre identity of *Esther* and whether or not the work continued to meet the needs of music education or religious observance. I consider these issues in the next chapter.

CHAPTER FOUR

GENRE INTRIGUE

Even as theatrical interpretations of *Esther* supplanted the original pedagogical and religious purposes Bradbury intended for his score, the public continued to refer to the piece as a "cantata" or "oratorio." Yet neither of these designations accurately accounted for the work's transformation into a staged musical drama and the rising prominence of the piece in the world of popular entertainment. In fact, uncertainty about *Esther*'s genre identity lingered for decades. Nearly forty years after R. W. Seager published his edition, author Eugene Wood humorously pondered the matter in this conversation with himself:

> There is acting in it, and scenery, and costumes, and you paint your face, and the curtain goes up, and all like that, but it isn't a the-ay-ter. Not at all.
> It's all singing. So it can't be a the-ay-ter.
> Well, if it's acting and costumes, and the curtain goes up and down, and it's all singing, it must be an opera.
> No, it's about the Bible, so it can't be an opera.
> Well, what is it then?[1]

Wood identified the two crucial and interdependent components of the overarching genre question: first, did the biblical source of *Esther*'s text determine whether or not the piece should be considered sacred? And second, what genre identity would best represent staged adaptations of the work? We should not underestimate the significance of genre, particularly among many conservative Protestants whose denominational creed forbade attendance at theaters or theatrical events. This prohibition often extended to staged enactments of narratives or texts originating in the Bible. In the discussion to follow, I evaluate various genre labels critics and audiences assigned to *Esther*.

Sacred or Secular?

Many nineteenth-century American composers employed a compositional process that relied upon considerable musical borrowing and recycling. George F. Root offered the following description of this method of creating new works from older material:

> Those who write the music, especially those who make the popular [tune] books and other music of our country, have, by steady practice and observation, stored their minds with such of the musical forms, combinations, and effects with which they have had an opportunity to become acquainted, [and] as seemed to them beautiful, striking, or effective. This may have been done to a great extent involuntarily, and the sources may be entirely forgotten. These, with whatever originality the individuals [composers] may possess, form the [musical] reservoir from which they draw.[2]

Bradbury confidently and unapologetically promoted this compositional strategy and he relied substantially on his keen sense of both marketplace viability and the public's taste when he created new compositions. As Bradbury explained in one of his tunebook prefaces, he

> made it his constant study to ascertain the present wants of the musical public at large . . . [composing] an unusual variety . . . of styles, rich and natural harmonies, and pleasing and graceful melodies . . . . While the artistic singer and choir have not been neglected, the wants of the people—"ALL THE PEOPLE" have been mainly considered and provided for . . . . A tune, to become a favorite . . . must be attractive to the popular ear. It must be a thing of life, possessing a character of its own . . . [I]t must please, not merely upon its introduction, but also upon more familiar acquaintance [solid capital letters original].[3]

Indeed, Bradbury frequently recycled melodic and rhythmic elements from a variety of musical sources. For example, his best-selling tunebook, *The Alpine Glee Singer*, included arrangements of opera and oratorio selections, previously composed British and American songs, Swiss, Alpine, and Tyrolese melodies, *ranz des vaches,* and German folksongs, or what he referred to as *volksmelodies*.[4] This eclectic list illustrates why musicologist Nicholas Tawa identified Bradbury as one of many "inspired" anthologists who consciously or unconsciously selected and then recombined innumerable melodic and rhythmic elements into a new song, employing just enough of a personal touch to convince audiences of its uniqueness and originality.[5] In his study of American hymnody, Peter Mercer-Taylor acknowledged the frequency with which "texts and tunes were mixed and matched" by many nineteenth-century US composers to create new pieces.[6] Yet as Tawa concluded about this process, "[w]hether the result was truly new concerned neither the creator nor the listener. Such a consideration had little significance for either."[7]

As Root confirmed, the contents of many composers' musical "reservoir" contained innumerable rhythmic motives and melodic formulae from secular and sacred sources, yet their origins may well have been largely forgotten or were considered irrelevant. This seeming ambivalence regarding the style and source of borrowed musical material made it possible for composers to routinely engage in what Mercer-Taylor calls a "distinct creative musical practice" characterized by a type of "translational action" whereby secular music could, unselfconsciously, be reconfigured for sacred or religious purposes.[8] The perceived attractiveness and potential marketability of a particular melodic or rhythmic configuration determined its usefulness in this regard and thus, many compositions exhibited an identifiable mixture of sacred and secular styles and idioms.

Not surprisingly, then, many melodies written in the United States during the nineteenth century for either sacred or secular purposes were often quite similar, even indistinguishable at times, from one another.[9] As one critic accurately stated of many religious songs, "[T]he themes [melodies] of some of our best Psalm-tunes are selections from popular Operas."[10] Bradbury turned to many classical composers' compositions for the melodies of some of his most famous hymns, and these sources included secular works by Beethoven, Haydn, Felix Mendelssohn, W. A. Mozart, and Weber.[11] Some mid-nineteenth-century American composers, including Bradbury, determined that the sacredness of a vocal work depended almost exclusively on the source of its text rather than the style and origin of its music.[12] In other words, Bradbury did not necessarily consider the selection of secular musical idioms to set sacred or biblically derived lyrics to be a violation of religious standards, taste, expectations, or intent.

Musical Example 4.1. Bradbury, *Esther*, "A Song of Joy" (Part I, no. 5), mm. 3–10, showing melodic contour.

Secular Music in *Esther*

As we will see, the practice of borrowing and rearranging music from secular sources is quite evident in the score of *Esther*. Manifestations of secular music can be detected in the score's melodies, some of which resonate with characteristics associated with parlor songs, glees, and ballads in circulation during the nineteenth century. One of *Esther*'s most prominent and audience-pleasing numbers, "A Song of Joy" (Part 1, no. 5), closely resembles melodies he used in his own earlier works or borrowed from secular sources. As such, this melody can be said to belong to a tune family, the members of which manifest common intervallic characteristics or contour, such as, in this case, a starting pitch on the dominant, a leap to the mediant, and a descent directly or gradually back to the dominant pitch (see musical example 4.1). (Or, if you prefer, a melody starting on the fifth scale degree, *sol*, a leap to the third scale degree, *mi*, followed by a return to the fifth scale degree.) To illustrate the contents of Bradbury's musical "reservoir" and the correspondence of "A Song of Joy" to the tune family just mentioned, the discussion to follow includes numerous music examples, transcribed in C major for ease of comparison.[13]

The eclecticism of *Esther*'s music and its relationship to other musical sources did not go unnoticed by a few disgruntled critics, one of whom heard Bradbury's score as a "wishy-washy concoction of more or less musical odds and ends."[14] Another critic perceived, unequivocally, that Bradbury assembled his score largely by "imitating" and "collating" a variety of preexisting musical ideas.[15] A New Orleans journalist also heard considerable borrowed and recycled material in *Esther* and identified a decided relationship between "A Song of Joy" and older melodies. Finding Bradbury guilty of producing musical "imitations, but no results," the reviewer then referred to *Esther* as "an *olla podrida* [literally "Spanish stew"] of light music" suffused with "snatches of popular ballads (Ethiopian [minstrelsy] especially) [italics original]."[16] Clearly, the musical miscellany Bradbury drew upon included melodic configurations with an identifiable relationship to blackface minstrelsy tunes.

Musical Example 4.2. Frederick R. Buckley (1833–1864), "Kiss Me Quick and Go" (New York: Firth & Pond, 1856), mm. 1–4.

Musical Example 4.3. Bradbury, arr., "Teachers and Scholars" (1849), its melody attributed to Ignaz Fränzl (1736–1811). Bradbury, *Musical Gems for School and Home* (New York: Mark H. Newman, 1851), 55, mm. 1–6.

Critics who detected a whiff of minstrelsy in *Esther* may well have heard a correspondence between "A Song of Joy" and Frederick Buckley's popular minstrelsy tune, "Kiss Me Quick and Go" (musical example 4.2).[17] Buckley composed this song for his family's minstrelsy troupe, Buckley's Serenaders, which frequented stages in New Orleans and New York during the 1850s. Quite possibly, Bradbury attended performances of this ensemble. Given his compositional deference to public taste, the inclusion of music in *Esther* suggestive of a well-known minstrelsy tune would come as no surprise. After all, minstrel shows became, arguably, one of the most popular types of staged entertainment during the nineteenth century.

Prior to the completion of *Esther*, Bradbury had previously published songs with discernible correspondences to the tune family discussed above. Quite likely, he had these melodies in mind when he composed "A Song of Joy." For example, the melodic contour of his parlor song, "Teachers and Scholars" (1849), resembles an unknown piece written by German concert violinist and composer Ignaz Fränzl (musical example 4.3). The evident relationship of Fränzl's melody to "A Song of Joy" indicates that Bradbury intentionally recycled this earlier tune for use in *Esther*.

In another example of musical recycling, Bradbury used the same melodic contour in a parlor quartette, "Song of the New Year," published by him in 1854.

Musical Example 4.4. Bradbury, arr., "Song of the New Year," melody attributed to Donizetti. *New York Musical Review and Choral Advocate* December 21, 1854, 432, mm. 1–4.

Musical Example 4.5. Bradbury, arr., "The Compact," with a melody Bradbury described as "from the German." Bradbury, *Singing Bird* (New York: Ivison and Phinney, 1852), 37, mm. 1–8.

Musical Example 4.6. Bradbury, arr., "The Goblet," from the German. Bradbury, *Singing Bird*, 168, mm. 1–4.

Although he attributed this melody to opera composer Gaetano Donizetti (1797–1848), its exact origin has not been determined (musical example 4.4).

Two more of Bradbury's earlier secular songs, both using a similar melodic configuration, bear the attribution "from the German" (musical examples 4.5 and 4.6), suggesting a possible origin of a *volksmelodie* for "A Song of Joy." It should be recalled that Bradbury spent considerable time while in Europe collecting examples of folk melodies and later published his arrangements of these songs in tunebooks.

In another manifestation of musical secularity, Bradbury used vocables or non-lexical syllables in *Esther* such as "a-ha," "ha, ha," and "la, la." Their very presence in *Esther* brings to mind mountain songs and minstrelsy tunes, both of which often made use of such percussive syllables. In *Esther*, Bradbury employed the syllable "la" for vocal accompaniment (musical example 4.7), as sometimes found in his arrangements of Tyrolean mountain songs.

Musical Example 4.7. Bradbury, *Esther*, "Go Thou Merrily" (Part I, no. 14), mm. 35–40. Male voices join in singing the vocable "la." Bradbury's notation for the tenor and bass voices also provided a left-hand part for a keyboard accompaniment.

Musical Example 4.8. Bradbury, *Esther*, "Hurrah" (Part I, no. 14), mm. 21–24.

Musical Example 4.9. Bradbury, *Esther*, "laughing song," (Part I, no. 5), mm. 39–42. Bradbury provided the left hand of a keyboard accompaniment, as shown here on the lowest staff.

He also incorporated two other secular song types in *Esther*—a "hurrah" song and a "laughing" song. Repeated exclamations of "hurrah, hurrah" were common in political oratory and military and patriotic songs of Bradbury's day. Bradbury set a "hurrah" text to accompany the announcement of Mordecai's threatened execution, the melody ascending in a word-painting cliché to symbolize the raising of the gallows (musical example 4.8).

Several "laughing songs" with their signature lyrics of "ha, ha" were in circulation in this era and their popularity surely encouraged Bradbury to include them in *Esther* (musical example 4.9).

One famous example of a laughing song, Jean-Paul-Égide Martini's "Laughing Trio" (musical example 4.10), described as "side shaking" by the press, inspired audiences to laugh "with all their might in concert with the singers."[18] This piece was enormously popular, and Bradbury would have been quite familiar with audience enthusiasm for Martini's "Trio."

Musical Example 4.10. Jean-Paul-Égide Martini, "Laughing Trio," mm. 39–48. George Kingsley, ed., *The Social Choir* (Boston: Crocker & Brewster, 1847), 156.

The opera *Der Freischütz*, written by Carl Maria von Weber, provided another probable source of inspiration for Bradbury's "laughing" song. Regular readers of the popular periodical the *New York Mirror* would have known of Weber's so-called "Laughing Chorus," a version of which appeared in the journal's pages as an accessible piano-reduction score quite suitable for parlor room entertainment (musical example 4.11). Because Bradbury was an astute observer of the public's musical preferences we can be certain that he would have been familiar with the acclaim for *Der Freischütz* among opera-loving audiences. Undoubtedly, he was also aware that minstrelsy singers

Musical Example 4.11. Carl Maria von Weber, *Der Freischütz*, Act I, "Laughing Chorus," mm. 7–10. *New York Mirror* 8, no. 20 (November 20, 1830): 160. Original notational scheme retained.

performed variants of Weber's "Laughing Chorus," as did celebrated troupes of touring siblings such as the Rainer Family Singers and the Hutchinsons.[19]

Bradbury's musical "reservoir" also included numerous dance rhythms, and he incorporated a few of these in his *Esther* score. Of *Esther*'s dance-like numbers, the spirited polka or two-step rhythmic gesture evident in the chorus "Call to the Banquet" set the mood in King Ahasuerus's court for impending frivolity (musical example 4.12).

In another instance of Bradbury's appropriation of dance motives, the martial quality of the rhythmic gestures in "Chorus of the Jews" resembles that of a polonaise dance (musical example 4.13).

Musical Example 4.12. Bradbury, *Esther*, "Call to the Banquet" (Part 1, no. 13), mm. 73–80, with an identifiable polka-like rhythm or a two-step dance. Note accompaniment cues in middle staff.

Musical Example 4.13. Bradbury, *Esther*, "Chorus of Jews" (Part II, no. 1), mm. 15–16, the text set to a polonaise-like dance rhythm.

The jovial duet between Haman and the king, "Long Live Our Beauteous Queen," can be heard as a jig (musical example 4.14). In fact, a New Orleans critic complained that "the jig," as an example of unequivocally secular music, was "most conspicuous" in *Esther*.[20]

The subsequent instrumental interlude, "At the Banquet," bears the incontrovertible subtitle "Waltz Movement" (musical example 4.15). Conservative audiences and religious leaders found the waltz particularly objectionable,

Musical Example 4.14. Bradbury, *Esther*, "Long Live Our Beauteous Queen" (reprise, Part II, no. 10), mm. 33–36, with the rapid, driving rhythm suggestive of a jig. This number first appears as Part I, no. 12.

Musical Example 4.15. Bradbury, *Esther*, "At the Banquet: Waltz Movement" (Part II, no. 11), mm. 1–8.

especially in a reputedly sacred work, owing to its potential for lascivious and morally dangerous temptation engendered by the face-to-face embrace of the dancers and their abandoned and dizzying swirl as they circle the room. Moreover, at a rapid tempo, centrifugal force caused waltzing dancers to cling ever more tightly to each other.[21]

Bradbury also evoked dramatic and musical devices associated with opera. For example, in the number "Do I Wake or Am I Dreaming?" (musical example 4.16) he set slightly variant texts simultaneously, granting the audience a brief intrusion upon the inner thoughts of characters as they react to Haman's sentence of death. In this quartette, Zeresh (Haman's wife) sings lyrics of mournful resignation juxtaposed with the celebration of Esther's successful intervention to save the lives of the Jews, sung by the queen's maid and Hegai. Mordecai, as the fourth voice, contributes a somewhat self-effacing response to the queen's triumph.

Musical Example 4.16. Bradbury, *Esther*, "Do I Wake or Am I Dreaming?" (Part II, no. 13), mm. 49–64.

Musical Example 4.17. Bradbury, *Esther*, "What Is Thy Petition?" (Part II, no. 12), mm. 43–50. Notation shown in its original configuration with accompaniment provided by Bradbury. Recurring dotted motive appears in the keyboard accompaniment.

Bradbury also anticipated dramatic events by employing motives to identify persons or emotions—a device found in some European operas. When Esther petitions the king, a recurring dotted figure derived from the waltz movement (see musical example 4.15) punctuates her lyrics (musical example 4.17).

Additionally, the melodic contour of the tune family discussed above appears several times, sung by the choruses to express joyous homage to Esther or to announce her banquet. A variant of this melodic formula also represents the king, and thus his presence becomes musically aligned with lighthearted celebration. Bradbury's reliance on identifiable motives and on the tune family discussed above lends a sense of musical and dramatic cohesion to the entire work in ways similar to that employed by composers of opera.

Ultimately, and as if to reiterate his conviction that *Esther* should be considered a sacred work, Bradbury concluded his score with a majestic setting of biblical texts absent any hints of secularity. Cady based the lyrics for *Esther*'s brief Finale (Part II, no. 15) on excerpts from Psalms 100 and 150. Bradbury employed the cantus firmus technique, setting the hymn melody, "Old Hundred," in augmentation, with choral accompaniment. He assigned the chorale of this familiar and popular hymn to the "tenors and as many sopranos as can be spared from the accompanying chorus." In addition, he recommended that "[t]here should be enough [singers] upon [assigned to sing] the 'Choral[e]' to have it distinctly heard above all the other parts. Brass instruments (well played of course) would be very effective here."[22] The

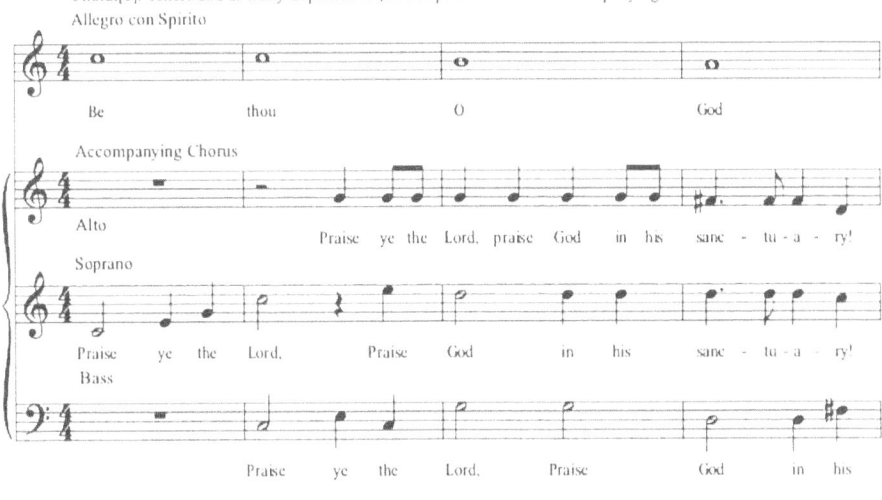

Musical Example 4.18. Bradbury, *Esther*, Finale, "Praise Ye the Lord" (Part II, no. 15), mm. 1–7.

remainder of the choral voices and all soloists sing Psalm 150 in a homophonic and largely syllabic setting (musical example 4.18).

Audiences and critics reacted with considerable enthusiasm to Bradbury's Finale. The *Musical Review and Gazette* posted this assessment:

> The closing chorus [of *Esther*], especially, is greatly and peculiarly effective. It is a Psalm of thanksgiving, a song of rejoicing sent up by the Israelites at their

deliverance. While in solemn exaltation rolls along the flood of harmony, suddenly the ear is arrested by a few familiar notes which the tenors give utterance to. The hearer listens doubtfully at first. Can it be? he queries; it is! High above all comes pouring forth the majestic measures of that glorious tune, "Old Hundred." The affect is as wonderful as the idea is beautiful.[23]

Bradbury could not have selected a more beloved sacred melody than "Old Hundred," and his choice to set this tune in the final number proved ingenious. An observation by the avid and prolific diarist and New York lawyer George Templeton Strong (1820–1875) summed up contemporaneous familiarity with this time-honored hymn melody: "Went to St. Paul's [Episcopal Chapel in New York]. They played 'Old Hundred' this morning .... That's the finest piece of church music I ever heard: noble, plain, simple, and majestic. Well played, with a good many voices (it wants a good many to give it effect), it strikes my ear more [favorably] than anything the people at St. Paul's ever play. And whenever it's played, everybody seems to join in."[24]

Cantata or Oratorio?

Inadvertently, Bradbury contributed to some of the uncertainty about the genre identity of *Esther* with his equivocal description of the work as "a cantata or short oratorio" found on the score's title page.[25] Yet for Bradbury, an insistence on *Esther*'s sacredness overshadowed, or even rendered moot, discussions of whether or not his piece should be regarded as either an oratorio or a cantata. He maintained that the characterization of *Esther* as sacred rested with the biblical origin of the narrative he set. In his mind, the musical material he borrowed from secular sources in no way detracted from the sacred purpose or religious sentiment of his score. So, too, he held directors and performers of the work responsible for secularizing *Esther*. Bradbury's resolute commitment to unstaged—and thus sacred—renditions of *Esther* resonated with his friend, Henry Clark Buell, a respected musician in the Beloit, Wisconsin, region. Buell reminisced about the time he played the part of Harbonah in 1859, under Bradbury's direction, in a production he enthusiastically recalled as being "entirely free of all stage effects, costumes, etc."[26] To complicate matters further, *Esther* initially became known as an instructional piece, and this purpose alone distinguished it from large-scale vocal works of

European origin, inspiration, and style such as cantatas and oratorios. In fact, aficionados of classical repertoire could not reconcile the work's pedagogical utility with the aesthetic purpose and often virtuosic demands of European musical models and precedence. More often than not, however, newspapers referred to Bradbury's score as the "cantata of Esther." At times, Bradbury favored this genre identity and offered the following explanation:

> The cantata, properly speaking, belongs neither to the oratorio nor the opera class of composition, being smaller, lighter, and of much less pretension in every way. We have both the sacred and secular cantata (so-called), by which is meant, first, such as take for their subject a story from the Scriptures, with the text chiefly as there found; and second, such as treat of [secular] subjects purely imaginative, or represent subjects, poetic or otherwise, as history, daily life, etc. It is, of course, unnecessary to say that *Esther* belongs to the first [sacred] of the two classes [of cantata] here enumerated.[27]

Moreover, Bradbury recommended a single, if unspecified, keyboard instrument for accompaniment, such as a melodeon, and this sparse scoring brings to mind the cantata genre. European composers of cantatas usually scored their works for fewer instrumentalists, sometimes writing accompaniments for a single keyboard instrument or basso continuo.

Yet a few attributes of Bradbury's *Esther* score suggested a genre designation of oratorio. First, the piece required a larger number of singers, along with solo parts, than was usually associated with the cantata genre. Second, the score contained two main sections, designated "Part One" and "Part Two," as reminiscent of some famous oratorios of European origin.[28] Furthermore, C. M. Cady derived much of his text from the Hebrew Testament, a traditional source for many oratorios. Nonetheless, even as *Esther* exhibited certain attributes commensurate with the oratorio genre, this category did not always mesh with reviewers. For example, the writer of the comment quoted below challenged the pretentiousness of assigning the oratorio designation to *Esther* and even enigmatically suggested a genre of "tragedy" for the work:

> If all the tom-foolery and nonsense of an Oratorio were taken away, and some of the common sense and human nature of the modern drama substituted, such a piece as *Esther* could be made one of the most magnificent tragedies ever placed upon the stage; but then it might be an offense against orthodox

morals to present it in such a manner, for in the latter case [modern drama], it would be a wicked theatrical exhibition, while in the former it is simply a Cantata, a splendid distinction without any difference, with the exception that the latter is called by its true name, while the religious drama is not."[29]

Those critics determined to deny *Esther* a genre classification characterized by a text taken from the Hebrew Testament sometimes compared, however unjustifiably, Bradbury's score to works by venerated oratorio composers. In so doing, they audaciously questioned the composer's sacred purpose and laid bare his employment of secular musical idioms. Not surprisingly, nothing favorable or constructive could possibly result from such comparison. For example, one journalist caustically dismissed Bradbury's score as a work inferior to Handel's first oratorio, *Esther* (1732): "Its title [*Esther*], being that of one of Handel's immortal productions, betokens no small temerity on the part of the composer. Shall we judge it by comparison with that great work? We will not be so cruel to Mr. Bradbury; we will not be so disrespectful to Handel."[30]

Writing about a performance in 1859, a New Orleans journalist altogether denied *Esther* the designation of "oratorio": "As to the work itself it did not strike me as an 'oratorio' at all . . . . The great characterizing feature of that class of composition, recitative, was entirely wanting, and the choruses were mostly of a light operatic style of work possessing but little of the sacred character of oratorio . . . . This, we may remark, is the besetting fault of the work."[31] In another review, the *Chicago Tribune* sarcastically poked at all the fuss about Bradbury's score and emphatically stated that, as an oratorio, *Esther* hardly communicated even a modicum of drama and religious feeling: "I can easier conceive how infants might play 'Macbeth' than adults play 'Esther.' I think the same brilliant genius which adapted *Esther* for . . . the dramatic stage might now go to work upon 'Mary Had a Little Lamb' with success. This song has just as much dramatic interest as the *Esther* cantata."[32]

Esther as Opera?

Bradbury insisted that *Esther*'s music and his score's text did not remotely suggest the categories of either secular entertainment or opera. Still, his compositional choices confirm a deference to marketplace viability, and in this way, he all but guaranteed *Esther*'s allure among a broad range of musicians' abilities and audience preferences. He vehemently denounced the prevalence of *Esther* performances that included the trappings of secular opera—a genre he considered inappropriate for biblical narratives. Apparently, in the minds of many, staging, acting, and costumes made all the difference when it came to genre identity. Only some three months after the publication of R. W. Seager's revision, a Connecticut newspaper boldly announced, of Seager's recasting of Bradbury's score: "how like a genuine opera."[33] Should we therefore categorize staged presentations of *Esther* as some type of opera?

More than a decade after the initial publication of *Esther*, a Michigan newspaper published a review that typified the lingering slipperiness and lack of clarity with the whole issue of genre identity. The writer quoted below attempted to draw distinctions between the genre categories of cantata and opera and to determine whether or not *Esther* exemplified the latter designation:

"Cantata" is defined by Webster as "a poem set to music; a composition or song intermixed with recitatives and airs [arias]." "Opera" is defined by the same authority as "a dramatic composition, set to music and sung on the stage, accompanied by musical instruments, and enriched with magnificent dresses," &c., &c., and more correctly designates such an entertainment as this [staged production of *Esther*]. Incidents related in the Book of Esther are arranged for the stage and set to music, the characters personated to give as near as possible the appearance of reality. Whether called Cantata, Opera or Theatre, does not change the character of the performance . . . . [B]ut, if strangled under one name it will crop out under another and take its would-be extinguishers as captive. So, too, the stage and its attractions are just as enticing by whatever name they are called. It is a natural appetite that cannot be smothered or extinguished.[34]

Writing in 1927, respected critic and opera historian Edward Ellsworth Hipsher offered insights about the staged performances of Bradbury's score. Hipsher held Bradbury in high esteem, referring to him as "one of America's most gifted melodists, at times almost Mozartian." Of *Esther*, he noted:

[I]t might well be rated [labeled] as folk-opera. It has surpassed similar works in many thousands of performances, most of these having been in the nature of opera, with costumes and scenery . . . . If not a master-work, it is good folk-music . . . . [P]robably no other single work ever reached so many of our people, especially in remote places, and awoke in them a taste for better music on the stage than had been commonly known.[35]

Hipsher's comments honor the popular-song configuration and ethos of many of *Esther*'s numbers along with Bradbury's evocation of folk-tune idioms. By "folk-music," Hipsher drew attention to the ability of Bradbury's melodies to captivate the "folk"—that is, the general population. Many of the melodic configurations employed by Bradbury to set Cady's text were already quite familiar to singers and audiences, and their additional dissemination via *Esther* performances only enhanced their public profile and overall universality. Yet as previously mentioned, Bradbury's score did not include any arias in the operatic sense of the term, and he intended his score to be most appropriate for, and approachable by, amateur singers.

The public's appetite for opera-like renditions of *Esther* knew no limits, and increasingly lavish approaches to performing the piece became the rage across the continent. Surely, the vogue for staging *Esther* derived impetus from performances of George F. Root's secular, staged and costumed piece, *The Haymakers* (1857). Root did not shy away from theatrical renditions of this work, and his score even bore the subgenre designation of "operatic cantata." Although *The Haymakers* never achieved the celebrity-like stature of *Esther*, communities nonetheless experienced the enjoyment and satisfaction of making costumes and stage accessories for performances of Root's piece. Also, we should not underestimate the influence of Seager and his edition of *Esther* that, after all, established the parameters for staging the work. So too, the rise in popularity of operatic interpretations of biblical stories also provided dramaturgical models for directors of *Esther*.[36] Beyond the construction of elaborate sets, some communities enhanced their staging of *Esther* with dancers along with realistic enactment. For example, in an Iowa production, "the drinking scene between the King and Haman . . . and the banquet scene . . . [were] the most real of any, especially so to the performers for there was real food and drink" on stage.[37] In a production in Sacramento's Metropolitan Theater, a special added number called for "thirty pretty little maidens" to "sing and dance for the entertainment of the King and strew flowers at the feet of the Queen."[38] A journalist lauded the set of a production in Illinois, noteworthy for its "very elegant throne, upon which his majesty, King Ahasuerus, sat in royal dignity attended by guards of very martial aspect and appropriately armed and accoutred." This reviewer also provided details about "the calamity howling scene, in which the Jewish captives bewail their unfortunate condition," additionally noting, in accordance with Seager's recommendations, "the chorus [of Jews] in solid black presented a strong contrast to the bright and varied costumes displayed by the Persian courtiers."[39] Some communities spared no expense and effort with the more technical aspects of a production, such as lighting. As one West Coast columnist exuberantly announced, "The stage in Roberts Hall [in Ferndale, California] is to be illuminated with three hundred candle power electric lights, put in the hall expressly for the great coming event, 'the Cantata of Esther.'"[40]

In a display of operatic extravagance, an undetermined number of directors even added horses to their productions of *Esther*. This level of spectacle tested the very limits and boundaries of amateur stagecraft, and of course, the patience of inexperienced stagehands.[41] Not surprisingly, directors dangled the prospect of onstage horses in *Esther* before the public in the form of newspaper advertisements and posters. For example, in 1877, director G. W. Jackson published notices alerting readers to his elaborate theatrical plan: "[I]n the fifth act there will be a grand triumphal march in which horses . . . will take part."[42] Reviewers neglected to mention just how many horses Jackson actually used in his production. In 1878, J. A. DeWitt, the director of a Chicago production, informed prospective attendees that "Mordecai will appear in the Grand Procession mounted upon the Royal Egyptian trained horse, 'Cleopatra.'"[43] Local newspapers printed dismissive reviews of DeWitt's production, and in particular, complained about the "scrub pony" that replaced the highly touted thoroughbred "Cleopatra," intended for Mordecai's triumphal appearance toward the end of the drama.[44] At least one horse could claim the distinction of having participated in multiple *Esther* productions. This honor goes to "Captain," who earned a reputation of acting "stage-struck" owing to his repeated appearances in *Esther*. Described as "one of the special features of the evening," Ahasuerus entered the stage astride Captain, the "magnificent horse in the triumphant march."[45] With commensurate enthusiasm, a Missouri newspaper reported, "The Tableau in which a beautiful Arabian horse appeared will never be forgotten. The scene was splendidly unique and elicited spontaneous and repeated applause."[46] But horses on stage sometimes presented untoward complications, such as occurred in Vernal, Utah, in 1907. The director of this production used a horse in some undisclosed capacity. Journalist Sue R. Watson wrote of the horse "that was supposed to be a magnificent steed [but] turned out to be a hang-tailed cayuse [Native American pony] and did what horses do when they get stage fright."[47]

Performances in 1922 in La Jolla, California, inspired detailed newspaper accounts of the entire production with special attention paid to the appearance of a horse on stage. I include a more substantial discussion of this production here as it attracted considerable publicity and was directed by a famous opera singer who also happened to be a member of a European royal family. Moreover, a photograph survives that includes the horse used in this production—the only known example of such an image.

The local chapter of the nationally influential Woman's Club sponsored the La Jolla production and appointed the celebrated Countess Laura de Turczynowicz as director. In advertisements for her production, the melodramatic Countess promised a "Pageant of *Esther*" and assured newspaper readers they could expect an event of unprecedented visual appeal and startling originality. Reviewers gushed about the "extravaganza," calling it "spectacular" and "the biggest affair ever presented in La Jolla."[48] According to one account, "rare scarfs" and "pieces of rich cloth" had been loaned to the Woman's Club for the dance scenes. The production's costumes, made by residents of La Jolla, culminated a "long study of the period and the characters" found in the Book of Esther.[49] This event also marked the dance debut of the Countess's fourteen-year-old daughter, Wanda Jolanda de Turczynowicz, who performed before the king.[50]

Adding to the pageantry of the event, the Countess proposed the inclusion of a horse, to be selected by her, personally. She initially insisted that only a totally white horse would suffice. When such a horse could not be found, she settled for a palomino with a white blaze. The chosen horse completed an arduous course of special training, grooming, and proper diet under the watchful attention and expertise of one of the Countess's many production assistants. A local journalist conferred the award for "most nervous actor" on "Capitan" the "gaily caparisoned steed" that enacted "the part of 'the horse the king rideth upon' [Esther 6:8–9]." Extensive training notwithstanding, Capitan required considerable coaching and constant handling during the performances, a task assigned to otherwise occupied Delano Cadman, who also happened to be playing the role of Haman.[51] An image of some of the production's cast (figure 4.1) shows the Prophetess standing to the right of

Figure 4.1. Cast, *Esther*, posed in the famous pergola of the Woman's Club, La Jolla, CA, 1922. La Jolla Historical Society Collection.

Capitan, attired in black and wearing her characteristic conical head covering. Queen Esther and King Ahasuerus stand to the Prophetess's left. During the photo session, the restless and incessantly "prancing" Capitan required "the combined efforts of Haman and the Captain of the Guard" to keep him under control so that he could appear in the photograph with the rest of the cast.[52]

Some productions of *Esther* took place during Lent, offering a Lenten alternative to opera in a manner similar to the function of classical oratorios—a practice associated, especially, with Great Britain. Yet staged versions of *Esther*, one Oregon writer sniffed, hardly differed from opera, and those who attended performances of *Esther* during Lent "imagined" they were, in fact, enjoying an opera performance. Unimpressed with Cady's lyrics and Bradbury's music, the same writer referred to *Esther* as a "moral muddle" and described the work as "magnificently weak and sublimely harmless" and thus wholly appropriate for Lent. "Talking about Lent," the writer sneered, "I think 'Esther' was a fitting finale to it, and I wonder that all those who were so bent upon being wretched [during Lent] didn't go to see it. I think if there ever was anything in the world which would conduce to make wretchedness more wretched it was 'Esther.'"[53]

Closing Thoughts

Even as some critics objected to the identifiable secular idioms in *Esther*, Bradbury never wavered from his insistence that his score satisfied the sentiments and purpose of a sacred work. For Bradbury, the accepted parameters of setting a biblically derived text using recycled secular music did not detract from its sacrality. His insistence that *Esther* was, indeed, sacred brings to mind musicologist Jake Johnson's assertion that "musicals themselves are religious texts covered in a thin veneer of entertainment."[54] Even with the addition of theatrical elements and the score's entrée into the world of staged entertainment, *Esther* maintained, in the opinions of most audiences and critics, an unquestionable allegiance to Bradbury's and Cady's sacred purpose.

However, even as the vogue of staging *Esther* came to dominate the work's performance history, the use of the genre designations of "cantata" or "oratorio" in reference to *Esther* continued. We should remember that directors presented the score as an unstaged cantata or oratorio for only a short period of time from the late 1850s into the early 1860s. Although the category "opera" was used in descriptions of *Esther*, the piece did not comfortably fit into this genre as its staged renditions shared few attributes in comparison to religious or sacred musical dramas written by European composers. At the very least, Bradbury wrote his score for amateur performers and pedagogical purposes, and furthermore, the piece does not display the characteristics associated with classical opera. As such, *Esther* strikes me as an early example of the subgenre of "religious musical theater" even as this category would not gain widespread currency until the 1960s. We are all familiar with more recent examples of musicals with texts derived from the Judeo-Christian biblical tradition, including *Godspell*, *Jesus Christ Superstar*, *Children of Eden*, *Joseph and the Amazing Technicolor Dreamcoat*, and *Rock Nativity*, among many others. These and other examples of this subgenre are often performed by amateur organizations, especially choirs associated with churches and schools. The musical language inherent in these pieces reflects popular and familiar styles of their day, as does *Esther*.

Some critics engaged in heated debates about the sacredness or secularity of *Esther* and therefore, they perpetuated unsettling questions regarding the score's actual genre identity. The content of these debates circulated widely, and the publicity resulting from these discussions only added to the public's curiosity about and intrigue with *Esther*. For many participants and audiences, however, the biblical source of the work's narrative rendered it undeniably sacred no matter where performed or whether staging and costumes were included. Others could not reconcile what they perceived as an irrefutable and intentional dismissal of the sacred purpose of the Queen Esther narrative no matter how resolutely Bradbury reiterated his original intentions. One need look no further than the music itself, some critics complained, as it evoked popular tunes, hints of minstrelsy, and even resembled opera in the minds of some. I devote the next chapter to consideration of the moral and religious controversy engendered by theatrical presentations of *Esther*.

CHAPTER FIVE

RELIGIOUS CONTROVERSY

Two reviews, published in the 1870s, illustrate the polarizing influence of theatrical interpretations of *Esther*. Writing in support of staging Bradbury's piece, a Chicago reporter gleefully announced, "At last the good people have an opera which they can attend without any detriment to their morals. It is 'Esther.'"[1] Yet the opposite point of view also occupied some critics, as in an item that claimed "the residents of Iowa have just discovered that the 'Cantata of Esther'—so frequently rendered by church choirs—is nothing less than an opera, and refuse [any] longer to countenance so sinful a thing. That it is an opera (not a big, fat opera, but a kind of lean one) there can be no doubt."[2] Significantly, both reviewers designated *Esther* as opera—the former finding no fault with the genre worthy of mention, the latter censuring opera as sinful. Potential sinfulness aside, the comments of these critics confirm the transformation of *Esther* into a staged musical presentation exhibiting characteristics associated with opera. Directors of such productions unintentionally added grist to arguments against theatrical performances of biblically derived narratives, especially as they followed R. W. Seager's directions for staging quite closely, including the literal enactment of the drinking and dancing scenes.

This chapter brings together a variety of religious and moral debates in circulation during the nineteenth and early twentieth centuries regarding theater attendance and staged entertainment. Many of these viewpoints reflected conservative objections to theaters as places of debauchery and their productions as morally suspect. Other viewpoints indicated a gradual and ongoing process of relaxation—even tolerance—among Protestant clergy and the religiously observant toward theaters. One thing is certain, however: staged performances of *Esther* provided, arguably, the most prominent lightning rod for ensuing debates about the moral status of theatrical entertainment and the venues where such events took place. So pressing and ubiquitous were these debates that hardly anyone could hope to avoid them or maintain neutrality in the matter. Some clergy and pious citizens voiced condemnation of staging *Esther* as tantamount to a sacrilegious portrayal of a biblical narrative. Yet many considered Bradbury's work to be sublime, harmless, instructive, and wholesome, even when staged. Still others viewed *Esther* as unequivocally secular entertainment—as an Oriental spectacle, even, and one delightfully imbued with supposedly authentic representations of life in the ancient Middle East. With the prevalence and popularity of Orientalist manifestations in *Esther*, audiences and critics came to expect an extravaganza depicting an autocratic and arrogant monarch, a resplendent palace, exotic attire, wild crowd scenes, and subtle titillation.[3]

Costumes, Acting, and Dancing

Writing in 1861 about an unstaged rendition of *Esther*, a reviewer baldly stated, "[H]ad the characters been costumed appropriately, it would have added much to the interest of the piece."[4] In fact, the earliest alteration to Bradbury's conception of *Esther* occurred when production directors added costumes. For some, this interpretive alteration alone threatened to defile or eclipse any sacred character the work possessed. Many Protestant clergy insisted on the preservation of a clear distinction between *Esther* and opera or staged entertainment, a goal rendered much more realistic and attainable if singers did not wear stage attire.

Some clergy voiced strong objections to costumes, as their very presence seemed to imply the inevitability of stage enactment and thus, by extension, the risk of moral depravity. Writing in 1873, Rev. James D. Eaton (1848–1928), a Congregationalist minister in Portland, Oregon, voiced opposition to theatrical attire for just this reason. He urged that "the *dress and acting*" be "left out of 'Esther' . . . and then it would not border so closely upon the Opera [italics original]."[5] Such an association with the secular attributes of opera presented a gnarly moral dilemma as, in Eaton's mind, the biblical origin of *Esther*'s text mandated strict adherence to an unstaged interpretation.

In 1879, Rev. H. S. Adams, pastor of the Methodist Episcopal Church in Chicago, wrestled with the possibility of allowing costumes to be worn in his congregation's proposed performance of *Esther*. As he summarized the situation, "[A]t first it was supposed that the oratorio was to be sung without any adventitious aids." Adams then consulted with his congregation's leaders and "the decision was reached that there could be no possible harm in the singers being clad in costumes in keeping with the characters they represented."⁶ Even as Adams reconciled the matter of costumes with an apparent absence of lingering divisiveness or angst, other churches and communities struggled mightily with this issue.

As costumes for *Esther*'s women participants sometimes displayed features or designs considered, by some, as indecent even for formal evening wear, the actual style and configuration of such stage attire occasionally elicited harsh criticism. More specifically, any low-necked women's costuming or that which exposed legs and arms violated standards of appropriate femininity, modesty, and decorum among more conservative-minded citizens. We should recall how R. W. Seager fanned these flames with his recommendation for dress length to be, ideally, "the shorter the prettier," thus risking a display of women's legs.⁷ The question of whether to perform *Esther* in purportedly indecent costuming caused a furor for the entire community of Chicopee Falls, Massachusetts, in 1891. A local Baptist clergyman, Rev. L. L. Hobbs, vigorously protested the participation of his congregants in the community's presentation of *Esther* largely because of the alleged risqué designs of the costumes selected by the production's director. As Hobbs argued, the "décolleté dresses, one foot short [in length] . . . without sleeves and low necked" assembled for the women singers were too revealing to be worn for any occasion.⁸ In opposition to Hobbs, the newly elected mayor of Chicopee Falls, George Sylvester Taylor (1822–1910), a member of a more tolerant Congregationalist church, defended the costuming choices. He admitted, however, that "the sleeves were short and the women's arms . . . exposed." Nonetheless, as Taylor reassured newspaper readers, "the cantata was certainly a religious one."⁹ A local newspaper critic sided with Taylor and found little fault with the costumes: "As to the skirts of the chorus—well, they were not so very abbreviated [short], but if they were, the girls had bandaged their shapely limbs in silken folds with gypsy-like effect."¹⁰ Emboldened by the sensuous intimation of this critic's comment, Hobbs delivered a sermon on the Sunday following the performances in which he vociferously reiterated his objections. The matter continued to attract widespread newspaper publicity far beyond the borders of Massachusetts. Even the New Orleans *Times-Picayune* weighed in on Hobbs's sermon and sniped, "[N]o amateur or other comic opera company can expect to get along [i.e., succeed] if a preacher is allowed to dictate" dramaturgical and artistic decisions. (Of significance, the *Times-Picayune* offered a genre identification of "comic opera" for *Esther*.)¹¹ Some four years after the Chicopee controversy, a Rocklin, California, newspaper issued a supportive comment about similar costuming and complimented the "short skirts and low-necked dresses" in a local production of the "opera Queen Esther." As the writer assuaged readers: "[T]he entertainment afforded in Queen Esther is good . . . and we advise all who haven't done so to see it. It is a change from our general local performances, the soloists are good, the costumes lovely, and the girls pretty."[12]

The appearance of dancing in *Esther* productions also caused much consternation. A Sacramento news item, published in 1877, highlighted the potential relationship between onstage dancing and the wearing of revealing costumes. However, the writer summarily dismissed the remarks of "stern churchmen" who refused to welcome innovative, wholesome entertainments into their communities:

[T]here is dancing in *Esther*, and the dancers are enveloped in drapery more scant than that of the modern conventional street dress! Well, there was dancing all through the Bible and the dancers were dressed in the costumes of their respective ages. God gave men and women ears and souls to enjoy music, and legs and muscles to dance with. Why should they not enjoy them in a rational manner? We have never had any sympathy with and very little respect for the ideas of those stern churchmen who rigidly frown down all amusements, and particularly those of a dramatic, musical or saltatory character, as being of the devil, brimstoney, and to be shunned as one would shun a mad dog or a den of rattlesnakes. If any considerable portion of the churchmen have relaxed in their opposition to harmless amusements it is a cause for joy, rather than censure, that they have come to see the light, and they have no reason to apologize because they have become rational.[13]

Dancing also stirred up a fuss two years later, in Chicago. In the fall of 1879, members of the city's Ada Street Methodist Episcopal Church began rehearsals for their performance of *Esther* scheduled for November 27, Thanksgiving Day. Preparation took place in the church and the production's director welcomed members of the community to attend. As rehearsals progressed, costumes, acting, and dancing were gradually added. The Methodist Episcopal denomination strictly forbade dancing and a disgruntled parishioner not only voiced strenuous protests about the entire production, but also audaciously, if guardedly, disputed the very parameters of what constituted "dance":

A religious question has lately caused much excitement in Chicago—namely, whether there has or has not been dancing in a certain Methodist church in that city. The dispute arose out of the performance of the cantata of *Esther* by members of the congregation. This performance led to the publication by an influential [church] brother of a card in which he said, "Vastly ennobling was the scene! The youthful members and probationers . . . dressed in gaudy theatrical costumes, performed their respective parts in dancing . . . . Does not the discipline of the Methodist Episcopal Church expressly and positively forbid dancing? . . . For several weeks prior to the opera [performances] the church has been open in the evenings for the rehearsal of its actor members. Very commendable, indeed, to see Church members engaged in taking their first lessons in dancing in the house of God. Alas! Alas! Has the time already arrived when the house of God is to be converted into a dancing academy and the church to be opened for theatrical performances?" . . . [T]he minister of the church denies that there was any dancing in the proper acceptation of the term. In a rejoinder which he has published he says, "In a certain part of the oratorio two young ladies, entering from different sides of the platform [stage], approached the King with a gliding motion. I am willing to confess that the motion was not a walk; but I am equally sure it was not a dance."[14]

Staging *Esther* in Churches

Some Protestant congregations permitted staged productions of *Esther* within their sanctuaries or social halls while others condemned theatrical presentations in church buildings as an unwelcome intrusion of sacrilegious entertainment. R. W. Seager often launched productions of *Esther* in churches and occasionally drew the ire of the religiously devout. As one press item complained of such a performance: "Prof. Seager is debauching the church morals of Medina, New York, with the grand comico-religious drama of Esther."[15] An Ann Arbor, Michigan, critic, writing in 1866, admitted "some persons were dissatisfied" that a staged performance of *Esther* had been allowed to take place in a local church. But "for ourselves," the critic explained, "we beg leave to dissent from this view. We believe that it is not only appropriate [for *Esther*] to be performed in a church, but that the church is just the place for its performance."[16] Another Michigan critic concurred, noting, "[T]he Church and the Stage have sometimes worked in harmony" and then concluded, "[T]he stage, [when] properly managed, is a most powerful instrument of good."[17]

Among the congregations and clergy who prohibited staged performances of *Esther* in their buildings, many did so primarily because of the realistic enactment in the banquet scene and in the drinking duet sung by the king and Haman. A review published in 1877 typified objections to these particular dramaturgical choices: "We liked the Cantata very much, except the drinking and dancing. Those, in the church, were out of place.... Drinking and dancing in a church of strictest total abstinence principles and discipline!!!! Comment is unnecessary."[18]

Other journalists entered the debate regarding the appropriateness of staging *Esther* in churches as in this objection from a Michigan critic: "Theatricals are insidiously insinuating themselves into day and Sunday school exercises and exhibitions as an effectual instructor and entertainer."[19] In another opinion, Evanston, Illinois, physician and occasional critic H. B. Hemenway decried the intrusion of staged performances in churches. As a theatrical drama, *Esther* joined Hemenway's list of questionable entertainments whose presence in places of worship disrupted concentration on spiritual matters. Hemenway thought it unconscionable "that those who find it very wrong to go to an opera are pleased to hear and see in their religious home a much inferior piece acted out if only the theme be taken from the Bible, as in the Cantata of Esther."[20] Rev. George A. Maston, who wholeheartedly agreed with the sentiments just quoted, made the following observations as he entered what he considered to be a "fine church" to attend a performance of *Esther*:

> Just look at the crowd of people going in! Having procured a ticket, we followed the crowd up to the auditorium [sanctuary], and the room is now filled with a fashionable audience; and the place which was formerly set apart for the worship of God is now changed into a modern theatre, with gorgeously decked stage, upon which ... are to be played celebrated pieces ... [such as] the Cantata of Queen Esther.... [During the *Esther* performance] there was dancing, which was done right then and there in a most artistic style.

Maston blamed the acceptance of secular entertainments in church buildings for a noticeable relaxation of religious piety among congregants: "The effect of these irreligious acts upon the spiritual lives of the membership of the church may be seen in their indifference to their religious duties, in their general tendency to disbelief, and in the utter disregard of sinners for things sacred . . . [along with] the decay of Protestantism . . . and [the] intemperate habits of both pastor and people, which are manifest."[21]

Esther in Theaters

As mentioned earlier, most pious citizens refused to attend any events that took place in theaters. Moreover, many Protestants rejected the idea, proposed by more tolerant Christians, that theater productions could, in actuality, offer moral lessons reasonably congruent with those presented during church services. A Rhode Island periodical drew attention to the potential for moral risk and temptation associated with attendance at venues where secular productions took place:

> People of late have labored to convince honest men that theaters are the best teachers of sound morality, but I, sitting at my fireside, have not yet become won to that belief. After questioning many good men on the matter and reading some pages of the history of the drama, I am surprised to find that the opinion of a majority of men of wisdom and sense agree with my own. I have been searching, too, for the benefits of stage instruction, and am compelled to say that I have been disappointed in my search . . . [T]here is danger . . . in attending a theater, [and] there must be wrong in leading one to desire to attend such displays.[22]

Yet during the 1870s, music directors increasingly launched *Esther* productions in local theaters or community halls, in part to sidestep the heated exchange of opinions regarding the staging of biblical dramas in churches. Moreover, such venues offered practical benefits as well as many such facilities had stages specifically designed for theatrical performance, and these could accommodate larger choruses. Also, a more substantial venue attracted more robust audiences along with the financial benefits of ticket sales and charitable fundraising. Even with these advantages, however, staging *Esther* in theaters created an outcry among devout citizens who usually shunned such places on moral grounds owing to the reputedly indecent entertainment they offered. Those opposed to theaters and the events presented in them vehemently insisted that nothing wholesome or spiritually uplifting could possibly occur at any venue where staged entertainment took place. A Michigan journalist who lamented the recalcitrant nature of protests against theaters admitted, "[T]he [Protestant] church has for a long time been arrayed against it" and acknowledged the unfortunate persistence of a "deadly hostility" between those who held conflicting viewpoints in the matter.[23]

So, too, audiences at events in theaters were known to engage, occasionally, in disruptive, even unruly, behavior. As documented by Lawrence Levine, indecorous audience conduct further exacerbated religious objections to theaters, and dramatic productions, more generally.[24] Although instances of rude conduct at *Esther* performances were apparently rare, a disturbance in 1880 received national newspaper attention. The incident unfolded when a loud verbal exchange between the actor playing King Ahasuerus and a member of the audience brought the performance to a standstill. As a Texas newspaper reported, "At a performance of the cantata of 'Esther,' at Dallas, Ahasuerus was advised by somebody in the audience not to 'cut it too fat.' [exaggerate or show off]. The personator of the great Assyrian went to the footlights and said, 'This is a religious show and you'll have to be decent. I'm Ahasuerus just now, but after the show I'm Sam Turner; and if any duffer [rude person] would like to cut it fat then I'll give him a mighty lively welcome.'" Clearly on the defensive, Turner offered to meet with anyone who hurled insults at him after the conclusion of the performance, quite possibly by way of some sort of physical altercation.[25] Various comments about this incident appeared in newspapers across the continent.

Objections to theaters even extended to operatic settings of sacred or religious libretti, especially those adapted from a biblical narrative. Of Gioachino Rossini's *The Israelites in Egypt*, a New York critic admitted its production "was a most hazardous speculation, for the public do not usually associate anything holy with the name of a theatre." Of course, the possibility of improper audience conduct, such as that described above, greatly influenced opinions regarding attendance at Rossini's opera. Decrying such notions as a "foolish feeling" that "should at once be dismissed," this reviewer assured readers that audiences at biblical operas acted with appropriate "propriety and decorum" and paid "deep and profound attention" to productions fully "imbued with the sacred character of the drama."[26]

Opera and Morality

Among the contentious nineteenth-century discussions of opera and morality, one in particular most effectively represented pertinent and contemporaneous arguments. In a heated exchange, Rev. William Weston Patton, a prominent and respected Congregationalist minister in Washington, DC, verbally sparred with Unitarian clergyman Robert L. Collier. Patton stalwartly maintained his opposition to opera in any form. Accordingly, he issued this statement:

> We reason about "the opera" as it is among us, and is described by its frequenters.... That the plots are, at best, frivolous, and very commonly loose in morality, is seldom denied, it being only claimed that they are of little or no account, the music being all that is sought. That a few attend simply for the music, may be granted; that a multitude go for the fashion, the display of dress, the excitement, and the sensual delight of song, dance and beauty, amid displays which appeal to one's lower nature and "moral weakness," is hardly to be denied.[27]

Rev. Collier offered this retort: "If the drama, if the opera, if dancing ... are sinful, if they are in any wise destructive of the religious sentiment and social order, let the clergy ... show wherein and why. Let them do this, not with mere wordy weapons, but with serious spirit and unanswerable logic, and the religious consciousness of the country will be on the side of the clergy."[28] Collier then expounded on the virtues of opera:

> [T]he legitimate [operatic] drama is to be endorsed. It is an educator. It is in no wise to be apologized for.... Anyone who objects to it on moral grounds must either be ignorant of it ... or there certainly must be a moral weakness in the nature of such objections.... [W]e who can enjoy it ... ought to feel a profound sorrow for such people because they do not know the infinite delights and joys of which, by their lack of musical culture, they are deprived .... It is a sorry religion that rejects it.[29]

Collier concluded his argument by equating drama and opera to a religious observance:

> "[I]f ... going to the theatre and going to the opera is healthful, refining, educating, and spiritualizing, if the soul is wafted heavenward upon the strains of the human voice as it expresses passion and power; if the setting forth, in elocution and eloquence, and acting ... is healthful and refining; if it lifts and enlarges the intellect, then God has sent these precious gifts to be used by you just as you would ... to His glory sing a hymn or say your prayers."[30]

Patton lashed out at Collier and accused him of audaciously delivering "a singular discourse in defense of theatre-going, which astonished even our secular papers, which are not often astonished at anything!"[31]

At first glance, a viewpoint expressed in 1877 by Rev. Dr. Israel E. Dwinell (1820–1890), pastor of the First Congregational Church of Christ in Sacramento, California, appears to coincide with Patton's. Specifically, Dwinell defined opera "as a kind of performance which 'sacrifices everything to music and action.'" Yet he also welcomed a more moderate view of staged biblical dramas, such as *Esther*, and gave due consideration to this enlightened opinion:

> We suppose, in our ignorance of the strides being made towards complete emancipation from old-fashioned religious views, that the presentation of the cantata of *Esther* with scenic and sensational accessories was quite phenomenal and in advance of our previous experience. If, however, as now seems to be the case, not only the cantata and oratorio, but opera and opera bouffe are included in the list of unobjectionable performances, we can only say that we had ludicrously failed in our attempt to estimate the pace [of change] of which the Church was capable.... [W]e have, at no time, found fault with the Church on relaxing its severity towards the stage.[32]

Only a day after the publication of Rev. Dwinell's remarks, a Sacramento journalist weighed in on the debate. Commensurate with a more relaxed approach to theaters, a writer, quoted at length below, cautiously recommended attending a theatrical performance of *Esther*:

> The recent representation of the *Cantata of Esther* at a theater in this city, with dramatic mountings and ballet accompaniments, for the benefit of a church and under the supervision and auspices of churchmen, has occasioned some discussion between the laity and clergy, churchmen and non-churchmen of

this community as to the position the church does or should occupy toward the stage. On the one hand it is contended that the production of *Esther* under the quasi patronage and for the benefit of one congregation, is an evidence that the church has shifted attitude toward the stage, which has hitherto been one of frowning opposition, and in this light those who introduced *Esther* to the public under the wings of the church are condemned for improper teachings. On the other hand, it is claimed . . . that the Cantata [*Esther*] is more of an oratorio than a dramatic performance and therefore is not to be confounded with the usual unrighteous follies of the stage. On the one hand there has been unrestricted hypercriticism of an unfair nature, and on the other a weak effort to apologize for that which needs no apology.

The productions of such compositions as "Esther," even by church members, clergy or laity, should not require apology except for faults manifested in the representation. The story of the piece is elevating, the music is intended to be good—and is so when well rendered—and although the dressing of the piece is not as sober as a Quaker meeting, it corresponds with history, and is therefore proper and morally correct, unless it be held to be morally wrong for the church to countenance anything that correctly reflects historical events.

If the churches would do more to encourage and bring out representations of the character of the [*Esther*] Cantata, they would do more than they have done to advance the cause of morality and elevate the public taste and character . . . . [C]hurchmen have become somewhat more liberal-minded and tolerant in the matter of amusements. In the interests of humanity it is to be hoped that this spirit of toleration will increase, and that thus the character of popular amusements will be elevated and made better, as well as the character and influence of religious entertainments and church teachings.[33]

In Portland, Rev. James D. Eaton also struggled with the controversy engendered by staged *Esther* performances and their resemblance to opera. However, he also allowed for the possible benefit of such theatrical productions if attendees approached these events imbued with "the right spirit" and remained receptive to the work's "noble sentiments":

[D]o you approve of the opera? I cannot say, just looking at the opera as it now stands, differing too little from the average theater [play]. Are you not afraid that the Oratorio [*Esther*] may glide into the Opera? . . . Dangers crowd about us on every side, and it is well to have a wholesome fear of them.... But it [*Esther*] must be judged upon its own merits, and not hampered with the weight of abuses, for which it is not responsible. The noble sentiments and emotions are there, and the noble music to express them is there, and I would that all the singers and the listeners might be moved by a noble spirit. Judge the Oratorio [*Esther*] by the same rules which I laid down in my sermon of this morning.... Does it unfit you for your proper work, either mentally or physically? Does it disincline you to public or private devotion? Does it induce in you a trifling spirit? Do you come away from the hall over-excited, heated, flushed, sensual? Then you will join me in saying it is wrong for you to go to the Oratorio of Esther.... But I believe you can be made better by going, if you will listen in the right spirit.[34]

For some, the aesthetic and musical characteristics of *Esther*'s score and lyrics rendered the controversy over whether or not the piece ought to be considered as opera moot. Opera required professional singers, a few critics argued, whereas Bradbury and Cady created a work for community music-making and instruction suitable for amateur performers and audiences of all ages and beliefs. Furthermore, some claimed, Cady's text and Bradbury's music could not adequately respond to or withstand the rigors of a fully operatic interpretation. Instead, blame for *Esther*'s performative ambivalence rested with Bradbury's and Cady's lack of experience in the realm of theatrical works and their inability to take sufficient advantage of the narrative's dramatic potential:

> The predominant passions involved [in the Book of Esther] are hate, pride, love, patriotism and religion. The story is simple and direct, with features so entirely probable and natural, and elements so highly dramatic and so nearly complete in themselves, as to leave very little to do for a satisfactory dramatist who should choose to take up this subject. It would be unjust to Bradbury to suppose that he was not... innocent of dramaturgy... and absurd to say that his work was, in any sense, a dramatic one. It contained the germ; but he did not know how to make it grow.... Bradbury, or whoever wrote his libretto, was simply incapable of forming an approximate idea of the converging treatment demanded by a strict and accurate dramatic conception of the plot. As a hymnologist he was successful, but his "Esther" was not composed for the stage; ... it was a good-natured amplification, and no more, of the

general idea of the goodness and sublime courage of the Jewess Queen, and the nobility of the King. Undoubtedly, the composer's motive was extremely praiseworthy, and the hold his little work has taken proves the success of his efforts to crystallize a point to the predominant religious taste and sentiment of the age. His score requires considerable modification, however, to be adapted to a satisfactory operatic presentation; but, at best, no surgery can ever extirpate his historical and dramatic defects, and retain any of the work . . . . These defects, nothing but a remanding of the whole subject, for treatment *de nove*, can ever cure. The secret of the popularity of his music lies in its smoothness, its religious feeling, the attractiveness of its rather limited melodic features, the scenic effects, imposing pageantry and contrasting costumes, where these are possible, and that spontaneous rallying of the human mind to the side of what is right, beautiful and distressed, and against what is wrong, repulsive and menacing. These principles reconcile the spectator to the . . . rather meager music; for, though Bradbury's melodies charm by their freshness and simplicity, [and] a certain originality and freedom from excessive vocal decoration, he was not a massive or varied harmonist, and his score is hardly strong enough to bear much superstructive orchestration. The lack of a central idea in the composer's own mind explains the liberties that are taken with his work; vagaries and interpolations being even suggested by the work itself, and interludes being frequently indispensable. This passivity is to be regretted, because it turns the book [Bradbury's score] over to what sometimes prove incompetent interpretations, and crude and amateurish business, from which, together with the inherent defects of the work, the powerful argument of the story so frequently suffers.[35]

Clearly, the mention of a need to supplement Bradbury's score with "interpolations" and "interludes" indicates the writer's familiarity with the original design of its music. Although the review lauded the moralistic sentiments conveyed in *Esther*, the writer nonetheless took serious issue with the goals of amateur performances and the style of music so essential to making such productions successful and relevant. Moreover, these comments confirm the writer's irrefutable preference for those interpretations of biblical narratives composed for, and performed by, professional opera companies.

However much controversy staged presentations of biblical texts ignited in the nineteenth century, such performances usually occupied higher moral ground than did operatic settings of libretti derived from fictive or secular sources. Just such a viewpoint informed a journalist's recollection and assessment of Emma Abbott's stage career and its moral trajectory, beginning with her performance of *Esther*'s title role in 1862.³⁶ Protracted discussions over the alleged immorality of opera assumed added gravitas when Abbott, famous by this time as the "Peoria warbler," announced plans to perform the title role of Rossini's *Semiramide* (1823), an opera renowned, or notorious, for its theme of incest:

> Emma Abbott, our ambitious and popular American prima donna, has just included the opera of *Semiramide* in her repertory. As we remember the story, Semiramide was a lady who manifested an ambition to get rid of her husband in order that she might marry her own son. If this is the kind of opera our Emma is coming to, we shall begin to regret that there ever was such a town as Peoria. When our Emma left Peoria, it was with the laudable determination never to lift up her tuneful voice in naughty opera. It was with great difficulty that she was persuaded to sing in any kind of opera at all. But alas! the descent from the cantata of *Esther, the Beautiful Queen*, to [such operas as] the *Chimes of Normandy* [by Robert Planquette], and thence to [Victor Massé's] *Paul and Virginia*, and thence to [Charles Gounod's] *Faust*, and thence to [Giuseppe Verdi's] *Traviata*, is gradual but sure. And now the pride of the prairies has so far forgotten her Peoria training, and is so recreant to the vows she registered in high heaven when she stepped from the concert platform [stage] upon the lyric [opera] stage, that she will boldly appear in public in the repulsive disguise of an immoral heathen queen who is enamored of her own son.³⁷

The author of this scathing critique might have had in mind the following attributes of the operas listed as irrefutable evidence of Abbott's alleged affinity for reputedly indecent repertoire: first, as *opéra comique*, Planquette's *Chimes of Normandy* (1877) features light music suffused with waltzes, jigs, and other dances of supposed loose morality; second, the plot of Massé's *Paul and Virginia* (1876) centers around the colonial slave trade and emergent female sexuality; third, Gounod's *Faust* dramatizes the temptations of the devil and the intractability of evil and sin; and finally, the central character of Verdi's *La Traviata* (1853), the tubercular courtesan Violetta, frequents glittery social events and eventually cohabitates with her lover. Incontrovertibly, Abbott's addition of the title role of *Semiramide* to her repertoire represented a watershed moment for some of her more religiously devout admirers who could not countenance the turn her career had taken.

The controversy over *Esther*'s disputed morality also revolved around another closely related issue: whether or not a biblically derived text could, or should, accurately retell events chronicled in a sacred narrative. To alter biblical content for theatrical or entertainment purposes constituted, in the eyes of many, a manifestation of blasphemy that only served to underscore the depraved nature of such efforts. In 1882, an incensed critic published a severe and vitriolic review of an apparently thoroughly distasteful *Esther* performance that took place in Montana. In addition to condemning *Esther* to the ultra-secular and sometimes bawdy entertainment genre of "burlesque," the writer castigated the production's director for the purportedly farcical depiction of a biblical queen:

> The cantata of Esther is sacrilegious because it burlesques one of the most beautiful female characters in the Bible. Of course, it is never expected that good singing and good acting can be mixed up in a burlesque, so about all the performers have to do is to stand up like a row of tree boxes, open their mouths, and howl. Yet in the face of all this, we have known some of the strictest ministerial divines [clergymen] to assume parts in it, particularly that of Ahasuerus.[38]

Historical allegiance occupied other critics who not only interrogated Bradbury's claim of sacred status for *Esther*, but also chastised Cady for his inaccurate retelling of the Book of Esther.[39] For example, Unitarian clergyman Rev. Thomas L. Eliot denounced Cady's omission of Queen Vashti's banishment in *Esther*'s text. (Cady began his text's narrative after the events precipitating Vashti's exit.) Eliot berated Cady, who "should by no means have left out Vashti, the deposed Queen—the representative woman, not only for her time, but for all time—who, rather than forfeit her womanhood by appearing at a drunken debauch at the bidding of her lord, chose to forfeit not only the King's favor and her throne, but even life itself, if need be."[40] Critic, editor, and suffrage activist Abigail Scott Duniway expressed a similar viewpoint and referred to *Esther* as "an ingenious distortion of facts." She singled out not only the absence of Vashti's role in Cady's version of the narrative, but also what she perceived as the centrality of Ahasuerus in *Esther*: "If one had never read the history of Queen Esther, and had the fact never been known that she became the wife of the old drunken debauchee, Ahasuerus, under very shocking circumstances, after Vashti, the real Queen, had been deposed for a reason very much to Vashti's credit, we might look upon the man who wrote up the drama, whose name shall be nameless . . . as a marvel of historical accuracy." In a subsequent comment, Duniway ranted about Ahasuerus and Haman and their unjustifiable dominance in Cady's version of the biblical narrative:

> Prominent among the actors in this Oratorical drama was King Ahasuerus, though why he should be prominent, except for the amount of bad whiskey he drinks, the horrid debauches he indulges in and the Bacchanalian songs he sings, deponent saith not. In the nineteenth century of the Christian era people set little store by kings, especially Ahasuerus. This old dotard, so the play [*Esther*] hath it, had a Prime Minister named Haman, of yours truly knows but little from what she saw and heard, except that he was a big-feeling, blustering fellow . . . [who] piled on the agony [histrionics] in the right places.[41]

However forthright Duniway may have been, she nonetheless revealed an absence of familiarity with the Book of Esther, noticeable especially when she admitted her seeming unawareness of the pivotal role played by Haman in the narrative.

The vogue of staging *Esther* for fundraising purposes also frustrated some clergy as such practices seemed to condone, however tacitly, the commercialization of a biblical story. For those earnestly engaged in promoting *Esther* as a legitimate, worthy, and artistic contribution to the world of stage and theater, questions of profitably actually confounded the issue of genre identity. Ultimately, the matter of whether a church should raise and accept money generated by a theatrical production, even one based on a biblical narrative, remained central to this component of the debate. Nonetheless, the more progressive among Protestants acquiesced to a resolution of the apparent contradiction between financial gain and religious piety as potentially beneficial to all concerned: "We have been prepared to expect some little inconsistency in the early periods of the new relations between Church and the stage," one writer admitted. "It is quite natural that they should produce some friction in the beginning. A judicious course of cantatas with scenic and other dramatic accessories . . . will no doubt soon remove the awkwardness, and bring the two seemingly discordant powers into a harmony of action which will beyond question be extremely profitable to both."[42]

In an editorial printed in 1900, the Trenton, New Jersey, *Evening Times* reflected on the nineteenth-century reception history of *Esther* and laid bare the most disquieting issues fueled and sustained by over three decades of theatrical interpretations of Bradbury's score. The comments quoted below concern a production sponsored by Rev. Emanuel B. Killinger (1848–1914), pastor of the city's English Lutheran Church. Benton, an accomplished musician, prepared the adult singers for these performances, while his wife, Alice Laura Killinger (1849–1935), worked with the children who participated. A local review of the Killingers' production offered this extended and astute summary regarding the status of *Esther* at the turn of the twentieth century:

> The recent presentation of the sacred cantata "Esther" in the [Trenton] Opera House and its repetition this evening [April 30, 1900] in the same place has been the cause of considerable criticism on the part of the church-going people of the city and some of the comments have not been kind to Rev. Mr. E. B. Killinger or the members of his church, under whose auspices the entertainment has been given.
>
> Church people as a rule are opposed to the theatre on general principles in some cases and in others because of the regulations of their denomination on the question; but in this case it is questionable whether opposition should apply, for the cantata is of a character far removed from that of the average production of the stage, although the latter is in many cases not as objectionable as some people think.
>
> The cantata of *Esther* is elevating in its character and ennobling in its influence and should not be classed with the average theatrical performance. The objection that it is being presented in the theater is met by the fact that there is no other place in the city where it could be held. The Opera House is the only building giving the required room and to criticize the entertainment on that account is hardly fair and more than likely the result of a lack of appreciation of a very meritorious production.
>
> The cantata is being given for a worthy cause, it is entertaining and instructive, it illustrates some of the great truths the disciples of the Bible are supposed to base their lives on, and it should, therefore, be patronized by all who can consistently do so without any compunction of conscience. The people of the present generation are a pleasure-loving people and if the

church is to debar them from innocent enjoyment there will be great temptation to throw the church overboard and indulge in pleasures even more harmful than the ones prohibited.

Some good results are already apparent from the production [of *Esther*]. A number of voices have been developed among a number of young people; there has been formed a permanent organization for the cultivation of their musical talents. The rehearsals which have been necessary [to prepare *Esther*] have kept the young men and women in refining and elevating influences and all have been benefitted morally and intellectually.

Rev. Mr. Killinger has done a good work in giving these young people musical training and the people of the city such a refining entertainment. He is to be commended and should be encouraged by liberal patronage.[43]

Orientalism

Writing in 1893, acclaimed author and editor Charles Dudley Warner asserted that a surprising number of persons attending *Esther* performances in his day regarded the Book of Esther "with some suspicion ... as an Oriental tale without religious significance."[44] In fact, a portion of the American population questioned the very biblical canonicity of the Book of Esther.[45] Warner's opinion struck a sensitive nerve as, to many Protestants, secularism permeated much of the ideology inherent in manifestations of Orientalism. By extension, then, some audience members considered *Esther* as Orientalist, and thus secular, much as they did the dramaturgical decisions made by directors of theatrical presentations of the work. However, the more progressive among Protestants thought as Warner did, that the Book of Esther offered virtuous lessons regardless of its Orientalist and secular—even profane—inferences, or its disputed presence in the Bible.[46]

Community residents who assembled costumes for *Esther* performances drew upon a collective acquaintance with the parameters of American Orientalism when they attempted to replicate the attire of the ancient Middle East.[47] Of course, this awareness of Orientalist expressivity had long predated *Esther*, as can be seen in architecture, clothing, home décor, literature, music, and the visual arts. To be sure, R. W. Seager capitalized on the prevalence of such a potentially Orientalist mindset in his prefatory essay concerning costuming and staging. He even stipulated that, as a director, his initial rehearsals of *Esther* would include informative "trips to the Orient" intended to enhance singers' knowledge and appreciation of life in the ancient Middle East.[48] The sheer vastness of King Ahasuerus's realm, extending "from India even unto Ethiopia" (Esther 1:1), presented countless possibilities for Orientalist appropriation.

In an article published in 1853 in the popular monthly *Knickerbocker Magazine*, venerated author and editor Washington Irving presented a vivid interpretation of Orientalist thought. Not only did Irving's account offer a nuanced view of nineteenth-century American Orientalism, but additionally, the general tenor of his analysis seems particularly apropos to discussions of *Esther*. Irving asks, "How then shall we define this thing of dreams and dirt, despotism and dignity called Orientalism?" As suggested by these paired alliterations, gnarly contradictions assumed no small significance in the US relationship with all aspects of Orientalist interpretation. The Book of Esther concretized such binary oppositions and their attendant anxiety as a polygamous monarch and his heroine queen, selected from his harem, constitute the two main characters in a biblical narrative. Yet Irving also attempted to offset the uneasiness provoked by mere insinuation of harems and polygamy by reminding his more pious readers of the centrality of the Holy Land as the unassailable source of biblical righteousness and truth:

> Ah, yes, there is a serener, because a more spiritual Orientalism. It is the more substantial, because spiritual, and because spiritual, no longer local. Who has not felt, rather than pictured that tranquil Orient: its silence full of the splendors and deep with the mysteries of the Infinite. It links our thoughts to earth by its enchantment; it lifts them to heaven by its revelation. The rich stream of poetry which flows through the Bible, and penetrates our best emotions, springs from the Orient.

Ultimately, Irving cautioned of his article's title, its historical references, and its predominant themes, "the subject needs restraint." Accordingly, the analysis to follow eschews polemics involving racial hierarchy, cultural domination, postcolonialism, and performative derision so often foregrounded in critical discussions of musical Orientalism. To impose on *Esther*'s reception the rigors of extended argumentation and theorizing would require employment of the very analytical methods that do a disservice to Bradbury's guileless spiritual and pedagogical engagement as well as the expectations of his vast audiences. As Irving concluded of the US's Orientalism in his day, "[T]o analyze it is to dissolve the charm."[49] Innumerable communities, singers, and audiences ultimately appreciated and respected the sincerity of Cady's text and Bradbury's music, and a recounting of *Esther*'s reception history should do no less. Thus, Irving's description of the Orient as the ultimate source of what he calls "spiritual Orientalism" guides the discussion to follow regarding *Esther* and Orientalist interpretation.[50]

Consistent with the ideology of "spiritual Orientalism," the majority of nineteenth-century American citizens presumed the unassailable messages of biblical texts could and would ultimately prevail. The Bible offered incontrovertible proof, even to those of no particular religious or denominational affiliation, that a system of ancient order and justice had operated for thousands of years, even within the profane worlds of harems and sumptuous palaces. As a young nation, the United States tended to heed the wisdom and lessons of these texts as the passage of centuries endowed them with time-honored credence and veracity. Moreover, the Esther story presented an account of triumph against improbable odds that resonated with Americans.[51] As biblical scholar Stuart W. Halpern summarizes, the Book of Esther, whether regarded as sacred, secular, or noncanonical, has nonetheless always held a persuasive position "in the American popular imagination." He continues: "Throughout our history, Americans have turned to the Scroll of Esther . . . as they navigated their liberties, morals, passions and politics. These recurring references are no accident. Rather, they reflect an appreciation of a story whose themes—freedom, power, fraught sexual dynamics, ethnicity, and peoplehood—continue to define American identity to this day."[52] As we have seen, Esther not only served as an agency of moral rectitude, but the piece also inspired secularized reactions to the narrative assembled by Cady. Historian John Tchen's characterization of "commercial Orientalism" applies here as well, as Bradbury, in a role commensurate with what Tchen terms a "cultural entrepreneur," created, in *Esther*, a potentially Orientalist phenomenon of extraordinary marketplace viability, however unintentionally he did so.[53] In staged productions of *Esther*, directors selected Orientalist tropes and images of irresistible appeal to an entertainment-loving public they knew well, even as they violated Bradbury's original intentions.

Among the most discernible of Orientalist interpretive attributes associated with *Esther* must be listed the following: first, a plot and characters from the ancient biblical Orient; second, the incorporation of costuming, staging, and other theatrical elements chosen to depict a biblical or Oriental plot and characters; third, the extreme distance, temporally and geographically, between the time of the plot, its location, and its place of reenactment; and finally, representation of Oriental ritual, a despotic monarch, and the power of an Oriental crowd. Certain additional, if more nebulous, features also contribute to Orientalist interpretative purposes, such as Western conception of Oriental emotions, character traits, and overly emphatic or histrionic behavior.[54] In *Esther*, for example, the queen's seductiveness and submissiveness endow her with an Oriental mystique befitting the occupant of a harem, while the king's wine consumption and general capriciousness satisfy many Westerners' visions of a hedonistic and self-indulgent tyrant of the ancient Middle East. Crowds, as extensions of powerful male characters represented by the choruses in *Esther*, reinforce various emotions, such as the king's rejoicing and his effusive praise of Esther as his new queen. So, too, many US Protestants also perceived Oriental crowds as obsequious sycophants, capable, for instance, of cheering Haman's rise through noble ranks and then, shortly thereafter, ecstatically celebrating, with macabre glee, his downfall and pending execution upon the gallows.[55]

Ralph Locke's extended analyses of musical exoticism, or what I interpret as representative of "Orientalism," yield another particularly useful lens through which to view *Esther*. Locke proposes a more expansive conception of the Orient in order to embrace not only musical gesture and elements, but cultural context as well. Even if staged works evince few or no musical references to Oriental places or practices, a setting in the Middle East and the presence of costumes, staging, and choruses representing ancient custom confirm the intention of enacting the Orient in some manner. For, as Locke stipulates, such interpretations manifest an awareness of "a place, people, or social milieu that is not entirely imaginary" yet "differs profoundly from the 'home' country or culture in attitudes, customs, and morals." More precisely, it is the process of evoking "a place . . . that is *perceived* as different from home by the people making and receiving the exoticist cultural product [italics original]."[56] Hence, not only did directors of *Esther* enthusiastically engage Orientalist interpretative elements, but as we will see, audiences came to expect such renderings. Furthermore, Bradbury also incorporated stylistic references to mountain songs—denoted by Ralph Locke as one of many "dialects of Western musical exoticism." Traces of their presence might have inspired some audience members to hear a relationship between *Esther* and other forms of comical—even demeaning—theatrical entertainment such as minstrelsy, albeit with a text based on a biblical narrative.[57] Certainly Bradbury's "laughing song" evoked this sentiment among some audiences and critics.

Most theatrical productions of *Esther* exhibited dramaturgical choices clearly reflective of an Orientalist ethos. For performances in Portland, Oregon, "the stage had been hung with choice Turkish and Persian rugs, which lent an air of Orientalism to the scenes."[58] An audience in Kentucky anxiously awaited the appearance of dazzling attire and a magnificent set: "At precisely eight o'clock the curtains rose, presenting to the . . . excited and expectant multitude, a scene of Oriental beauty and splendor."[59] As a California newspaper enthused, "No one can question, when considering the royal, magnificent, Oriental costuming and grand choruses, that a wonderful display of unequalled brilliance and splendor will meet the astonished gaze of fortunate beholders on the evenings of rendering *Esther*."[60] Examples of overtly Orientalist interpolations also included choreographed evolutions of scarves, ribbons, and cymbals along with the ceremonial scattering of flower petals. As renditions of such scenes sometimes involved females clad in revealing costumes (at least for their time), their visual appeal contributed to the sensuality and potential titillation of staged *Esther* performances. Among the productions incorporating such scenes, an Illinois performance, in 1892, included "two very pleasing and heartily applauded innovations" consisting of "the marching of the king's and queen's pages."[61] Director Martin E. Robinson (1866–1936), who masterminded performances in Dayton, Washington, supplemented Bradbury's music with a number performed by "dancing girls": "[T]he beauty of their poses and graceful manner made a decided hit with the audience," an enthusiastic reviewer confirmed. To the banquet scene, Robinson added "a cymbal dance" performed by the king's and queen's pages, rendered in "graceful and well-trained movements."[62] Similarly, a production at the Crescent Theatre in Hillsboro, Oregon, included several "king's maidens" who entertained the monarch with "a ribbon drill" along with a "scarf dance" (figure 5.1).[63]

However, efforts to replicate Oriental and biblical authenticity, especially through costume design, sometimes resulted in humorous—even embarrassing—blunders. In fond recollections of *Esther* productions in Pennsylvania, syndicated columnist Henry W. Marden (1850–1920) elaborated on such occurrences. Referring to *Esther* as "the ever-pleasing cantata," Marden

Figure 5.1. King Ahasuerus's maidens posed for their scarf dance in a production of *Esther* in the Crescent Theatre, Hillsboro, Oregon, unknown photographer, 1904. Five Oaks Museum, Portland, OR.

focused some of his comments on the "comical sides" of amateur performances. He wrote of one performance he attended:

> The costumes for the King, Haman and the other notables, as well as "the royal apparel" for Mordecai and his promotion, were borrowed from the Masonic brotherhood . . . . [Some of the actors] being much shorter and broader than the parties for whom the outfits had been designed, were at a loss to dispose of the wealth [excessive size] of sleeve and skirt, and went through their respective parts burdened with the sensation of being very much over-dressed.

In another reminiscence, Marden lauded a group of participants who assembled all the costumes for the choruses. Constructed of thin, silky "black serge or bombazine," these garments, as described by Marden, employed loosely gathered sheer fabric held in place with waist sashes. An unanticipated problem arose, however, with the belated discovery that lights at the rear of the stage caused the dark cloth to appear translucent and all present could thus enjoy a unique view of players' undergarments and legs. In the ensuing humorous debacle, "the [reaction of the] male members of the Jewish chorus on the occasion referred to were truly 'a sight to see,' and the audience was not slow to catch on."[64] The potential for sexualized gazes directed at Orientalist costuming did not go unnoticed by author Eugene Field, who reviewed performances he attended in 1870 in Galesburg, Illinois, and in the nearby towns of Abingdon and Kewanee. Given by the Philharmonic Club and comprised mostly of Knox College faculty, the performances created quite "a sensation" as their "Oriental costumes" showed off, to considerable visual appeal, the "shapely shanks of some of the faculty ladies." The risqué costumes provoked Field's quip about a sequel: "[E]mboldened by their success . . . it was understood they [Philharmonic Club members] were planning shortly to produce a cantata to be called *Adam and Eve*, also in original costume."[65]

Beyond R. W. Seager's prefatory essay on staging and costuming, many sources of inspiration for Orientalist interpretations of *Esther* were in circulation in the United States. Such sources provided communities with images, verbal and visual, from which ideas for costumes, props, and stage action might be gleaned. Those responsible for assembling costumes may have even turned to descriptions of harems and life in the Middle East more generally, published in popular travel memoirs.[66] As one enterprising *Esther* performer recalled, communities consulted a variety of sources as they conceived of, and made, costumes out of materials available locally: "Besides studying the Bible for information concerning ancient costumes, habits, and manners, many suggestions can be gained from collections of famous pictures and illustrated books describing Oriental countries. Oriental rugs and curtains, brass and copper vases, and a heavy curtain add to the stage effect. The costumes can all be easily made at home."[67] In her memoir, historian Sarah Pratt (1853–1943) remembered *Esther* in bygone Indiana as a "dignified and colorful" work suffused with the virtues of biblical "Jewish history to back it." She, too, reminisced about the process of creating homemade Orientalist costumes:

> Ambition, aided by imagination and the pictures in the back of the big Bible enabled the skilled needle-women of the day to attire the stars [of *Esther*] in Hoosier-Persian costuming which was highly acceptable to an eager and uncritical audience. If not entirely correct, it still served to make everybody gasp at the sceptres, the turbans, the sashes, breastplates and sandals. These were worn by the principals while the riotous chorus was draped in sheets and light-colored wraps.[68]

Advertisements for and reviews of *Esther* performances document the vogue of such Oriental paraphernalia. For example, a review of a performance in Milwaukee praised "the singers . . . dressed in oriental costumes," yet hastened to reassure readers of the "tasteful" and "elegant" nature of this attire.[69] Similarly, a performance in New Hampshire in 1867 elicited a description of such costumes as "at once appropriate and brilliant . . . [as] devised and made by the ingenious hands of the ladies connected with this enterprise."[70]

As mentioned above, Bible illustrations yielded ideas for creating costumes, scenery, and props for productions of *Esther*—a trend that continued well into the twentieth century. A review of a production that took place in 1922 noted, "It is quite possible that many a weighty family Bible has been disturbed from a peaceful and dusty repose and is furnishing forth quaint plates . . . . [Biblical] oriental settings [illustrations] give opportunity for gorgeous colorings and graceful draperies."[71] Among the many illustrated Bibles in print in the mid-nineteenth century, several contained images depicting the most familiar scenes in the biblical Esther narrative.[72] The New York publishing firm of Harper issued its expansive three-volume set, *The Illuminated Bible* in 1843, quickly selling the first printing. This set included the complete Hebrew and Christian Testaments intermingled with hundreds of engravings. Prolific artist and engraver Gustav Doré published his *Holy Bible with Illustrations* that yielded another source of imagery and inspiration for scenery and costumes. For a run of three performances in the Eureka, Kansas, Opera House, the director procured "an exact reproduction of Gustav Doré's celebrated engraving of the Court of Ahasuerus" that provided an enormous onstage backdrop.[73] That this and other images originated in a Bible seemed to convey sanctified approbation of their usage elsewhere, including transference to the stage. However, Bible illustrations also occasionally drew caustic disapproval: in a review of Harper's *Illuminated Bible*, clergy protested the juxtaposition of ornate engravings with biblical text, castigating the publisher for inclusion of "objectionable designs" and condemned them as "revolting indelicacy, if not obscenity."[74]

I return now to Halpern's mention of "fraught sexual dynamics" as one of many charged narrative components found in the Book of Esther. Such undercurrents not only drew attention to the sensuous nature and implications of the *Esther* plot, but they also rattled many clergy and devout Protestants during the late nineteenth and early twentieth centuries. However inadvertently, Cady's text nonetheless subtly alluded to the profane, polygamous, and exotic realm of the harem. In the minds of some audience members, harems conjured up titillating fantasies of odalisques as they luxuriated under the proprietary and watchful eyes of eunuchs. We should also remember that the very existence of eunuchs and their presence in a harem, along with attendant polygamy, presented potentially troubling images for many devout Protestants.[75] As author Henry Van-Lennep reminded readers of his popular publication, *Bible Lands*, "the Book of Esther contains a pretty full account of the polygamy practiced by Persian kings."[76] *Esther* opens with the Messenger recounting the king's selection of Esther from among hundreds of harem occupants to be his new queen (Esther 2:16–18). Although Cady omitted details of Queen Vashti's humiliation and dismissal, audiences at all familiar with the biblical narrative would have recalled that Esther spent considerable time in the king's harem in preparation for her brief opportunity to impress Ahasuerus. With his erotic gaze and voyeuristic pleasure riveted on Esther's virginal beauty, the king proclaims that she exhibits "grace and favor in his sight" (Esther 2:17). As a harem potentate, King Ahasuerus wields his golden scepter as a representation of absolute power, masculinity, and virility. After all, insists biblical scholar Shimon Levy, "on stage the scepter is a heavily charged prop."[77] In staged productions of *Esther*, the king extends his scepter to the queen as she approaches him, and she touches its tip in an act of humility and sexual submission. Such gestures symbolize one of the many ways gender, power, and hierarchy played out in Orientalist depictions and texts: males impose dominance while females exist as seductive, penetrable, and malleable beings.[78]

Esther was not entirely devoid of stereotyping, and certain, if measured, doses of caricaturization were noticed by a few of the work's critics quoted earlier. Illustrative of one incident of Orientalist stereotyping in *Esther* can be appreciated in the scene of sheer buffoonery during which King Ahasuerus and Haman engage in ritualized male bonding as they share laughter during the consumption of wine (Bradbury's version, Part I, no. 5). Laughter in *Esther* becomes communal catharsis for everyone present as each individual audience member experiences the attendant heightened cultural escape amid the suspension of reality. As socially condoned expression, these boisterous outbursts disguise and shield private critique of pompous and despotic authority figures. That Bradbury did not anticipate a negative reaction to the so-called "laughing and drinking scene" between Haman and Ahasuerus underscores not only his spiritual engagement with the biblical narrative he set, but also his optimism and sheer naiveté.[79] Some reviewers berated Bradbury for his inclusion of laughter in *Esther*, deemed as decidedly secular and thus wholly inappropriate: "It would seem to us an outrage upon the decent proprieties of religious feeling to hear a jolly *laughing duet* performed by a couple of men representing [the] King and Haman, interspersed with boisterous 'ha, ha, ha' [italics original]."[80] Not surprisingly, Bradbury attempted to deflect such comments with this explanation: "In introducing a merry laughing song, designed (musically only) to represent the hilarity of these two personages, we have gone quite as far as seemed to us proper, and by older and doubtless wiser heads, have been gently reprimanded even for this. And do any ask, 'Why not—it is such a capital place for a funny effect, and for causing the audience to laugh and clap their hands?'"[81] Clearly Bradbury appreciated the mirth quite evident in portions of the Book of Esther for, as clergywoman and biblical scholar Debbie Blue summarizes, "[H]umor is the essence of the book." Blue especially cites passages that satirize Ahasuerus's decadence and the foibles of the Persian elite. She also singles out the biblical characterization of Haman as a "comic villain" who exhibits the "slapstick quality" of a person who readily displays overweening expressions of "self-importance."[82]

Historian Susan Nance ponders why so many Americans readily volunteered to perform "in the guise of persons from the Orient" as they eagerly did in productions of *Esther*. The possibility of benign cultural engagement and exchange constituted a compelling allure for singers who portrayed characters in *Esther* and the audiences who raved over their performances. And as Nance concludes, entertainment such as *Esther* offered audiences one of many "sites of incredible riches, romance and happy endings" of irresistible appeal, pleasure, and reassurance.[83] We should recall that Cady's text presented just such a "happy ending" as the Jews in his version of the narrative do not contemplate the vengeful slaughter of Persians as they do in the biblical Book of Esther. Instead, Persians join with Jews, and together, they engage in a peaceful, reverent, and celebratory Finale of thanksgiving.

Closing Thoughts

What attributes of *Esther* managed to shield the piece from total condemnation regarding its purported sinfulness? At the very least, innumerable performances in countless locations buoyed and energized the work's popularity, and this groundswell of endorsement held at least some sway with even the most devout members of the US public. Certainly, many enthusiasts of *Esther* who perceived the work as sacred heard in the score's melodies a correspondence to Bradbury's familiar and beloved hymns and religious songs. With increased tolerance and open-mindedness, objections to *Esther* on purely moral grounds gradually became intermittent and substantially unsustainable against the tidal wave of the piece's enormous appeal.

As we have seen, even as some critics obsessed over questions of genre identity and the work's reputed sacredness or secularity, *Esther*'s signature and overarching themes of courage, loyalty and righteous conduct prevailed. No amount of staging could obliterate Bradbury's and Cady's heartfelt and sincere commitment to genuine moral purpose. Furthermore, on virtually every page, Bradbury's conscious choice of American music idioms and musical accessibility remained apparent, no matter how lavishly staged and costumed. If, as Richard Crawford argues, nineteenth-century musical taste does not necessarily mesh with that of the twenty-first century, Bradbury nonetheless composed, in *Esther,* melodies that remained extraordinarily popular and memorable for decades.[84] The educational aims he intended for his score endured as amateur singers continued to rise to the arduous task of learning and memorizing their music and attendant dramatic action. In the end, Bradbury succeeded in creating a moralistic entertainment he fully intended to be enjoyable, elevating, and spiritually rejuvenating. *Esther* performances continued to be produced for over one hundred years after the work's premiere—a fact that attests to Bradbury's unimpeachable sincerity and his score's overwhelming success.

CHAPTER SIX

INTERLUDE
Esther Images

On April 9, 1896, Seattle's *Post-Intelligencer* urged readers to stroll down to an unnamed local drugstore to admire a series of "large photographs" displayed in the building's windows. The images, deemed "a credit to any photographer," featured "many well-known citizens of Seattle" in costume for an upcoming presentation of the "cantata of Esther." Obviously delighted with the display, a Seattle journalist expressed confidence the images would "undoubtedly produce a strong desire to view the performance."[1] In a similar announcement, the Cambridge, Massachusetts, *Chronicle* recommended the viewing of "a group of photos" of cast members, the images providing ample justification for a critic's designation of the production as a "grand pageant." Located in the window of the Odd Fellows Hall, the photos "well set forth the magnificence of the costumes" and documented the enormous size of the production's cast, comprised of "cup-bearers, queen's attendants, maids of honor, chamberlains, ladies of the court, Persian and Median princesses" and a chorus of two hundred singers.[2] The practice of photographing *Esther*'s singers became surprisingly commonplace as innumerable communities went to the trouble and expense of creating images of individual players, cast groupings, or entire choruses. Some of these images were produced by well-known photographers who evidently found their subjects inspiring and worthy of their expertise. To generate additional enthusiasm for *Esther* performances, many local newspapers printed photographs of cast members. These images not only document the choices communities made regarding stage accessories, they also confirm the widespread influence of R. W. Seager's recommendations for costumes. In addition, they illustrate some of the hot-button issues that fueled debates about the appropriateness of staging *Esther*.

This chapter offers a selection of photographs of participants in *Esther* productions from a variety of locations and time periods. Although *Esther* images appear elsewhere in this book, my purpose here is to draw attention specifically to costuming, staging choices, and dramatic action. The criteria for choosing these images included one or more of the following (listed here in no particular order): first, the quality of the photographs; second, the participation of persons well-known locally or regionally in the performance; third, the reputation of the photographer; fourth, the existence of information about the production, especially reviews; fifth, evidence of Orientalist representation; and finally, the ways these photos illustrate adherence to and popularity of Seager's revision.

However much insight photographs of cast members reveal, their poses often communicate little about the players themselves. So too, these images do not necessarily reveal the humorous situations that sometimes arose when amateurs appeared on stage for the first time. For iconography that does not shy away from these and other matters, I turn to the drawings of famed cartoonist William Ely "W. E." Hill. In his illustrations, Hill conveyed the charm of an *Esther* production, allowing us to appreciate not only the personalities of those who portrayed principal roles, but also the blunders that can occur in a community-based amateur production. Hill's candid portrayals reflect his obvious familiarity with and affection for *Esther* and confirm how popular the piece remained well into the twentieth century.

1868, Minneapolis, Minnesota

Bradbury's objections to staging biblical narratives notwithstanding, Minneapolis audiences and critics expressed wholehearted enthusiasm about theatrical renditions of *Esther*. During the years 1864 to 1866, over 5,000 area residents attended staged *Esther* performances in various theaters and community halls.[3] In fact, a well-known local musician, Alfred M. Shuey, singled out *Esther* as the city's "first musical event of importance."[4] During his Minneapolis residency in the fall of 1866, an ailing Bradbury urged local musicians to inaugurate plans for future performances of *Esther* in accordance, of course, with his stipulation that the work be presented in a formal concert or church setting. Apparently, he remained blissfully unaware that the city had already established itself as a regional center for staged productions of *Esther*. Nonetheless, at Bradbury's suggestion, some seventy local singers founded the Musical Union as a permanent choral organization dedicated to the performance of large-scale vocal works.[5] The Union presented its inaugural staged performances of *Esther* that same year in Minneapolis's Harrison Hall to capacity audiences. According to the *Winona Daily Republican*: "The first production of the Oratorio of Queen Esther by the Minneapolis Musical Union was given on Wednesday evening last [February 20, 1867] in that city. The papers speak of it as a great success and bestow much praise upon the dress and singing of the performers."[6]

However, none of Minneapolis's early staged versions of *Esther* attracted more attention than performances on the thirteenth and fourteenth of November 1868. These performances took place in the city's Pence Opera House, a facility opened and dedicated in June 1867. Financed by wealthy businessman John Wesley Pence (1829–1893), the performance space occupied the third floor of the Pence Building. Pence spared no effort or funds to obtain fashionable decor and state-of-the-art theatrical accessories for his theater. Equipped with the latest in "mechanical stage appliances," the venue also included an elaborate proscenium curtain deemed "a masterpiece of art."[7] The builders also installed rather unusual seating for audiences consisting of moveable and backless "upholstered settees each made to hold five persons comfortably." With room for some one hundred settees, the opera house could accommodate an audience of around five hundred.[8]

For the production of *Esther* in Pence Opera House, local school music teacher, keyboardist, and singer James Benjamin "J. B." McGibney directed a cast of some fifty members of the Musical Union.[9] Two highly respected local musicians, Charles Marsh (1830–1878) and German native Ludwig W. Harmsen (1839–1915), improvised the accompaniments on a Burdett pump organ and piano, respectively.[10] With the assistance of eager volunteers, the singers made costumes and stage props, spending the enormous sum (for the time) of five hundred dollars for materials.[11] The *Star Tribune* fairly gushed about the whole affair. As one reviewer remarked, "The audience [size] was remarkable for the condition of the streets—so muddy as to be almost impassable, and so dark as to be quite invisible. Nearly or quite five hundred people were present [each night] . . . and probably no other musical entertainment could have drawn one thousand people to the Opera House during the past two evenings."[12] For the opening scene, the *Tribune* had this to say: "Up goes the curtain, and down to the front come over fifty adult singers, Babylonian in face, dress and song. Who they were of our quiet domestic citizens, thus, in one short week's preparation transformed into the Court of King Ahasuerus, we don't know; but gleaming in [costumes of]

Figure 6.1. King Ahasuerus and his guards, from a stereograph by Alonzo H. Beal, photographer, 1868. Author's personal collection.

scarlet, white and gold . . . all swept down to the front of the stage singing [the opening number], 'Haman, Haman, Long Live Haman.'" In actuality, the singers must have entered via the stage and then assembled in the orchestra space in front of the settees. Although the hall boasted a stage of 30 ½ by 63 feet, box seats and dressing rooms took up much of the space on the sides of the stage, leaving insufficient room for fifty singers and stage accessories.[13]

This production remains unique among early staged presentations of *Esther* as it was, most likely, the first to be photographed extensively. The Musical Union selected Minneapolis photographer Alonzo H. Beal, respected in his day in the upper Midwest, to memorialize the performances.[14] As the local press gleefully announced, "Beal has [created] stereoscopic views of some of the most striking scenes in the cantata, which give one a very good idea of the dress and groupings upon the stage." An enterprising entrepreneur, Beal displayed the photographs at his "Premium

Figure 6.2. "Prayer Tableaux" (Part I, no. 9), from a stereograph by Alonzo H. Beal, photographer, 1868. Author's personal collection.

Gallery" for the public's viewing and enjoyment, and not surprisingly, made copies available for purchase.[15]

Although R. W. Seager would not publish his edition of *Esther* for another six years, many of his ideas for staging and costuming can be seen in Beal's photographs. For his series of images, Beal selected a few of the familiar moments in Cady's version of the Esther narrative. His first photograph (figure 6.1) shows Ahasuerus in the back of the stage, occupying a throne resting on a raised platform. The king's elaborately layered costume, accessorized with a large cape and sash, denotes his exalted status. He cradles a scepter on his right arm and looks sternly toward the camera. Four helmeted guards, armed with spears and battle axes and holding shields, flank Ahasuerus. Admittedly, the guards' kilts, assembled from what appear to be table clothes or drapery fabric, look more whimsical than martial or threatening. A local critic, clearly amused by the guards' appearance, described them as "bearded like pards," a reference to the scruffiness and excessive length of the actors' facial hair.[16]

Figure 6.3. One of the queen's maidens before a palace guard, no descriptive title provided. From a stereograph by Alonzo H. Beal, photographer, 1868. Author's personal collection.

Figure 6.2 illustrates the chorus of Jews enacting the "Prayer Tableaux" (Part I, no. 9). The High Priest, rendered eminently identifiable owing to his long white beard and the miter adorning his head, leads the kneeling crowd in prayer after the threat of total annihilation. Some members of the Jewish chorus bow their heads and clasp their hands in reverence and supplication. With arms outstretched, the Priest's towering figure lends unequivocal drama and emotionalism to this scene. The women of the chorus wear costumes consisting of gowns draped with bedsheets. Notice, too, that the women allowed their hair to flow down over their shoulders, in a manner Seager would later recommend.

In figure 6.3, one of the queen's maidens kneels before a palace guard. Although Beal did not label this photograph, the scene undoubtedly occurs immediately prior to the queen's initial encounter with Ahasuerus. The maid's

Figure 6.4. Esther's approach to the king, from a stereograph by Alonzo H. Beal, photographer, 1868. Author's personal collection.

facial expression reveals her anxiety about the queen's fate. This photograph offers a close-up view of the guard's attire, noteworthy for its patterned kilt, frilly shirt, and faux sandals fashioned from strips of cloth wound over socks. The guard's shield looks like a repurposed parasol.

For the scene in which Esther approaches Ahasuerus (immediately following Part I, no. 10), Beal posed the king on his throne with Esther kneeling before him (figure 6.4). The king holds out his scepter to Esther as armed guards and the queen's entourage look on.

In figure 6.5, a stoic and resolute Zeresh urges Haman to erect gallows for the execution of the insolent Mordecai. She underscores the profound significance and vehemence of her declaration with a dramatically raised arm and extended finger. This photograph allows us to appreciate additional details of the players' costumes. For example, what began as drapery material

Figure 6.5. Zeresh demands of Haman, "build thou a gallows" for the execution of Mordecai (*Esther*, Part I, no. 14), from a stereograph by Alonzo H. Beal, photographer, 1868. Author's personal collection.

or a furniture cover suffices admirably as royal apparel when the edges of the cloth have been frayed or fringed. Seager would later make this recommendation in the preface to his edition. Notice, too, how effectively a white bedsheet serves as an ankle-length veil when draped from Zeresh's crown.

Haman is shown, in figure 6.6, on bended knee, after receiving word of his impending execution. A court attendant consoles him by resting her hand gently on his shoulder. His wife, Zeresh, standing next to another of her courtiers, receives the news disconsolately. Note the decorative stars stitched onto the women's gowns—an embellishment that Seager would later recommend.

The queen and her guests celebrate at her banquet, shown in figure 6.7. In the foreground of the photograph, the pages serve wine. Additional goblets

Figure 6.6. Haman's defeat, from a stereograph by Alonzo H. Beal, photographer, 1868. Author's personal collection.

rest on a table draped with a small Persian rug, located center stage. Armed guards stand in readiness at the very back of the scene, their plumed helmets visible. The stage of Pence Opera House barely accommodated the cast and quite likely, additional singers in this scene assembled just in front of the settees during performances.

In the closing scene of the production, the cast assembles on stage to celebrate the triumph of the Jews (figure 6.8). Even with this photograph's small group of participants—around only twenty-five in total—the stage appears prohibitively cramped. The imposing High Priest stands on the right, with Esther and the king seated on their thrones in the center. Mordecai stands on the left, two pages sit in the front, with the guards barely visible at the rear of the stage.

Figure 6.7. Esther's banquet, from a stereograph, Alonzo H. Beal, photographer, 1868. Author's personal collection.

Figure 6.8. *Esther*, Finale. From a stereograph by Alonzo H. Beal, photographer, 1868. Author's personal collection.

Figure 6.9. *Esther*, Duhem Brothers Studio, photographer, Denver, Colorado, April 1874. Denver Public Library, Western History Collection, # X-18515.

1874, Denver, Colorado

Most likely, the earliest production of *Esther* in Denver took place in 1874, just after the publication of Seager's edition in March of that year. A local newspaper enticed readers to gather for the purpose of organizing an April performance of "Bradbury's masterpiece . . . to be soon produced in full Median, Persian and Jewish costume, representing the Oriental splendors—the dress, manners and modes of government at the court of King Ahasuerus and Queen Esther." Denver musician and director James Diggett promised audiences "thrillingly interesting dramatic action."[17] The daily newspaper accounts of rehearsals reflected considerable regional enthusiasm for this production. On opening night, huge crowds flocked to the city's Grand Opera House, with many turned away owing to lack of seats. A critic observed, of the homemade costumes, "though mostly were tinsel, were brilliant and showy, and made a fine impression."[18]

A subsequent newspaper announcement instructed the Denver cast to report to the Grand Opera House in costume for a series of photographs to be taken by the respected Duhem Brothers Studio, Victor M. Duhem and Constant Duhem, proprietors.[19] A single image from the session survives (figure 6.9). In this photograph, taken outdoors rather than on the Opera House stage, the Duhem Brothers simulated a theatrical setting by assembling

Figure 6.10. *Esther*, September 1891, photographer unknown. Pages kneel before the throne and salute the king and queen with raised wine goblets. Oakham, MA, Historical Association.

the cast in front of tall flats painted to show trees with leaves. The highest branches of Denver's actual trees, without leaves, are barely visible above and behind the flats. Esther and the king stand in the back row of the cast, in the center, the queen clutching the tip of Ahasuerus' scepter. Pages, played by the smallest children, with girls seated and boys kneeling, occupy the front row. Exotic-looking plumed helmets, "borrowed from the Knights of Pythias" for the king's guards, can be seen in the very back.[20] The imposing guard standing in the left front of the photograph wears an elaborate, most likely rented, costume, his socks wound in leather thongs.

1891, Oakham, Massachusetts

Regional singers presented *Esther* in Oakham on the first and second of September 1891, in the town's Memorial Hall. Local jewelry store proprietor and church choir director Frank S. Conant conducted the rehearsals and performances. The singers, accompanied by a small ensemble consisting of two violins and double bass, featured local favorite Clara M. Plummer as pianist. Unfortunately, no reviews for these performances have been located, but the Oakham Historical Association has preserved a program and a few cast photographs.[21]

Figure 6.11. *Esther*, September 1891, photographer unknown. The Prophetess gazes upward. Oakham Historical Association.

Gaslights, mounted at the very front of the stage, illuminated the entire space sufficiently for the photographs in this series. In figure 6.10, Conant and Plummer, located offstage, gaze at the principal players in the cast. A placard mounted above the right proscenium announces the "brilliant cantata of 'Esther.'" Seager's instructions for stage accessories clearly influenced Conant. The king and queen occupy their thrones, centered at the very back of the stage, mounted on a raised platform. Above and behind the thrones, filmy curtains and a canopy reinforce the Oriental appearance of this scene. Ahasuerus holds his scepter slightly raised, in a gesture of irrefutable power. The group to the queen's right consists of the Prophetess and various court attendants. To the king's left, two guards stand in readiness, their spiked helmets barely visible. The photographer posed Haman, prior to his downfall, crowned and attired in royal regalia. Four pages appear in the center, facing the king and queen, with two of them kneeling before the throne. They raise wine goblets in tribute to the monarchs.

In figure 6.11, Conant sits on a raised stool. The Prophetess stands center stage, her upward gaze endowing the scene with unequivocal drama. Various astrological and alchemy symbols, affixed as appliqués, decorate her gown. These symbols, recalling pre-Christian and ancient Oriental belief systems, reinforce the mystique of the Prophetess and her function in the narrative.[22] Ahasuerus stands in the front, his scepter in his left hand and a wine goblet

Figure 6.12. *Esther*, September 1891, photographer unknown. The principal players and conductor Frank S. Conant (1856–1926) face the audience. Oakham Historical Association.

in his right. Standing to the king's left, Haman also holds a goblet. This scene occurs immediately after the laughing duet sung by Ahasuerus and Haman. The entire cast looks toward the Prophetess just prior to her solo, "Lo, o're the Wicked" (Part I, no. 6), the lyrics of which warn the multitudes of the threatened destruction of the Jews.

Figure 6.12 shows many of the principal players as they might have been assembled for applause after the Finale. Four elaborately uniformed guards flank the stage, battle axes in readiness, while the captain of the guard stands immediately in front of Esther and Ahasuerus. Mordecai sits on the left attired in a rumpled homemade robe. Similarly, the costumes of the female court attendants also appear to be assembled out of household materials, gathered with drapery cords.

1896, Libertyville, Illinois

In 1896, singers in the village of Libertyville, located near Chicago, presented two performances of *Esther* in the community's Union Church. A regionally popular singer and music teacher, M. Alice Davis (1865–1913), directed the production and also assumed the title role. The cast consisted of what a local newspaper referred to as "the most prominent young people in town" who promised "to produce something startling in the way of amateurism." A glowing review included these comments:

Figure 6.13. Cast principals, *Esther*, Libertyville, IL, 1896, unidentified photographer. Image courtesy of the Libertyville Historical Society, Libertyville, IL.

> Both evenings as the curtain rose a melodious and powerful chorus of "Haman, Haman, Long Live Haman" burst forth from a group of thirty-seven voices in perfect harmony . . . . Queen Esther came forth, in the person of M. Alice Davis, and it would be folly to give this lady more or better laurels than have heretofore been won by her. All Lake [C]ounty's people know her to be an excellent vocalist and, as in all her past performances, Miss Davis was the star . . . . The costumes were elaborate and were furnished by a Chicago costumer. The chorus girls were attired in beautiful robes except when sorrow reigned over their nation, and deep mourning apparel clothed them.[23]

An unidentified photographer captured an image of the principals in the cast (figure 6.13). The photographer posed the actors in front of a stage flat on a boardwalk leading to the entrance of the Union Church. In the back row, four guards, identifiable by their plumed helmets, spears, and shields, flank the king and queen. Mordecai stands to the left just in front of a guard, while pages and the queen's attendants crowd the center of the image. A uniformed and rather formidable-looking Herald stands to the right. Haman reclines on the boardwalk, in front of the cast, in a pose symbolic of his eventual fall and execution.

1897, Norman, Oklahoma

The music department at a fledgling University of Oklahoma, founded in 1890 and located in Norman, presented *Esther* in 1897 as a fundraising initiative. New Orleans native Grace Adelaide King (later Maguire, 1879–1951) rehearsed the cast and conducted the performances. King had already earned regional acclaim for her soprano voice and inspired the newspaper sobriquet "Oklahoma Nightingale." Having joined the University's faculty at the tender age of sixteen, King assumed responsibilities as head of the music department only two years after her initial appointment.[24] A local newspaper anticipated that this *Esther* production would offer yet another display of her extraordinary talent, as "Miss Grace King never goes before the public with anything that is not first class."[25] Another newspaper echoed this assessment, adding, "Miss King never does anything by half."[26] The enthusiastic regional press kept readers apprised of preparations for the performances, such as the reassurance that rehearsals were "progressing nicely."[27] Newspapers also enticed potential audience members with promises of "an up-to-date entertainment" to include lavish staging.[28] King scheduled her production to commemorate Oklahoma Day, still celebrated annually on April 22. The date coincided with the initial stirrings of an unprecedented migration known as the "Land Run of 1889," during which thousands of European settlers flooded into what was then the Oklahoma Territory, inhabited, at the time, mostly by Native Americans.[29]

King selected all the singers for her production from the University community. For principal roles, she carefully considered musicality and candidates' "peculiar adaptation for their respective parts." The chosen players and chorus members represented the "cream of the musical department of the University." Rehearsals consumed several weeks, and King reportedly worked with the cast "almost incessantly."[30] A Norman daily published a verbose review of King's opening performance, excerpted below.

> On Thursday evening April 22, the celebrated cantata, "Queen Esther," was presented in the [O]pera [H]ouse.... The pleasant evening marked well the celebration of the eighth anniversary of Oklahoma and all things conspired to render that excellent exercise a culminating success while one of the largest audiences ever assembled in the halls of our city filled the house to over flowing to witness this the Queen of Cantatas, the brightest jewel of modern reproductions. The attention of all was eagerly fixed upon the stage and every

face gleamed with admiration when, at 8:15, the curtain was rolled up, revealing Haman, the King's favorite, triumphantly walking immediately in front of a host of thirty Persians whose voices rang out with praise and adoration while they repeatedly shouted with great emotion, "Long live Haman, the son of Hammedatha!" When the vision of the expectant audience dawned upon the second scene, they beheld King Ahasuerus arrayed in purple and fine linen, seated upon his richly decorated throne, having a golden scepter in his hand . . . while the royal guards were stationed on either side, living aspects of all the dignity and pride of Oriental custom . . . . [Participants in the banquet scene] were seated around the wine table, full flowing glasses were clinking with perfect regularity for the success of the undertaking till, flushed with the royal nectar . . . the jovial guests and superiors began to grow clamorous and to smash their glasses in their confusion, and the great company of Persian singers rushed in to join in the Bacchic revelry with "A Song of Joy." But all were startled and hushed in fright, starting backward as the Prophetess entered in front singing in sad tone a warning to the throng. This was one of the best scenes of the play and it brought down the house with showers of applause. Next was the triumphal march, by twenty-four Jews and Persians . . . [and] the attractive march of select maidens . . . . Everything passed with such perfect good harmony that if the grand old historian, Josephus himself, had been present he could not have offered a single criticism. The entire play was a success from the beginning and many desire to have it repeated in the city. This excellent work on the part of Miss King, assisted by the faculty and students, has brought untold honor upon the University and emphasizes the fact that this, Oklahoma's highest educational institution, has the best organized department of music in the Territory. May the University continue its good work for the upbuilding of our state.[31]

The mention of Josephus in this review suggests that King had the first-century historian's essay printed in programs distributed at the performances. Her elaborate staging of the work generally followed Seager's instructions, albeit with liberties taken in the interpretation of the banquet scene. In addition to the "clinking" of wine glasses, King dramatized the frivolity and abandon of the occasion and the effect of considerable wine consumption by having the actors smash their goblets.

King cast C. Ross Hume, a student at the University, as both the Herald and Hegai. A member of the first graduating class of the University and eventually a respected Oklahoma lawyer, Hume also became a well-known and enthusiastic chronicler of regional history. He later published some of the diary entries he wrote while he participated in King's production. On April 18, 1897, he informed his diary:

> Have been out five nights the last week with the cantata, and will be out every night this week until Thursday. I can't do justice to my studies so will be glad when this thing is over. This cantata was "Queen Esther," and a cut [photo] of the cast was in last Sunday['s] *Oklahoman*. The play [preparation] was started in the Winter, and many [University] students were in the chorus. It was the most elaborate undertaking of the Music Department, and practice and worry over costumes took much of our time. A solo which I undertook marked the beginning of my gray locks.[32]

On May 2, Hume recorded details in his diary of King's plan for the entire cast to travel to nearby Purcell, Oklahoma, some twenty miles distant, to perform for that community's residents: "We expect to go to Purcell Friday night and repeat the cantata, give it here [in Norman] Saturday night again, so I don't expect I will feel very lively." In his diary entry for May 9, Hume referred again to the performance in Purcell and remarked on the overall financial gain realized from the entire production: "We . . . made our [production] expenses which were about $75 or $80. Our receipts for the three nights were a little over $200."

One photograph of the principal cast members of Grace King's production survives (figure 6.14). This image reveals some of the eccentric choices her players made in assembling their costumes. Hume, attired as the Herald and identifiable by the long ceremonial bugle resting in his right hand, stands to the far left in the photo. He accessorized his uniform with numerous unidentifiable badges or buttons, his metal helmet fitted with an outsized dark feather plume. Following Seager's instructions, he simulated sandals by winding, somewhat haphazardly, wide strips of cloth over his socks. Note, too, the curtain draped about his waist. Directors sometimes cast a local child as the daughter of Zeresh and Haman, and in this photograph, a charming little girl, cast for this role, stands to Hume's left.[33] Esther's multiple necklaces and spangles accentuate the Oriental aspect of her costume. The king's scepter, hardly convincing, resembles a twirling baton or curtain rod. Additionally, Ahasuerus's oversized collar brings to mind the costume usually worn by the

Figure 6.14. Norman, OK, 1897, unknown photographer. C. Ross Hume Collection, University of Oklahoma Libraries, Norman, OK.

clown Canio in Ruggiero Leoncavallo's opera *Pagliacci* (1892). As occasionally seen in other photographs of this time period, both monarchs wear crowns constructed of cardboard. Little thought apparently went into Mordecai's costume, as the man playing this role wears an unadorned black choir robe and pillbox hat. Only one guard appears in this photo, cradling a sword in his left hand, a tasseled drapery cord wound casually about his shoulders. The prize for the most ludicrous costume must be awarded to the High Priest, who wears a silly Halloween mask and bug-eye glasses, his face framed with an implausibly large and fluffy white wig and faux beard.

1907, Vernal, Utah

Vernal citizens pooled their talents and resources to produce *Esther* for the purpose of funding the community's first public library. Local politician, amateur archeologist, and portrait photographer Leo C. Thorne produced

Figure 6.15. Lucille Goodwin Bassett (1879–1952), soprano, as Queen Esther, Vernal, UT, 1907, Leo C. Thorne, photographer. Uintah County UT Library Regional History Center.

Figure 6.16. David Manwaring (1862–1912), bass, as Ahasuerus, Vernal, UT, 1907, Leo C. Thorne, photographer. Uintah County UT Library Regional History Center.

images of several of the cast principals.[34] The surviving images from this session illustrate the resourcefulness of community players in their creation of inexpensive and eye-catching costumes. No review of this performance has been located, but local historian Sue Ruple Watson recorded her recollections, published a newspaper article about the production, and preserved the photographs shown here.[35]

A seated Lucille G. Bassett, cast as Queen Esther (figure 6.15), was the wife of Ernest Knight Bassett (1861–1944), a respected local music teacher who directed this production. Appropriately, she wears an elaborate Orientalist layered costume of embroidered fabric, a fringed sash, and a headdress and crown decorated with stars. Thorne posed the queen on her throne, her arms positioned in such a way as to reveal her metal bracelets. Watson credited Bassett's acclaim in her role as Esther to her extraordinary voice and likened her regal bearing to that of "England's Queen Victoria."[36]

Figure 6.17. Thomas Edward Birchell (1886–1930), baritone, as Haman, Vernal, UT, 1907, Leo C. Thorne, photographer. Uintah County UT Library Regional History Center.

Figure 6.16 shows David Manwaring attired as what Watson described as a "magnificent" Ahasuerus, with fists clenched in a gesture of arrogant power, his face conveying a menacing expression. He wears a long gown draped with a fringed shawl, resourcefully and inexpensively assembled from what Watson identified as a "couch cover." His accessories include a beaded necklace, bracelets on his forearms, and a rather peculiar head cover held in place with a modest crown. According to Watson, "[A]ll the mistakes and makeshifts [of this production] were forgotten when Manwaring lifted up his mighty voice and told his court enemy off in wrathful arias, that for me still reverberate ... more than 60 years since I heard him sing them." Manwaring's powerful and rich bass voice attracted offers of college scholarships to study singing and opera, but family obligations and scant financial resources precluded such a pursuit. He nonetheless enjoyed a successful career as a local music teacher and frequenter of the stage.[37]

Thorne's photograph of Thomas E. Birchell as Haman depicts the king's overseer reacting, in utter disbelief, to the conviction of treason and his sentence to the gallows (figure 6.17). Exposed arms allow us to appreciate Haman's signature arm bracelets but otherwise, Birchell's costume bears no

Figure 6.18. Alta Newcomb (later Hughes, 1883–1966), alto, as Zeresh, Vernal, UT, 1907, Leo C. Thorne, photographer. Uintah County UT Library Regional History Center.

Figure 6.19. John Robinson (1850–1927) as the High Priest, Vernal, UT, 1907, Leo C. Thorne, photographer. Uintah County UT Library Regional History Center.

resemblance to the attire expected of Ahasuerus's once-exulted court official. He wears a sleeveless woman's dress of patterned cloth extending only to his knees, accessorized with a hat, necklaces, and large coin earrings. Watson fondly remembered "tall, handsome, young" Birchell as a most fitting choice for the role of Haman.[38]

In figure 6.18, Alta Newcomb, as Zeresh, pleads for the life of her husband, Haman. Her costume, distinguished by dramatic layering, flounced sleeves, large earrings, forehead ornament, arm bracelets, headband, and beaded necklaces, all subtly evoke an Oriental image.

British native John Robinson, cast as the High Priest (figure 6.19), used a sash as a decorative and functional element to secure what looks like a nightgown. The censer he carries denotes his religious function. His elaborate headdress, resembling an Oriental fez, reinforces the mystique of his hand gesture and stoic gaze. Watson fondly remembered Robinson's "voluminous, long white beard"—his own—and described him as "old" at the time of the production and "a natural" for the role of the priest.[39]

Figure 6.20. Francis Fern Dillman (1888–1973) as the Prophetess, Vernal, UT, 1907, Leo C. Thorne, photographer. Uintah County UT Library Regional History Center.

Figure 6.21. Edward William Evans (1869–1966) as Hegai, Vernal, UT, 1907, Leo C. Thorne, photographer. Uintah County UT Library Regional History Center.

Francis Fern Dillman as the Prophetess (figure 6.20) also employed a lengthy fringed sash to accessorize her gown. Her raised arms show off flounced sleeves and arm bracelets to fine advantage and with equal effectiveness lend drama and tension to her upward gaze. In contrast to Seager's recommendation for black attire, she created her costume from a white bedsheet.

Thorne's photograph of Edward W. Evans, who played Hegai, the eunuch in charge of Ahasuerus's harem (figure 6.21), accentuates the actor's stern countenance. Evans wears a calf-length costume assembled from a rumpled woman's housedress, accessorized with a sash and broad waistband. He used wound leather straps over socks to simulate sandals and completed this Orientalist image with head attire consisting of a fez-shaped turban adorned with braided tassels. Watson did not indicate whether or not Evans's rather unusual forked-style beard was natural or contrived for the stage.

Thorne photographed Pearl J. Christensen, dressed as Mordecai's sister, in a thoughtful pose with downcast eyes (figure 6.22). Her head turban and

Figure 6.22. Pearl Johnson Christensen (1882–1946) as Mordecai's sister, Vernal, UT, 1907, Leo C. Thorne, photographer. Uintah County UT Library Regional History Center.

Figure 6.23. Hazel Imogene Harmston (1891–1960), soprano, as the Herald, Vernal, UT, 1907, Leo C. Thorne, photographer. Uintah County UT Library Regional History Center.

large hoop earrings lend an Oriental aspect to her otherwise rather generic attire consisting of a black gown and shawl. The choice of a black costume identifies her as Jewish, as recommended by Seager.

Watson described Hazel I. Harmston as a "cute and clever Herald complete with trumpet and pleated kilt."[40] In figure 6.23, Harmston wears sandals fashioned out of wrapped strips of fabric and an Orientalist head covering. A scarf, draped haphazardly, nearly covers the instrument she holds to her lips. She appears to be fully prepared to perform the bugle call that will summon courtiers to the banquet.

The Beggar presented stark contrast to the appearance of the residents occupying the palace of King Ahasuerus (figure 6.24). His bare feet and unadorned clothing accentuate his abject poverty. With a stance suggestive of a halting, compromised gait, he leans on a walking staff for stability. He begs for alms with an outstretched, beseeching hand as his cowering gaze underscores the utter hopelessness of his circumstances.

Figure 6.24. Brigham Charles Christensen (1877–1968) as the Beggar, Vernal, UT, 1907, Leo C. Thorne, photographer. Uintah County UT Library Regional History Center.

Figure 6.25. Hazel Johnson (later King, 1886–1918), Persian Princess, Vernal, UT, 1907, Leo C. Thorne, photographer. Uintah County UT Library Regional History Center.

In figure 6.25, Hazel Johnson, cast as the Persian Princess and therefore, a member of Zeresh's entourage, smiles enigmatically for the camera. She adorned her costume, assembled from a nightgown, with a forehead ornament, dangling strings of beads, arm bracelets, and hoop earrings. Her pose accentuates the dark veil she lifts coquettishly above her head. The presence of the roles of a Persian Princess and a Beggar in this production confirms director Bassett's use of Leon Keach's edition of the *Esther* score.

The Vernal production of *Esther* took place in the local, spartan, wood frame community hall built in 1893 by Jacob Reader Workman and known variously as the Vernal Opera House or Workman's Opera House (figure 6.26).[41] Workman equipped the facility with an ample stage, curtains, and scenery flats. During the performances discussed above, Workman operated the theater's coal-oil lamps, the only available stage lighting. Watson related how "a skinny" Workman, "his buckskin pants tucked into the tops of his rawhide boots, flitted quickly by . . . to turn the lamps high or low according to the mood on stage."[42]

Figure 6.26. Vernal Opera House, undated photograph. Uintah County UT Library Regional History Center.

1911, Valley City, North Dakota

On February 9, 1911, regional talent sang *Esther* at the cavernous Valley City Armory. A local newspaper provided a brief review of the production and praised the community's effort with special focus on the performances of principal roles.[43] To memorialize this event, an unidentified photographer posed cast members outdoors in the snow, the reflection from which enhanced available lighting. Of this photographic session, two of the three surviving images appear here. In one of these photographs (figure 6.27), the king and queen stand in the middle of the cast, all of whom huddle close together for warmth. Groups of children who augmented the crowd scenes and served as pages for the queen's banquet flank the principal players. The singers made their own costumes, most of them assembled from white bedsheets. For the pages' costumes, drapery cords tied around the boys' waists decorate their robes, while the girls wear sashes across the shoulders of their white dresses.

In figure 6.28, principal players crowd together, and a few have pulled their hands up into their sleeves to fend off the cold. Male actors in this photograph wear head attire representative of Orientalist inspiration. Note the appliqués decorating Ahasuerus's robe to simulate ermine trim. The woman playing Queen Esther has gathered her robe more closely about her for warmth.

Figure 6.27. Choruses and principal cast, *Esther*, unknown photographer, February 9, 1911, Valley City, ND. Photograph courtesy of Lloyd D. Witter Scrapbook, Barnes County Historical Society, Valley City, ND.

Figure 6.28. Principal players, *Esther*, unknown photographer, February 9, 1911, Valley City, ND. Photograph courtesy of Lloyd D. Witter Scrapbook, Barnes County Historical Society, Valley City, ND.

1911, RICHMOND, VIRGINIA

A brief review of an *Esther* performance in Richmond on June 16, 1911, singled out the players of the king and queen for "stellar honors." The event took place at the City Auditorium under the direction of local music teacher Frank R. Hufty. Organizers of the production hired the Borjes Orchestra, a touring ensemble based about one hundred miles away, in Norfolk, to accompany the

Figure 6.29. Elizabeth Crenshaw Monell (1872–1965) as Queen Esther, Richmond, Virginia, 1911, Walter Washington Foster, photographer. Glass negative located in the Foster Collection, Virginia Historical Society, Richmond, VA.

Figure 6.30. John Andrew Poole (1865–1950) as King Ahasuerus. Richmond, Virginia, 1911, Walter Washington Foster, photographer. Glass negative located in the Foster Collection, Virginia Historical Society, Richmond, VA.

singers. Funds realized from the performance benefited the Sheltering Arms Hospital, the Pine Camp of the Tuberculosis Society, and two local churches.[44]

Famed Richmond portraitist Walter Washington Foster photographed members of the cast; of this session, three images survive.[45] Cast for the role of Queen Esther, soprano Elizabeth Crenshaw Monell wears her "hair down, flowing" in the style suggested by Seager (figure 6.29). She assembled a simple gown of gathered white bed linens fastened by a braided satin drapery cord. Arm bracelets add subtle Orientalist mystique to her appearance. Although Monell's crown might have looked convincing from a distance, Foster's studio lighting betrays its simple cardboard construction. Monell, a favorite with regional audiences, accumulated accolades and respectable fees as the "highest priced church soloist" in Richmond.[46]

No doubt Seager would have approved of the costume worn by John Andrew Poole for his role as Ahasuerus. Foster's photograph of Poole (figure 6.30) shows the imposing monarch wearing a cape of bedding material

Figure 6.31. Esther and Ahasuerus, Richmond, Virginia, 1911, Walter Washington Foster, photographer. Glass negative located in the Foster Collection, Virginia Historical Society, Richmond, VA.

trimmed with faux ermine, clutching his golden scepter. His costume also included a cardboard pendant and crown, with fabric strapping wrapped around his feet to simulate sandals. Note, too, Poole wears his trousers tucked into high socks just below his knees, as recommended by Seager.

Foster beautifully captured the dramatic and poignant scene when Esther approaches the king. With hands clasped in prayerful reverence and evident trepidation, Esther kneels before Ahasuerus as he holds his scepter for her to touch (figure 6.31).

1911, Los Angeles

In 1911, the Los Angeles school district's Parent Teacher Association hired respected choral director George Leonard Howes to produce *Esther*. Three performances were given, and the funds generated from ticket sales supported the area's schools. Howes was well known in the world of theatrical

Figure 6.32. Banquet scene, *Esther*, Los Angeles Auditorium, 1911, photographer unknown. The seated king and queen, played by George Leonard Howes and Myrtle Gladys Jones, occupy the center of the image. Photograph originally published in the *Los Angeles Herald* on October 27, 1911, 12.

productions and had previously directed *Esther* in several other major cities. The cast of this production included professional singers and regional teachers in the principal roles along with several hundred schoolchildren who sang in the choruses. Composer and touring concert organist Charles H. Demorest (1881–1950) provided what a critic described as "skillful adaptation of the accompaniments to [meet] the needs of solos and choruses." Local music teacher and occasional stage actress Myrtle Gladys Jones added her signature excellence in dramatic conception along with her well-trained voice to portray the "beautiful and royal looking queen" who "bore herself triumphantly." Howes assumed the role of Ahasuerus, and according to a reviewer, "sang excellently." The choruses were attired in colorful costumes, assembled from rich "scarlet and gold" fabrics.[47]

A photograph taken of a cast grouping in the banquet scene of this production was published in the *Los Angeles Herald* (figure 6.32). In this image, large numbers of courtiers crowd around the enthroned king and queen, laughing and obviously enjoying the celebratory mood of the event. Some of the revelers clutch bouquets of flowers while others hold wine goblets. In contrast, the rather unexpectedly stoic facial expressions of the monarchs suggest their inadvertent and fleeting lack of engagement with the frivolity of the moment.

Figure 6.33. Chorus members and principal players, *Esther*, Price, UT, 1912. Clarence Stevenson Photograph Collection, J. Willard Marriott Library, University of Utah, Salt Lake City, UT.

1912, Price, Utah

An advertisement for an *Esther* production in Price enticed local citizens to avail themselves of the performance's "sweet singing children, elegant costumes and bewitching triumphal marches."[48] The performances took place on January 31 and February 1, 1912, in the auditorium of the local Town Hall. To prepare the chorus and oversee details of staging, the community hired A. G. Bixler, an itinerant and sought-after choir director. In addition, he possessed a fine bass-baritone voice and sometimes assumed the role of Ahasuerus in performances he directed.

One photograph of the principal players of this production survives (figure 6.33). In the image, Bixler is seated in the foreground with cast members crammed on the small stage of Price's Town Hall. Given the lack of space, the "bewitching triumphal marches" referred to above must have taken place off-stage. A handwritten note accompanying the photograph indicates Bixler's adherence to one of Seager's recommendations: "[T]hose [dressed] in black are Jews; those in white, Persians." Most of the cast members created their own costumes, made of white bedsheets gathered at the waist with sashes. Seager's suggestions also influenced the costume makers who decorated the women's gowns with multiple appliqué stars. The women wear their hair down over their shoulders, plaited, or held in place with headbands.

In this photograph, Esther and the king sit in the second row, fifth and sixth from the left, respectively. Bixler cast two prominent local educators for these roles: teacher M. Edith Walker as the queen and Don Carlos Woodward, school superintendent, as the king. Two of the king's guards stand in the back, their battle spears crossed menacingly. A defiant Haman sits in the second row with arms folded, his characteristic wide metal bracelets clearly visible. Bixler selected a local prominent industrialist, John A. Hendrickson, to operate the lighting and curtains. Hendrickson stands out from the rest of the cast, dressed in a suit and tie, standing in the back to the right. With little room for stage decorations, Bixler propped flats against the stage walls upon which were painted trees. Brief mention of these performances in a local newspaper remarked that capacity crowds "packed" the hall both evenings. Calling the production "a most pronounced success," the press concluded, "[T]he ability displayed by many of those who took part would have done credit to a trained theatrical troop."[49]

1917, REEDLEY, CALIFORNIA

Regional singers of greater Reedley performed *Esther* several times in the city's Grand Theatre during the month of February 1917. Originally, only two performances were scheduled, but overwhelming public enthusiasm prompted repeated presentations. A local newspaper applauded the fifty choral members and players of principal roles "composed of talent of exceptional ability." The press complimented the stage set as being quite "in keeping with the Oriental atmosphere in which the cantata is presented, showing the excellent taste of those upon whom fell the task of decorating."[50] Yet the canopy suspended over the throne hardly looks regal as it rather resembles an old ship's sail or a parachute.

Public school music teacher Lewis W. Harvey, who had previously produced *Esther* several times in the region, selected the players, rehearsed the singers, directed the production and assumed the role of King Ahasuerus.[51] Harvey appointed respected civic leader, Christian F. Mueller, to play Haman. For a subsequent *Esther* production in Reedley in 1924, the talented Mueller served as music director. Mueller spent much of his career working for the regional YMCA and provided the first opportunities for public outdoor recreation in the area. He also sang in numerous regional performances, some

Figure 6.34. *Esther*, cast members, Grand Theatre, Reedley, CA, 1917, photographer unknown. Reedley Historical Society.

of them directed by Harvey. To commemorate Mueller's contributions to the region, the Reedley city administration opened a park in 1963, bearing his name. Of this decision, a city councilman explained, "The reason we bestowed this honor on C.F. Mueller is that we think he has done more for the youth, not only of Reedley, but the country, than any other man."[52]

Figure 6.34 is the only known photograph of the 1917 Reedley production of *Esther*. Compared to most photographs of cast groupings, the actors in this image appear authentically engaged with the scene they enact. In particular, the poses, gestures, and facial expressions of the singers, especially those in the foreground, convey the emotional tension of the moment. The king, identifiable by the scepter he clutches in his right hand, reacts with astonishment as Esther raises her arm to identify Haman as a traitor. Zeresh clasps her hands in horror in reaction to the queen's gesture. Hardly able to maintain composure in the face of such an accusation, Haman turns away from the Persian crowd, his fists clenched in fury. All the while, the king's guards stand in readiness in the back of the stage, their battle axes quite visible.

Figure 6.35. Four cast members of an *Esther* production, Palm Garden, Kellogg Sanitarium, Battle Creek, MI, 1922, photographer unknown. Left to right: King Ahasuerus, Chamberlain, Haman, and the Prophetess. This image originally appeared in *Adventist Heritage* 15, no. 3 (Winter 1993): 45. Photo courtesy of Loma Linda University, Loma Linda, CA.

1922, Battle Creek, Michigan

During the summer of 1922, Mahon H. Serns (1880–1957), head of the music department at Battle Creek Academy, began preparations for a production of *Esther*. Some forty students, members of the Battle Creek Academy Players, sang in the choruses, while regionally prominent singers assumed principal roles. The first in a series of several performances took place on November 12, 1922, in the Gymnasium of Battle Creek's world-renowned Kellogg Sanitarium. A capacity crowd of 1,500 greeted the cast. An enthusiastic local critic praised the "freshness" of the actors' voices and their "fine regard for dramatic possibilities." The critic added that the gymnasium had been "beautifully decorated with ferns, palms and flowers, and the bright costumes were enhanced in attractiveness by the judicious use of a spotlight." Director Serns expressed considerable satisfaction with the performances, and in particular, singled out the principal players for praise.[53]

One photograph of participants in this production has been located (figure 6.35). For this image, taken in the magnificent glass-domed Palm Garden of Kellogg's Sanitarium, exotic vegetation provides a stunning backdrop. A group consisting of the king, a court chamberlain, and Haman occupies the left side of the image. Both Haman and the king hold wine goblets, and thus we can assume that the scene shown here occurs at the conclusion of their drinking duet. To the right, the Prophetess, attired in her characteristic black gown, gestures accusingly toward Haman.

The Sanitarium's founder, famous nutritionist, physician, and cereal industrialist Dr. John H. Kellogg, designed the garden as a recreational and meditation facility for his institution's patients. He selected all the garden's flora and released his personal collection of exotic birds and butterflies into the space. The astonishing display featured twenty-foot-tall banana trees that actually bore fruit.[54]

1920, Drawings by W. E. Hill

The humor and charm of *Esther* productions captivated William Ely "W. E." Hill, a nationally renowned satirist and cartoonist.[55] In a retrospective about Hill's highly successful and lengthy career, New York's *Daily News* reminisced in 1960 about the artist spending "the better part of each week for the past 40 years seated at the drawing board in his first-floor bedroom. There, in pen and ink, he created the weekly gallery of candid cartoons that have appeared under the W. E. Hill byline in the Sunday news and client newspapers of the *Chicago Tribune-New York News Syndicate* across the country. A collection of Hill's sketches would be a veritable family album of everybody's neighbors penned in affectionate satire."[56] As comic strip artist and historian Bill Griffith so astutely observed, Hill's drawings "provided millions of people with shared cultural references."[57] Certainly Hill's illustrations of an *Esther* performance fulfilled this role exquisitely. In a series titled "Presented by Local Talent," Hill's sketches occupied an entire page of the *New York Tribune*. His drawings celebrate an amateur performance in the small town of Slaughterville, Oklahoma, with candid portrayals of the players' homemade costumes along with their onstage spontaneity.

Hill drew Slaughterville's piano accompanist wearing a determined and rather severe facial expression as she wends her way through the score (figure 6.36). Her countenance reflects the considerable effort often required to blend and sustain ensemble integrity with a large group of amateur singers who, owing to the jitters and lack of experience, may momentarily lose contact with the music and conductor.

Figure 6.36. The piano accompanist. W. E. Hill, *New York Tribune*, October 3, 1920, Graphic Section, 69.

Figure 6.37. Middle-aged chorus member. W. E. Hill, *New York Tribune*, October 3, 1920, Graphic Section, 69.

Figure 6.37 depicts a middle-aged chorus member, her droopy eyes and hooded lids suggesting fatigue or ill health. As Hill recounts, this member of "the local talent chorus" blames her wan appearance on overindulgence after the previous evening's rehearsal. Hill's caption quotes this singer: "[L]ast night after the dress rehearsal I went home and ate three dishes of apple sauce and a soda biscuit, and I *never* will again—I had indigestion *all* night long! [italics original]." Her facial expression betrays an admission that she brought the lingering effects of this seemingly benign flight of late-night snacking to the stage the following evening. If it seems that Hill cannot resist poking fun at this distracted singer, he also admires her fortitude as she soldiers on, even if somewhat incapacitated. To be sure, the presence of all participants in the crowd scenes, even if one or two cannot deliver an optimum performance, would be preferable to a reduced number of choral singers. Besides, a variety of facial expressions adds zest to the overall visual appeal of the onstage crowd and Hill excelled in capturing this sort of detail.

Figure 6.38. A dog's stage debut. W. E. Hill, *New York Tribune*, October 3, 1920, Graphic Section, 69.

Although blunders will happen during amateur stage productions, Hill always saw the humor and fun in such occurrences. Any number of situations kindled Hill's imagination, such as the possible intrusion of, say, uninvited quests appearing on stage—a distinct possibility if a stagehand propped a back door open for much-needed ventilation. With just this sort of circumstance in mind, Hill drew a dog wandering onto the stage, no doubt having entered through an unattended door (figure 6.38). As Hill described this scene, "[T]he dog, in a chummy mood, greatly interferes with the lamentation of Uncle Mordecai's followers." Indeed, the facial expressions of the female members of the chorus in the foreground convey a variety of reactions to this intrusion ranging from amusement to surprise. The singer on the far right seems oblivious to the dog's presence and continues to sing. A stagehand peers from behind a curtain, having only this moment discovered the dog and seemingly perplexed as to how to remedy the situation.

Hill drew a bespectacled Haman, laughing mockingly, while a resolute Mordecai sits stoically at the palace gate (figure 6.39). As Hill wrote of this drawing, "Haman, the proud and haughty, giving a nasty 'Ha, ha, ha!' to Mordecai, the Jew."

Hill's depiction of the Herald shows a young girl clad in what resembles an Elizabethan costume gingerly raising a ceremonial bugle to her lips (figure 6.40). She seems a bit bewildered, with eyes downcast, as if waiting for the conductor's cue to play the bugle call signaling the opening of the banquet scene. As Hill explained: "'Haste to the banquet hall! Haste ye to Esther's

Figure 6.39. Mordecai and Haman. W. E. Hill, *New York Tribune*, October 3, 1920, Graphic Section, 69.

Figure 6.40. Klara Weeks as the Herald. W. E. Hill, *New York Tribune*, October 3, 1920, Graphic Section, 69.

Figure 6.41. Esther's maidens in retreat. W. E. Hill, *New York Tribune* October 3, 1920, Graphic Section, 69.

call!' brings Klara Weeks to the fore in the guise of the Herald. Klara holds her trumpet a little as though she feared it would bite her, and she missed out on the period stuff in dressing the part, but these were mere details." True to Hill's caption, little Klara wears a costume more appropriate for a Shakespeare play.

Hill illustrates another blunder in figure 6.41. Following a premature entrance onto the stage, Esther's spindly-legged young attendants attempt a hasty retreat. Of this scene, Hill writes: "The child dancers, down on the program as favorite maidens of Queen Esther, have missed their cue and have come on too soon. They can't seem to get back." Indeed, the little girl on the left appears crushed by the accumulated reverse momentum of those in front of her. The girls clutch garlands and enter the stage to perform a dance before the king.

In a drawing of Esther, Ahasuerus and their courtiers (figure 6.42), the queen energetically gestures as she pleads for Mordecai and the fate of the Jews. The children in the foreground appear a bit unimpressed or disinterested in the scene's purpose. In keeping with the spirit of creating stage attire from repurposed items, Esther wears a sleeveless flapper outfit accessorized with a sash, arm bracelets, and beaded necklaces. Hill's caption describes the costume of the bespectacled king as a drapery from a "Turkish cozy corner" combined with an old "Sunday-school Santa Clause get-up." Hill's mention of

Figure 6.42. Esther, Ahasuerus, and courtiers. W. E. Hill, *New York Tribune*, October 3, 1920, Graphic Section, 69.

a "Turkish cozy corner" would have resonated with *Tribune* readers, as many middle- and upper-class households of the nineteenth and early twentieth centuries set aside just such a space as an alternative to the more formal parlor area where families received guests. Designs for such social spaces featured Oriental rugs and elaborate draperies representing Middle Eastern fabrics and patterns held in place with oversized tassels and garlands of beads.[58] Hill's humorous suggestion that Ahasuerus's costume consisted of repurposed items reflected staging choices still quite current in 1920.

Hill drew a bespectacled local physician and chorus singer, and offered this description: "Dr. Simms, being hastily summoned from the wings to extract a hairpin from the foot of one of the child dancers" (figure 6.43). With raised arms, the doctor expresses his utter exasperation at being called offstage as "he is in the middle of one of his big scenes."

Keenly aware of the mishaps that can occur in amateur productions, Hill could not resist including a drawing of an uncooperative stage curtain (figure 6.44). Of this image, Hill writes, "The curtains won't come down without some member of the cast leaping at them and dragging them down by force." In fact, this particular curtain required the combined strength and determination of two players.

No photographer captured the humor, charm, and occasional mishaps of an *Esther* production quite like Hill. Rather than focusing solely on the

 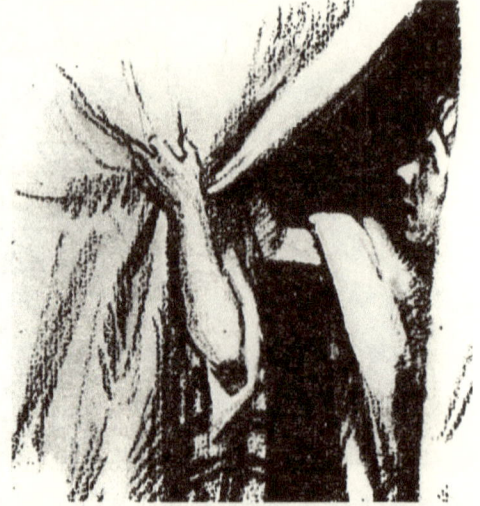

Figure 6.43. Dr. Simms is called offstage. W. E. Hill, *New York Tribune*, October 3, 1920, Graphic Section, 69.

Figure 6.44. An uncooperative stage curtain. W. E. Hill, *New York Tribune*, October 3, 1920, Graphic Section, 69.

idealization of the characters in *Esther*, Hill strove to reveal the personalities of the actors themselves. Even as a few of the chorus members in Hill's drawings appear somewhat disengaged, those playing major roles exhibit a level of spontaneity and dramatic interaction quite in contrast to the formally posed cast groupings shown in many photographs. His drawings offered newspaper readers an opportunity to experience the nostalgia of reliving their association with *Esther* as performers or as audience members. That a newspaper of the *Tribune*'s prominence and influence devoted an entire page to *Esther* underscores the enormous popularity that this work still enjoyed well into the twentieth century.

Closing Thoughts

Photographs and drawings of *Esther* participants illustrate the ways communities conceived of *Esther* as a theatrical work. These images also document the influence that R. W. Seager, and the communities themselves, exerted on the transformation of *Esther* into a staged extravaganza suffused with Orientalist imagery and spectacle. We can appreciate the sincerity of community productions of *Esther* through these images and the evident pride they exude, borne of musical and dramaturgical self-determination. Ultimately, as these images confirm, amateur performers succeeded in maintaining the dignity and religious sentiment of a biblical narrative even as they overlaid Cady's text with secular theatrical elements. No other nineteenth-century work of popular, amateur musical theater composed in the United States attracted this amount of iconographic interest. That so many images of cast members survive and are held in numerous regional historical collections and appear in newspapers speaks to their cultural value and the significance of the events and times they preserve.

CHAPTER 7

ESTHER AND MINORITIES

The most publicized renditions of *Esther* by American minorities took place in African American and Asian immigrant communities. Beyond serving as entertainment, these performances helped raise funds for charitable causes and projects of considerable interest to minorities, especially those quite outside the purview and concern of whites. In preparing and performing *Esther*, minorities not only strengthened their own community and ethnic cohesion, but also reinvigorated their determination, courage, and resiliency in the face of white discrimination and racism.

African Americans and the Book of Esther

For African Americans, the biblical trials and triumphs of the ancient, displaced, and enslaved Jews have always held special significance. Through music, Black people renew their relationship with Hebrew Testament heroes and prophets and endow them with a living presence and familiarity quite beyond the comprehension or appreciation of whites.[1] In his discussion of nineteenth-century biblical exegesis, Albert J. Raboteau asserts that African Americans interpreted certain narrative settings in the Hebrew Testament, especially Egypt and Ethiopia, as references to Black Africa and their own ancestral Africans. Because the story of Queen Esther occurred in the territory "from India even unto Ethiopia" (Esther 1:1), Black people and persons of color resided in this vast region and were, therefore, the participants in the Book of Esther.[2]

The Queen Esther narrative has often provided solace, wisdom, and strength for African Americans, particularly during times of political strife. For example, in 1870, Black state legislators in North Carolina referenced the Book of Esther in an address they published as a broadside. In their address, the authors decried the state's "system of disenfranchisement," designed and enforced by whites with Haman-like "deception, fraud and intimidation." The representatives identified correspondences between the Jewish diaspora in Ahasuerus's realm and the US Black population as an "analogy between our case and that of the Jews at that time." Similar to the Jews, who faced certain annihilation, "the colored people are the great victims appointed for the slaughter." The image of Queen Esther assumed metaphorical importance for the legislators who concluded, "We as Representatives, occupying the place of power, as did Esther, feel it our duty to warn you of the impending danger and arouse you to such action as may tend to avert, if possible, the threatened evil."[3]

In another activist appropriation of Esther imagery, Rev. Dr. Francis J. Grimké, the celebrated and outspoken pastor of Washington, DC's African American Fifteenth Street Presbyterian Church, turned to the Book of Esther as an empowering source for Black resistance and survival amid the humiliations of segregation. In a sermon he delivered, subsequently published in 1913, Grimké wrote an elegant statement about the application of Esther to contemporaneous racial politics:

> I have just been reading over the Book of Esther.... We as a people would do well to ponder, carefully, the words of Esther to Mordecai in our struggle against the enemies in our country that are bent on our destruction just as truly as Haman was bent on the destruction of the Jews, and for the same reason, because we are not disposed to bow and cringe and debase ourselves before them.... And at the bottom is the same spirit against which we have struggled in this country.... The thing that offends, that excites the ire of whites is the assertion or exhibition of manhood on the part of the Negro; it is because he has the temerity to claim for himself what they claim for themselves, and precisely on the same ground. The thought of the Negro as a slave has so taken possession of them as to entirely obliterate from their minds the thought of him as a man and as a citizen. And these are the people who are in the seat of power; these are the people who have the ears of the country, the people who control, largely, the press and pulpit, the business and labor organizations, and who command, in virtue of their wealth, the best legal talents of the country.[4]

Queen Esther also symbolized and embodied the potential power of biblically sanctioned female leadership, activism, and courage among Black people. As biblical scholar Sidnie White writes, "African American women reading Esther as their own wisdom literature were continuing a tradition of transforming Biblical, particularly . . . Jewish texts of bondage, to explain and negotiate American Black experiences of enslavement and subordination. When African American women turned to the Book of Esther and its royal subject for wisdom, they discovered virtually 'a dictionary of survival techniques.'"[5] Moreover, as historian Evelyn Brooks Higginbotham concludes, during the nineteenth century, Black women "likened their role to that of the biblical Queen Esther, who had acted as an intermediary between the king and her own people. They envisioned themselves as intermediaries between white America and their own people."[6] To foil Haman's genocidal plan, Esther employed strategies associated with an African trickster such as denial, subterfuge, manipulation and delaying tactics.[7] Cultural critic and poet Kevin Young ranks the trickster persona, rhetoric, and attendant actions of considerable significance in African American culture tantamount to "rituals of church or prayer."[8] Several prominent African American female leaders adopted Esther's trickster persona and rhetoric for their public addresses. To cite but a couple of examples, orators Maria W. Stewart (1803–1879) and Sojourner Truth (1797–1883) interwove their speeches with Esther imagery and biblical quotations in order to enhance and disseminate their activist rhetoric and strategies.[9] Writing in 1916, E. Azalia Hackley (1867–1922), noted Black singer, educator, and activist, encouraged African American mothers to impress upon their daughters the significance of Queen Esther: "Each colored child must be a race missionary and prove her worth and powers, thus winning friends for the race . . . . Her education must be a process of the development of powers not only to fit her for citizenship and life, but it must fit her for her race's burden . . . . She must be taught the application of the story of Esther to her race. Tell her that each colored girl may be an Esther . . . to advance and change the prevalent opinion of the Negro."[10]

For many African Americans, Bradbury's so-called "Laughing Song" (Part I, no. 5) presented potential for cultural catharsis. Cady's laughter lyrics not only facilitated celebration, on a literal level, of redemption and vindication, but they also provided an opportunity, however subtly, to collectively experience solidarity against white oppression. In a now-classic theory of humor, Henri Bergson identified laughter as a primary means of implementing social "inversion" and initiating "reciprocal interference" aimed at unjust laws and practices. As Bergson asserts, "[L]aughter is, above all, corrective," especially when it functions as "a revolt on the surface of social life."[11] In applying Bergson's thesis to Black audiences at *Esther* performances, laughter episodes can be interpreted as a metaphor for and manifestation of sarcasm, resistance, and defiance directed toward racism. *Esther* performances offered African Americans a safe haven for eruptions of laughter, mockery, and hilarity without the threat of suspicion, retaliation, or punishment.[12] Theologian Jacqueline Bussie advocates a related viewpoint to consider when evaluating the reception of *Esther* and attendant laughter in Black communities. She postulates that the very unexpectedness and seeming absurdity of certain secular situations in a biblical narrative create an intense aura of paradoxical disbelief. Hence, the scene in which Haman and Ahasuerus drink and laugh together need not necessarily be judged as sacrilegious or amoral in and of itself. Rather, the very presence of such a seemingly secular event actually freshens, rejuvenates, and accentuates the overarching spirituality of Bradbury's music and Cady's lyrics.[13]

Bradbury's score presented opportunities for African American performers to employ vocal improvisation in the unique ways associated with their cultural expression. It should be remembered that Bradbury did not set all of Cady's text to music as he reserved excerpts from the Book of Esther for the Messenger to declaim.[14] In the absence of specific performance directions, the Messenger could enunciate these lines as if preaching, chanting, or telling a story. In other places within the score, Bradbury set text using sparse notation (for instance, see musical example 2.1), where, once again, a performer might employ a nuanced and syncretic blend of rhetorical heterogeneity. These verbal episodes can function as partitions between sung numbers in a format suggestive of a performed sermon in which religious songs alternate with quasi-spoken or chanted text.[15] *Esther* opens with a Bible recitation (Esther 2:16–18), and this passage lends itself to an interpretation resembling the introductory section of a performed sermon. Opportunities to exploit the aesthetic and cultural nuances of Black sermonizing resurface throughout the piece. In this way, the Messenger and the performers of *Esther*'s chant passages function similarly to a preacher who not only engages in a transformative and hybrid style of vocal and dramatic declamation, but also assumes the responsibility of delivering spiritual and socio-political messages. As Albert Raboteau describes the attributes of this style: "At a certain stage, the preacher's chanting takes on a musical tone . . . . Dramatic ability, as much as a sense of timing, is a necessity for the successful preacher, who may play several parts at once . . . as he retells one of the familiar Bible stories. The relation of music and preaching has, traditionally, been symbiotic. There is a vocal continuum between speech and song in the sermon, as speech becomes rhythmic chant, and chant in turn becomes tonal and shades into song."[16]

Composer, musicologist, and critic Olly Wilson (1937–2018) published astute comments about African American vocal practices characterized by the interactive nature of song and preaching. He wrote of the ways Black musicians reiterate a core of pragmatic and spiritual beliefs representative of the uniqueness of their lived experiences: "For several hundred years now, since our forefathers' involuntary departure from the homeland . . . black people have been adapting . . . everything from food and dress to language and religion . . . to conform to an essentially African way of doing things. Nowhere has this adaptation been truer than in music."

The expression of these beliefs draws upon what Wilson identified as a rich "kaleidoscopic repertoire of elements and practices" derived from African sources. Such practices include "a heightened sensitivity" to "immediateness of expression" as manifested in improvisatory techniques. Wilson also singled out the African-derived "tendency to create a high density of musical events" and to place paramount value on music as a "ritualistic, interactive, communal activity." To create their signature "multidimensional" style of singing, African Americans often rely on a continuum of vocalization and consider "rhetorical strategies of speech" as integral to the overall aesthetic of their music making.[17] Linguist Geneva Smitherman labeled this performance practice as simply "talk-singing."[18]

The Fisk Jubilee Singers and *Esther*

The Fisk Jubilee Singers performed one of earliest and most noteworthy African American renditions of *Esther* in the later nineteenth century.[19] From its founding in 1866, Fisk University struggled financially. The institution's treasurer and music teacher, George Leonard White (1838–1895), proposed taking the school's vocal ensemble on a concert tour to raise money from ticket sales. Prior to their now famous inaugural tour of October 1871, White and the Singers, augmented with some forty additional students for the choruses, prepared *Esther* and presented the work in Nashville and nearby Memphis.

Figure 7.1. Maggie L. Porter, ca. 1871. New York Public Library.

White invited soprano Maggie L. Porter (figure 7.1), then a former Fisk student, to sing the title role.[20] During the process of selecting a singer for the role of Queen Esther, White considered assigning the part to a young woman of lighter complexion than Porter, but eventually changed his mind. Porter later recalled, "[H]e selected me for the queen and it raised Cain!" Upon hearing of this decision, someone remarked that they "had never heard of a Black queen before," but Porter responded with evident pride, White "kept the black queen just the same."[21] Porter's selection for the title role aroused prejudices associated with a Eurocentric view of the Hebrew Testament that denied the biblical presence of Black people in positions of virtue, royalty, and influence.[22] It is for this reason I believe Porter's association with *Esther* assumed activist significance. She clearly knew how extraordinary it was for the famous role of Queen Esther to be portrayed by an African American woman of dark skin hue, especially in the South. Whether or not her self-identity as a Black Queen Esther affected her performance cannot be determined from surviving documentation. Nonetheless, keen memory of her selection for this role and the attendant issue of skin color remained so vivid in her mind that she readily recalled the circumstances in detail during an interview over sixty years later.[23]

Owing to prevailing racist hostility, White encountered difficulties when he attempted to secure a venue for the Singers' production of *Esther*. An article reprinted in the *New York Tribune* detailed the unfortunate circumstances:

> Prof. White, an excellent musician and teacher at Fisk University, has succeeded in organizing a splendid choir among the pupils. He has made all preparations for [the presentation of] . . . *Esther*. There is no other choir in the city [of Nashville] capable of succeeding in the production of a great musical work, but the [University's] managers are unable to provide a hall for their performances. There are several halls used by wandering stars or native amateurs for concerts, performances, and the like, prominent among them "Masonic Hall." But the trustees of Masonic Hall refuse to let [rent] the Hall for the concert of Fisk University because "the citizens of Nashville would not like to see the Hall used by n*****s." For the concert of the best organized, best managed choir of the city, containing among its members the best cultivated male and female voices, the Hall could not be rented. They are colored, and must not contaminate Masonic Hall. The few lesser halls in the city followed suit, and the concert cannot be held.[24]

Eventually, the Masonic Hall management relented, and the Singers performed *Esther* on March 9 and 10, 1871 (figure 7.2). Enthusiastic audiences filled the 1,200-seat hall on both nights. Ticket sales netted some three hundred dollars for the university's fundraising campaign.

A Washington, DC, newspaper printed the following review of the Singers' performance:

> To say that all who attended these concerts were delighted is not sufficient to express the pleasure evinced by those who listened to the representation and were thrilled and moved by the solos, duets, quartets and choruses given with spirit, taste and due regard to musical laws. . . . We were especially impressed by the freshness and mobility of all the voices. . . . Mr. T[homas] Rutling, who enacted the part of Mordecai the Jew, has a pure tenor of good compass furnishing nearly two octaves of chest tones of rich quality and possessing *timbre* sufficient to make the fortunes of half a dozen opera singers. It is the best tenor we have ever heard in Tennessee. . . . If Rutling were in Paris or

Figure 7.2. Poster, Fisk Jubilee Singers' performance of *Esther*, 1871. Fisk University, John Hope and Aurelia E. Franklin Library, Special Collections, Photograph Archives.

Figure 7.3. Fisk Jubilee Singers touring ensemble, ca. 1871. From left to right: Minnie Tate, Greene Evans, Isaac Dickerson, Jennie Jackson, Maggie Porter, Ella Sheppard, Thomas Rutling, Benjamin Holmes, and Eliza Walker. Courtesy of Fisk University, John Hope and Aurelia E. Franklin Library, Special Collections, Photograph Archives.

> Leipsic, in spite of his color, they would put him in the Conservatoire, and *presto*! . . . the world would have an Othello . . . . Miss Minnie Tate [as Zeresh, Haman's wife], a child [age 13], astonished us by the pure rich *contralto* tones she poured forth to the delight of all who heard her. In her solos to Haman she evinced rare dramatic talent, by her inimitable reading and action. The voice of Miss [Jennie] Jackson [as the Queen's First Maid of Honor], *soprano*, is remarkable, possessing much power and with all, very sympathetic in its tones, while she managed it with skill . . . . [Isaac P.] Dickerson, as Haman, sang his solos with spirit, and possesses a baritone voice of pleasing quality . . . . Miss Porter as Esther was fully up [to commendable standards] in [the performance of] her part, and rendered it with much quiet dignity . . . . Mr. [Greene] Evans as the King was dignified and possesses a bass voice of good compass . . . . Miss [Georgia] Gordon as the Prophetess is entitled to more than passing notice, the careful earnestness with which she rendered her part deserves commendation. The choruses were well sung with marked effects; we were much pleased with the *diminuendo* . . . and also the vivacity and spirit . . . . To Mr. White and his coadjutors, we extend our thanks for the rare treat afforded [see figure 7.3] [italics original].

In addition to praising several of the Singers individually for their performances, the reviewer quoted above also singled out accompanist Ella Sheppard, whose ability to improvise at the keyboard contributed substantially to the overall quality of the production.[25]

Fisk University's principal, Adam Knight Spence, expressed enthusiasm for White's efforts while he also acknowledged the ambitious and challenging nature of *Esther* performances: "A fine concert given entirely by colored people is a new thing. It encourages the colored people themselves and tends to lift them into respect with others [whites] . . . . We must do something to keep [the Singers] before the people. This [production of *Esther*], I think, is a good way to accomplish that."[26] In his comments, Spence singled out the significance of a performance by Black people of a piece associated wholly with white singers and audiences, particularly in the South. The meteoric rise in popularity of *Esther* took place largely in white communities with few performances of the work by African Americans recorded by the press prior to 1871. Spence would, therefore, have been quite aware of the identity of *Esther* as a white work. Furthermore, white audiences associated Black stage performers with minstrel shows, vaudeville comedy, and the singing of spirituals but not with a work categorized as either a sacred oratorio or staged biblical drama.

Two months after their successful debut in Nashville, the Singers traveled by train to Memphis and performed *Esther* on June 28, 1871. For this performance, White had secured the expansive Greenlaw Opera House with seating for 2,200. Owing to unusually hot weather, audience attendance was less than hoped. A positive, albeit brief, review in a local newspaper lauded the Singers' costumes as most "appropriate" and praised the ensemble's "fine conception of the characters."[27] The Singers never performed *Esther* in its entirety again, but selections from the work remained in their repertoire during their first extended concert tour through the northeastern United States and eventually in Europe.[28]

Surviving documentation illustrates the ways the Fisk Jubilee Singers' performances of *Esther* served specialized African American artistic and activist purposes. At the very least, Maggie Porter's performance took courage as her interpretation of the title role was one of the earliest by a Black woman. Furthermore, the Singers had to maintain composure and determination amid the heated controversy over whether or not an African American ensemble should have been permitted to perform in Nashville's Masonic

Hall. It must be remembered that the same racist practices and attitudes that denied African Americans access to European concert music also applied to lighter works such as *Esther*. The Singers faced the very real possibility that no matter how exquisite their rendition of *Esther*, they nonetheless risked derision and ridicule from white audiences and critics. Thus, through the proving ground of *Esther* performances, the Singers established themselves as a music ensemble of considerable persuasion, ability, and polish.

Esther in Washington, DC, and Montgomery, Alabama

In May 1881, African American soprano Amelia L. Tilghman (1856–1931) traveled from her native Washington, DC, to Louisville, Kentucky, to sing as the invited featured soloist for the prestigious *Saengerfest*, an enormous music festival organized by the city's Black community. While in Louisville, she attended a performance of *Esther* given by Cincinnati's premier African American ensemble, the Queen City Choral Society. A newspaper reporter took notice of Tilghman occupying a box seat and manifesting "great interest in the performance." The event impressed her profoundly, and she returned to Washington determined to organize a similar production in the nation's capital.[29]

Tilghman (figure 7.4), a Howard University graduate and elementary school teacher, is best remembered for editing the first African American music periodical, *Musical Messenger*, published by her from around 1886 until 1892. Tilghman toured during the 1880s in the northeastern United States as a soloist and ensemble singer, earning positive reviews. She also sang as the featured soprano at DC's Fifteenth Street Presbyterian Church.[30]

By 1881, a newspaper item confirmed that *Esther* had become "a very favorite work, by the way, with colored people."[31] Not surprisingly, then, Tilghman's desire to produce *Esther* in Washington, DC, met with considerable enthusiasm in the Black community. Her plan was unprecedented as she may well have been the first African American woman to direct such a production. Among her local supporters, John Wesley Cromwell (1846–1927), editor of the influential African American DC newspaper, *People's Advocate*, provided her with ample publicity. Tilghman presented *Esther* as a theater piece and reviews of her production confirm that she used Seager's edition and followed his recommendations for staging the work.

Figure 7.4. Amelia L. Tilghman. Irvine Garland Penn, *The Afro-American Press and Its Editors* (Springfield, MA: Wiley, 1891), 403.

We should not underestimate the challenges Tilghman encountered as she prepared to launch her *Esther* production. According to surviving press accounts, she had no prior experience as a director of staged musical productions. In addition to the daunting task of assembling a cast and choruses, she also oversaw the creation of costumes and stage accessories. She recruited seventy-five singers from area church choirs, including twenty-eight children. As a respected soprano soloist, she maintained strong connections with the directors and members of Black church choirs along with the region's school music teachers. Her familiarity with these musicians' abilities provided her with considerable information from which she could make informed decisions regarding personnel, especially in the selection of players for *Esther*'s principal roles.

For her production of *Esther*, Tilghman not only assumed the title role, she also conducted the choruses and played piano accompaniments during rehearsals. The *Evening Star* joined the *People's Advocate* in promoting the production, and in their notice, promised an unusual spectacle to be sung "by the best musical talent of Washington."[32] Tilghman wisely selected bass Philip James Ferguson (1852–1885), the singer in the Louisville performance she attended, to reprise his role as King Ahasuerus for her production. A Washington, DC, native and Ohio resident, Ferguson had long taught music in Cincinnati's public schools. Of his performance in Louisville, the press noted that "his talents as a singer and intelligent actor are as great as those that have made him such an able teacher."[33] Tilghman also cast respected Washington, DC, singers with previous concert experience, including Mamie Nichol (as Mordecai's sister), Tillie J. Somerville, soprano (as the Prophetess), baritone William T. Benjamin (as Haman), and tenor Richard W. Tompkins (as Mordecai). Both Benjamin and Tompkins had previously performed with Washington's short-lived Colored American Opera Company in the early 1870s. Tilghman and her cast presented *Esther* twice in the city's famous Lincoln Hall. A popular venue for speeches, drama, and concerts, the hall boasted a seating capacity for 1,000 attendees.[34] Owing to the theater's small stage, the more substantial scenes must have taken place in the ante-proscenium area.

Tilghman's production did not completely sell out Lincoln Hall, but sizeable and enthusiastic audiences attended both evenings, on November 24 and 25, 1881. The *People's Advocate* hailed Tilghman's *Esther* as "the grandest musical effort made here by our people." According to press accounts, she was the first Black woman to direct such a production, an endeavor that becomes that much more remarkable when we remember that she also sang the title role. Tilghman's experience as a teacher and a soprano soloist served her well, as this comment from the *People's Advocate* confirms: "Considered in its entirety it was a grand success, it being the first time that a company composed so largely of younger persons without previous experience in operatic or oratorio music, had essayed the rendition of so beautiful a cantata as Queen Esther. The result has proven that there is talent which needs but to be intelligently and thoroughly trained to produce really artistic performances."[35]

Tilghman's visually appealing staging and costumes did not go unnoticed by an *Advocate* critic who wrote: "Let it be stated that the costumes were *beautiful and appropriate* [italics original]." The *Advocate* reviewer continued with these comments about the performance itself:

> The piece opened with the Persian chorus. The obsequiousness of the Persians and the haughty manner of Haman (W[illiam] T. Benjamin) were well displayed both in song and acting. The next scene shows King Ahasuerus (Philip James Ferguson, of the Queen City Choral Association), on his throne of state, entertaining and approving Haman's plot [to annihilate the Jews in the realm]. There is a song of joy between them [Haman and Ahasuerus], but they were appalled by the song of the prophetess (Miss Tillie J. Somerville) ["Lo o'er the Wicked"] whose full contralto notes were distinctly heard all over the hall. [The petite] Miss Tilghman (Queen Esther), it must be remembered, has not the physique we look for in a queen—especially in one who is chosen for her *commanding* excellence; but she made up in sweetness of appearance what she lacked in other respects. Her first appearance was in the third scene, with the Jews bewailing their impending destruction. The duet which followed between her and Mordecai (R[ichard] W. Tompkins) [Act II, "Go Thou unto the King"] was quite realistic. The chorus which followed ["To Thee, O Lord"] was full and strong, but not deadening [overpowering] the clear voice of the Queen. The tenor obbligato was a gem ["Prayer for Success"]. "In Thee Do I Put My Trust" [conclusion of Act II], accompanied by the chorus, was very acceptably rendered by Mordecai's sister (Miss Mamie Nichol). The duet between Queen Esther and King Ahasuerus ["Long Live Our Beauteous Queen"] gave excellent opportunity for the shrill [well-projected], clear soprano of Miss Tilghman and the excellent voice of Mr. Ferguson. Zeresh, the wife of Haman, has an alto voice not very strong, but sweet and true, which was displayed to better effect on that account in duets than in solos. She was one of the very best, if not the best, lady actors. She seemed to enter into the very spirit of the occasion. The Grand March of boys and girls was very well done, eliciting hearty encores both nights. The invitation to the banquet, the banquet scene, and the *denouement* were all quite realistic. The duet between Mordecai and Zeresh, "Do I Wake, or Am I Dreaming?" [Act V, scene 3] after the exaltation of the former and the humiliation, of the latter, one of the sweetest and at the same time one of the most touching airs of the cantata—the notes of one were those of mingled

rapture and those of the other were of pain and remorse; but they blended as perfectly as if they had been attuned for the same sentiment. With the grand [Finale] chorus "Praise the Lord" which brought out distinctly all the leading voices, the curtain fell [italics original].[36]

Tilghman left Washington, DC, in 1885, pursued conservatory music studies in Boston and then moved to Montgomery, Alabama, where she resided for two years. While in Alabama, she again produced performances of *Esther* and also sang the title role.[37] Montgomery's white daily newspaper, the *Advertiser*, printed this item about Tilghman's production:

> The American negro has always been credited with a large natural gift for music. There seems to be very little known in this section [of the country] as to his ability to skillfully execute in the musical [realm] . . . . They [the performers] will, as far as Montgomery is concerned, at least, have an opportunity tomorrow night . . . to exhibit ability in that direction. There is to be put on the . . . beautiful Cantata of Queen Esther. Those who know this cantata know that it combines most beautifully the musical and dramatic, and the additional interest in this case is that the performers are all colored from the king to the peasant girl, orchestra and all, about sixty persons being in it.

The writer readily acknowledged Tilghman's musical expertise and unequivocal qualifications to direct this production: "The manager [Tilghman, as director] has had a great musical experience and the benefit of some training in the Boston Conservatory of Music, so quite a novel treat awaits those who go to McDonald's [Opera House] tomorrow evening [May 17, 1886]."[38] George Freeman McDonald (1839–1905), owner and manager of the facility that bore his name, promised directors of stage productions "all modern improvements," including a "complete stock of elegant scenery" and audience seating for 1,000.[39] According to a review in the Black press,

> Miss Tilghman represented the beautiful queen, and she manifested that solemn, pathetic [emotionally charged] and dramatic force throughout the play, which gave it life-like appearance, as one would picture it . . . in the Bible. The highest praise is due her for the presentation of this cantata. She was the sole organizer, and deserves the thanks of the citizens generally for her interest in everything which tends to the improvement and elevation of our race.[40]

The *Advertiser* published a measured evaluation, calling the event "very creditable and greatly enjoyed by all who witnessed it."[41] A regional Black newspaper, the *Huntsville Gazette*, stated glowingly, albeit briefly, "the Cantata of Queen Esther . . . was brilliantly rendered and largely patronized."[42]

Tilghman's productions of *Esther* were extraordinarily significant events for Washington, DC, and Montgomery audiences and these cities' Black communities. Her performance in the title role, along with the singers in her cast, elicited considerable support and acclaim from the regional press. Not only did these performances garner community enthusiasm, they also proved personally inspiring for Tilghman herself. That she reprised her DC production and her performance in the title role in Montgomery speaks to the activist intent and artistic fulfillment she undoubtedly felt.

The Hampton Singers and *Esther*

The Singers of Hampton Normal and Agricultural Institute (now University) first performed *Esther* on April 8, 1889, as part of the school's annual commencement celebration. Frederic G. Rathbun, a New England Conservatory graduate, organist, and composer, and the Institute's music teacher rehearsed the Singers and directed the production. The cast, comprised of students and alumnae, performed on campus in Virginia Hall (figure 7.5). Little documentation of this performance survives aside from a brief article in the institution's monthly publication, the *Southern Workman*, praising the effort. Audience members were said to have commented, "If you could only transport all this to a New York or Boston concert hall!"[43]

The hope for a New York production of *Esther* by the Hampton Singers, as expressed in the *Southern Workman*, became a reality only a few years later. Following in the footsteps of the Fisk Jubilee Singers, the Hampton Singers responded similarly and eagerly to their institution's severe budgetary shortfalls and a dire need for fundraising. Such campaigns were usually coordinated by General Samuel Chapman Armstrong (1839–1893), founding president of Hampton Institute. But the onset of debilitating illness in 1892 precluded Armstrong's participation in any public functions. Members of the Institute's Board of Trustees determined that some sort of ambitious effort to secure funding needed to be implemented immediately and they inaugurated the Armstrong Association to pursue these goals. This organization proposed

Figure 7.5. Hampton Institute Singers, 1880s. Collection of the Hampton University Archives, Hampton, VA.

fundraising events in the New York City area beginning with an evening gala featuring presentations for well-heeled philanthropically minded benefactors to take place in the spacious concert hall of Madison Square Garden. As a follow-up to this event, Hampton's fundraisers scheduled performances of *Esther* by the institution's Singers in New York and nearby East Orange, New Jersey.[44] According to the *Southern Workman*, the choice of *Esther* "seemed especially appropriate" for this purpose as its text expressed the "plea of a downtrodden people for an opportunity to rise."[45]

The gala at Madison Square Garden took place on January 18, 1893, the evening before the Singers' first performance of *Esther* in the New York area. A surviving press account of this event yields a sense of prevalent opinions, held by prominent white New Yorkers, of contemporaneous race relations and of efforts to educate African Americans. It also brings into focus the considerable weight of expectation and responsibility brought to bear upon the Singers, as their performances comprised the centerpiece of these urgent fundraising efforts. Regarding the evening of January 18, the *New York Sun*

Figure 7.6. Touring ensemble, Hampton Institute Singers, 1890s. Collection of the Hampton University Archives, Hampton, VA.

observed, "[A]mong the audience, naturally, were not a few negroes, well dressed as a rule, although they did not wear evening clothes like their white neighbors." The evening's program consisted of addresses given by invited speakers interspersed with performances by the Hampton Singers' touring ensemble (figure 7.6) consisting of what the *Sun* referred to as "weird plantation spirituals." With the exception of Booker T. Washington, all who spoke were white.[46] In the first address, Columbia University President (and former Brooklyn Mayor) Seth Low (1850–1916) complimented the ways Hampton Institute "illustrated how the two problems which confronted American civilization—the negro and the Indian problems—could be solved." (During this era, the student body at Hampton Institute included both Black people and Native Americans). Next, Rev. William S. Rainsford (1850–1933), a Social Gospel activist and pastor of New York's St. George's Episcopal Church, spoke. Citing as a credential the experience of having "lived among both the Indians and the negroes," he concluded, "[Y]ou must educate through the fingers to the brain. You can't cram nineteenth-century civilization down the throats of the barbarous races without preliminary training in the mechanical arts."[47]

To secure a venue for the Hampton Singers' first performance of *Esther*, the Armstrong Association approached impresario Augustin Daly (1838–1899), who agreed to donate the use of his famous Daly's Theatre located in the heart of the entertainment sector of the city at Broadway and 30th Street. A well-known playwright as well as an internationally renowned director and producer, Daly enjoyed celebrity status in New York and in London, where he also operated a theater. In choosing events for his theaters, Daly selected "novel, original, entertaining, and unobjectionable" works and productions.[48] He undoubtedly regarded the Hampton production of *Esther* as a benign novelty and therefore quite in keeping with his theatrical philosophy and mission.

An entry in the box office journal of Daly's Theatre for January 19, 1893, lists the Singers' "charity matinee" for 2 p.m. and confirms sponsorship for the event by Emily Smith Putnam (1865–1944), Fanny Garrison Villard (1844–1928), and Charles Dudley Warner (1829–1900).[49] These individuals brought to this project considerable philanthropic commitment along with persuasive financial and social connections. Putnam, a prominent educator and historian, served as secretary of the Armstrong Association.[50] Fanny Villard, a civil rights activist and daughter of famed abolitionist William Lloyd Garrison (1805–1879), was a member of the Ladies Committee of Hampton Institute. She convinced the *New York Times* to publish a plea for funds for the Institute and to advertise the Singers' performances.[51] Her husband, Henry Villard (1833–1900), a Civil War correspondent, journalist, financier, and wealthy railroad magnate, served as vice president of the Armstrong Association. The third sponsor, Charles Dudley Warner, a member of the editorial board of *Harper's New Monthly Magazine*, maintained frequent contact with the New York theater world. Warner voiced considerable sympathy with and support of Booker T. Washington's educational principles.[52] (Washington became indoctrinated in the industrial model of education when he attended Hampton Institute. He incorporated the same approach at Tuskegee Institute, founded by him in 1881.)

Edith Armstrong (1872–1941), General Armstrong's daughter and biographer, accompanied the Singers to their only rehearsal in Daly's Theatre, which began at 9 o'clock the morning of their performance. "The spirits of the Troupe were irrepressible," she reported. "[I]t was all we could do to keep our *prima donna* [who played Queen Esther] from singing all the time." She described the stage set used by the Singers, left in place from the previous weekend's performances, as an "armorial hall with black far-reaching recesses, hardly Biblical, but most effective." Members of the Armstrong Association gathered to watch the dress rehearsal with Augustin Daly "looking curiously on."[53] Owing to "softening" milder weather, a capacity crowd of 1,500 attended the matinee. The total amount of money raised at this performance, an astounding $2,700, included box office receipts and donations.[54]

Two reviews of the Hampton Singers' performance at Daly's Theatre, published in the *New York Sun* and *Harper's New Monthly Magazine*, survive.[55] According to the *Sun*, two addresses preceded the stage entrance of the Singers. In the first of these, Booker T. Washington spoke "most eloquently and earnestly upon the subject of the condition of southern Negroes and the best methods of helping them." Charles Dudley Warner then took the stage to introduce, with "clever remarks," the Singers and their performance. Among the few comments concerning the Singers, the *Sun* made condescending reference to their "untutored talent," "childish simplicity," and "naiveté" and concluded, "[E]verything was done and sung in the crudest possible fashion." Clearly, the *Sun* critic witnessed an interpretation of *Esther* that differed substantially from the expectations of a Eurocentric performance and the assumptions of a white audience.[56]

The second extant review of the Singers' performance, written by Warner, appeared in *Harper's*. In his review, Warner commented:

> The Muse who is watching out for the American drama, or rather for that variety of the modern drama which is made up of music, spectacle, and smart timely remarks, must have winked her eye when she looked down on an afternoon performance [by the Hampton Singers] . . . in New York in January [1893] . . . . [For, at that performance] there were indications of a . . . racial, poetic conception of life which must have set the Muse reflecting on new possibilities for the stage . . . . [T]he Muse . . . may have got a hint of an undeveloped talent in this race, some instinct, some imaginative conception, for something new in dramatic representation.

Warner clearly perceived something quite unexpected in the Singers' performance. What did he mean by "a racial, poetic conception of life"? What indications of "new possibilities for the stage" did he witness?

To begin with, Warner confirmed that the production, rendered "according to the unaided conception of the Hampton students," manifested many "remarkable features." Of the students' voices, he wrote: "[T]hey put into the music their own minor pathos. Many of the voices were exceedingly sweet, and some of them remarkable in range and sympathetic quality. Untrained except by themselves, without a conductor, with no orchestra, they sang with a nice ear for harmony and effect. Used to singing spirituals and plantation melodies, they carried into the rendition of the cantata the simplicity and the primitive pathos of their musical natures." The Singers' ability to perform without a conductor convinced Warner of their unassailable musicianship and polish. To maintain ensemble integrity, accuracy of intonation, and rhythmic cohesion, they relied solely on each other for cues. Thus, unhampered by the imposition of a conductor, they could respond freely, in a rhapsodic and improvisatory manner, to spontaneous inspiration. The resultant "nice ear for harmony and effect" Warner heard could only have originated with choral practices they perfected while "singing spirituals and plantation melodies"—practices they "carried into the rendition of the cantata." As to the Singers' acting, Warner made these telling observations:

> They were perfectly at home also in their Oriental costumes, which did not seem to be put on for stage effect. Fully impressed with the reality of their parts, they moved and acted with entire grace and dignity, and their [stage] groupings were always pleasing and picturesque. In it all they were simple and never betrayed self-consciousness. The representations were not aided by scenery and all the illusion of time and place had to be created by the performers. It is not too much to say that in the conception and rendition of this old story they showed that their race has a genuine dramatic instinct. It is doubtful if any other school in the land, of the same grade of scholarship, could have given this story with such simplicity, such absence of self-consciousness, and so much musical ability. This may have much or nothing to do with the question of the general capacity of the race just emancipated; but the Muse of whom we have spoken may have got a hint of an undeveloped talent in this race, some instinct, some imaginative conception, for something new in dramatic representation that will be as pleasing as it is primitive.

Of the audience's familiarity with the Book of Esther, Warner wrote: "[I]t is well known that a metropolitan audience spends so much of its leisure time in the study of the New Testament that it is obliged to neglect the Old .... The story of Esther was therefore new to many present" at Daly's Theatre. He noted that, in contrast, with the [Hampton] performers it was quite otherwise. To them the Old Testament, with its marvelous legends and unpronounceable names, is as real as modern history, and it is stamped to its least letter with religious meaning, and divine authority. Their vivid imaginations kindle at the sight of the remote and almost spectral personages, and the Oriental pageantry and color appeal to them.... They had, indeed, the first element of successful dramatic presentation, faith in the story, and profound realization of the characters. Their semi-tropical natures lent fervor to their conceptions;... they were royal persons and courtiers. The large chorus were, for a time, inmates of the palace, born and living in an Oriental atmosphere.[57]

The "fervor" of the Singers' "conceptions," as explicated by Warner, also reflected their relationship with Cady's lyrics, especially as certain passages provide a vehicle for social and political commentary. The convincing quality of the performance Warner witnessed can be attributed, in part, to the Singers' own realization that the biblical characters they portrayed were ancestral Africans. In addition, the designation of Jews as "a race despised, forlorn," (Seager, ed., *Esther*, Act I, scene 1) summarized how African Americans perceived the ways they were regarded in the 1890s by the dominant white population. Black people felt a kinship with Jews of the Hebrew Testament as a people who had been forcibly uprooted and displaced, especially when they sang the lyrics, "There is a certain people, scattered abroad, and dispersed among the people in all the provinces of thy kingdom" (Act I, scene 2). Of the texts in *Esther* selected from other books of the Hebrew Testament, the phrase "snare of the fowlers" doubled as a metaphor for slavery and the yearning for emancipation (Act V, scene 3): "Our soul is escaped as a bird from the snare.... The snare is broken, and we are escaped" (Psalm 124:7). Such passages allowed Black performers and audiences an opportunity to express and contemplate, communally, their frustrations with race hierarchy and to reinforce collective resolve to resist, deflect, and transcend the denigrations of segregation and racism.

Although Warner's review offered seminal and unprecedented insights, some of his comments also typified the discourse of contemporaneous white critics who tended to sidestep serious musical criticism of Black performers and defer to patronizing rhetoric. His unfortunate choice of condescending prose included references to the performers' "semi-tropical natures," their "untutored" musicianship, and their "primitive pathos." To be sure, he did not deny he heard a decidedly African American interpretation of *Esther*, nor did he refute the performers' unequivocal affinity with both the music itself and the Book of Esther. Yet the discernable performance practices and aesthetics he witnessed were, otherwise, almost totally beyond his critical acumen and vocabulary.[58]

Among more recent African American performances of *Esther*, the Beth Eden Baptist Church, located in Oakland, California, presented a staged production in 1950. The church's website states: "One of the highest and most acclaimed Youth Choir productions was on December 29, 1950. The choir performed *Esther, the Beautiful Queen* at the Oakland Auditorium Theater." As Rev. Dr. John P. Hubbard (1883–1955), pastor of the congregation at the time, confirmed, "[T]he main purpose of the life of Beth Eden Baptist Church is to serve the community in the very highest capacity. This includes the cultural development in every department of human life. In sponsoring *Esther*, we hope to more intensely enshrine the nobility of self-sacrifice."[59] No additional information about this event has been located.

In another performance in 1960, students at the historically Black Oakwood College (now University), located in Huntsville, Alabama, staged *Esther*. Established in 1896 by the Seventh-Day Adventist Church as Oakwood Industrial School, the founders of the institution closely aligned its curriculum and values with the pragmatic and gradualist philosophy of Booker T. Washington. The largest and most prestigious vocal ensemble on campus, the Aeolians, came under the direction of Joni Mae Pierre-Louis (1927–2009) in the late 1950s. Pierre-Louis's tenure as conductor attracted accolades for the "Aeolian Renaissance" she launched, during which the choir increased in size, expanded its repertoire, and embarked on lengthy tours. In this era, the college inaugurated an ambitious fundraising campaign for the purpose of expanding the campus's infrastructure in support of an application for enhanced accreditation.[60] The college's performance of *Esther* occurred during the time period of this initiative. Although no reviews of Oakwood's production of *Esther* have been located, yearbook photographs offer a view of costuming choices (figures 7.7, 7.8, and 7.9). An unidentified photographer posed cast members in front of the signature stone walls of the institution's famous Moran Hall, one of the most significant historic buildings on campus. The students shown in the cast photos most likely made their own costumes in the college's "clothing lab," an instructional facility furnished with sewing machines and other equipment used by those pursuing vocational training in preparation for careers in the garment industry.[61]

Figure 7.7. Lewis Henderson as Mordecai, Patricia Dent as Queen Esther, and Henry Fordham as King Ahasuerus. *Acorn* (Oakwood University yearbook), 1960–1961, 189. Oakwood University Archives, Huntsville, AL.

Figure 7.8. Ahasuerus extends his scepter to Queen Esther. *Acorn* (Oakwood University yearbook), 1960–1961, 189. Oakwood University Archives, Huntsville, A

ESTHER IN SAN FRANCISCO'S CHINATOWN

Why would Chinese immigrants, who brought to the United States their own rich operatic repertoire and tradition, choose to perform *Esther*? This question becomes particularly compelling when we consider the significance and frequency of Chinese opera performances in America's Chinatowns.[62] Yet however much San Francisco's Chinatown residents valued and perpetuated their native country's operatic tradition, they also found in *Esther* a work of unique and considerable appeal and purpose. Performances of English-language vocal works constituted a component of Chinese immigrant efforts to establish an American identity. Through such performances, they could demonstrate to white audiences their ability to learn and effectively perform, in English, what had become an extraordinarily popular piece of musical theater. So too, when seeking donations from friendlier and more sympathetic whites, fundraising for Chinese causes could better be accomplished through the vehicle of a persuasive and familiar work such as *Esther*.

Immigrant members of San Francisco's Chinatown's Presbyterian Church performed *Esther* more than once before large audiences. The church, founded in 1853 by Rev. Dr. William Speer (1822–1904), was the first of its kind in North America. Beyond providing a venue for Protestant services, the church opened a dispensary and school, worked toward the repeal of discriminatory laws targeting Chinese immigrants, and published *The Oriental*,

Figure 7.9. Left-hand photo: Paul Brantley as Haman; right-hand photo: Esther denounces Haman. *Acorn* (Oakwood University yearbook), 1960–1961, 189. Oakwood University Archives, Huntsville, AL.

the country's first Chinese English bilingual newspaper. Speer also worked tirelessly to mediate tensions between Chinese and white residents of San Francisco. He regularly delivered lectures "to explain the character, customs and wants of the Chinese, to remove misapprehensions, and to enlist . . . benevolent persons in efforts to instruct and befriend them."[63]

During the nineteenth and early twentieth centuries, large numbers of Chinese immigrants joined Protestant churches for both religious and social reasons. Churches assisted immigrants with acculturation while simultaneously encouraging the preservation of traditional Chinese customs, languages, and values. As members of a Protestant church, recent immigrants, especially, could continue to associate with ethnic Chinese and speak their native language. Churches also provided opportunities for congregants to learn English in a nonthreatening, supportive environment. By participating in the practices and beliefs of an American denomination, they not only engaged, spiritually, with other congregants, but they also had access to social services, such as schooling and procurement of employment. Chinese members of Protestant churches also raised funds for charitable causes and relief efforts in their native land and sent missionaries overseas to facilitate these projects.[64]

Figure 7.10. Cast, *Esther*, Chinese Presbyterian Church, Chinatown, San Francisco, Suen's Studio, 1924. The baby in this photograph, second row toward the left, was probably the daughter of Haman and Zeresh. Historical Documentation Project, Bancroft Library, University of California, Berkeley, CA.

On May 9 and 10, 1924, members of the Chinese Presbyterian Church performed *Esther*, quite likely the first production of this work by Asian Americans. The performances were conducted by Boston native Walter B. Bartlett (1870–1943), at one time a singer at Italy's celebrated La Scala Opera House, and the founder of an opera company in Martinez, California.[65] Figure 7.10 shows the cast of Bartlett's production of *Esther*, photographed in the Chinese Presbyterian Church sanctuary. The presence of an organ and grand piano in the photograph's foreground suggests the modes of accompaniment Bartlett had at his disposal. Bartlett, in evening attire, stands in the center of the photograph holding a baton. All of the performers, posed on a crowded stage, wear costumes assembled from easily draped materials. The accessories and stage set typify theatrical presentations of *Esther*, including a canopied throne in the back of the stage. Esther and Ahasuerus stand in the middle of the photograph to Bartlett's right. The Prophetess, wearing her characteristic conical head covering, stands on Bartlett's left. Another woman in the photograph, standing in the second row, holds a toddler aloft. As it was fairly common for directors to include a child in the cast—as the child of Zeresh and Haman—we might assume that this woman played the part of Zeresh. The banner suspended above the stage boldly announces, in embroidered Mandarin characters, words meaning, approximately, "the emotions deep and the music pure."[66] Contrary to the traditions of Chinese opera, in which men—as "male actresses"—often played female characters, the men of Bartlett's production portrayed only male roles.[67] Hence, Asian American performances of *Esther* in which women enacted their own characters actually contributed to what Gary Okihiro calls the "recentering" of women. Such adherence to European expectations of staged gender roles, rather than reliance on traditional male impersonations of females, represented acquiescence to Western assumptions of behavior and interpretation.[68]

San Francisco's Chinatown residents staged *Esther* again in 1932 under the director of voice teacher and conductor Lawrence B. Reeder (1890–1943). According to newspaper accounts, Reeder had long "been identified with progressive musical activities." One of his students, Maud Dunn, performed the title role in this production, and Tsw Wing, a baritone who traveled to California from China, sang the part of Ahasuerus.[69] An unidentified photographer posed three of the production's singers for a publicity image. The actors shown in the image assembled their costumes using native fabrics accessorized with stunning headdresses and draped veils (figure 7.11).[70]

Reeder's production raised money for the Shanghai Relief Committee, one of many philanthropic projects sponsored by the Chinese Chamber of Commerce along with charitable organizations such as the Chinese Six Companies and the Chinese Consolidated Benevolent Association.[71] Four major events in China motivated relief organizations to greatly increase their activities in 1929 and the early 1930s: economic hardship (exacerbated by the Great Depression), drought, flooding, and war. During the years 1929 to 1931, China experienced a severe and unprecedented drought. Heavy snowfall and torrential rains followed, causing the China Floods of 1931—arguably China's worst natural disaster of the twentieth century. An estimated 140,000 people drowned, and countless others lost their lives from famine and disease resulting from the catastrophe. Over one million persons were displaced and some five million required relief in order to survive.[72] In early 1932, the Japanese invaded flood-ravaged Shanghai

Figure 7.11. Left to right: Lily Lum (a courtier), Lucy Tom (Prophetess), and Mary Chung (another courtier). Unknown photographer, Chinatown, San Francisco, May 3, 1932. San Francisco History Center, San Francisco Public Library. http://sflib1.sfpl.org:82/record=b1012199.

and bombed civilians. The Shanghai War, as the ensuing conflict came to be known, lasted some three months. Estimates of casualties varied from 6,000 to 13,000 civilians, and some 230,000 residents fled to refugee camps. The war also disrupted manufacturing, farming, and commerce, resulting in further economic devastation for the region.[73] Reeder contributed all funds raised from his production of *Esther* to the causes just mentioned.

A "United Nations-like" Cast

During the 1950s, several Seventh-Day Adventist Church choirs, located in California, combined to perform *Esther* under the direction of Philippine native Rev. Dr. Ulysses M. Carbajal (1922–2016). Trained as a physician, opera singer, composer, conductor, and ordained as a Seventh-Day Adventist clergyman, Carbajal first became acquainted with *Esther* while a student at Philippine Union College. During the years 1949 to 1951, he not only directed many productions of *Esther*, but also sang the role of Ahasuerus several times.

Carbajal and his cast gave their first performance of *Esther* in Loma Linda in 1959 and then in several other California locations, including Antelope Valley, Berea, Glendale, Lancaster, Long Beach, Los Angeles, National City, Riverside, San Diego, and Van Nuys.[74] He went to considerable effort to recruit an ethnically diverse, multiracial cast comprised of "Filipino, Negro, Chinese, Japanese, Mexican, Guamanian and Palauan" singers, described by newspapers as "United Nations-like."[75] In addition, Carbajal cast his wife, Jovita Dela Cruz Carbajal, a classically trained soprano and Philippine native, in the title role. One color photograph taken of Carbajal's cast survives, but unfortunately, it is not of sufficient quality to reproduce here. (This photograph can be viewed online in the journal *Ectopic Murmurs* Vol. 23, no. 1 [January 2012], page 5.) Unlike the characteristic stage attire associated with many productions, Carbajal's cast did not employ dark costuming to designate members of the Jewish crowd. Instead, the players selected sheer fabrics of pastels, bright hues, and white for their garments, reflecting their country's native dress. The most striking head attire in this cast, a particularly dramatic conical golden headdress, was worn by the High Priest. Two African immigrants, dressed in elaborate costumes and cast as Chamberlains, sit in readiness on either side of the monarchs.

Carbajal's goals were evangelical, to be sure, but he also embraced racial heterogeneity, and he continued to select representatives of many minority communities for his casts in all of his productions.[76] His performances of *Esther* bring to mind historian and cultural theorist Bill Mullen's conception of "Afro-Orientalism." With a view toward creating a potent counterdiscourse to racist rhetoric, Mullen conjoins notions of Orientalism with Asian, African, and Black American identities, thus recognizing the shared, global struggles of subjugated people of color.[77] The common interests of Africans and Asians recalls a speech delivered by Frederick Douglass in which he articulated the power of this hybrid view of the world's citizenry when he described, in 1868, the potential of interracial cultural contact and interaction to "remove mountains of prejudice."[78]

CLOSING THOUGHTS

Productions of *Esther* by minorities served some of the same purposes as those launched in White communities—fundraising, music instruction, entertainment, and spiritual engagement. However, minority identification with the biblical Queen Esther extended beyond a Eurocentric interpretation of the Book of Esther to embrace not only a more nuanced context, but also served as an expressive vehicle for confronting and critiquing life in a diaspora. As a symbolic figure, Queen Esther lived as an exile and her deeds conveyed the imperative of remaining loyal to one's people at any cost. American minorities identified with the oppressed Jews in the Book of Esther who, like themselves, were continually threatened with discriminatory, violent, and racist white behavior. Performances of *Esther* provided a public musical forum through which minorities could engage in a communal exploration of biblical themes, especially courage, resiliency, and the possibility of redemption. By recruiting singers from a variety of racial and national origins and identities, conductor Ulysses M. Carbajal extended the activist significance of *Esther* to include a blend of Asian immigrants and African Americans. His productions provided a model and a means for cultural exchange and mediation in a racially heterogeneous and cooperative setting.

CHAPTER 8

AN INTERNATIONAL MEGAHIT

A mere three years after Bradbury published *Esther*, a New York music journal announced, "We hear of Mr. Bradbury's *Esther* being performed in so many places that we can scarcely keep our readers posted. It seems to give universal satisfaction."[1] How astute a comment as, by the 1870s, copies of the score had traveled northward to Canada and then overseas to Africa, Asia, Australia, the Caribbean, Great Britain, and New Zealand. In this chapter, I follow a trail of reviews that documents the enthusiastic reception for *Esther* in foreign locations. While many of these performances provided theatrical entertainment and helped raise funds for local charitable causes, others served missionary and evangelical purposes, especially in more remote areas.

Canada

Even before R. W. Seager published his edition in 1874, communities in eastern Canadian provinces staged *Esther*. Residents of Burford, Ontario, celebrated Dominion Day (July 1) with a production in the local military "drill shed." The performance, which took place in 1870, included some thirty singers. Members of the region's 7th Fusilier Band supplied incidental music along with an organist who played accompaniments. We can only begin to imagine what this production may have been like as the drill shed did not actually have flooring, in the true sense of the word. Instead, a mixture of soil and chipped bark sufficed to accommodate horses and marching soldiers, the principle users of the structure. Additionally, the town's public works crew flooded the area in the winter to create an indoor skating rink, and therefore a temporary floor had to be laid for this theatrical presentation of *Esther*.[2] A Burford correspondent published an enthusiastic and lengthy review of this production. The writer expressed pleasure and not a little relief that the drill shed had been "fitted up with much more than ordinary taste and care."

A "highly appreciative and intelligent audience" filled the facility to capacity. The correspondent then continued:

> [E]ven the most sanguine scarcely anticipated the complete success [this production] attained. It is a matter for congratulations ... that we have the taste and ambition to provide an entertainment so rational and ennobling.... The programme opened with a beautifully arranged tableau ... in which all the performers, numbering over thirty, took place.... King Ahasuerus, arrayed in purple robes, wearing a golden crown, sitting upon the throne, holding the golden sceptre, surrounded by his chamberlains with battle-axes drawn, was the very impersonation of a despotic Persian monarch; and with the advantages of a bass voice seldom equalled, and a bearing dignified yet not severe, rendered the illusion perfect.... [T]he heroic queen, enveloped in a robe of green, her head encircled by a crown of golden beauty, partially concealed by an ample veil studded with brilliant ... stars in miniature, rendered her appearance graceful, attractive and prepossessing. Her voice is powerful, yet sweetly musical, thoroughly cultivated, and under perfect control.... The light and joyous garb of Haman's friends make up a picture of Oriental grandeur which must be seen to be appreciated.... [Especially noteworthy were] the changes of character, incident and dress, the turbans and robes of eastern lands, the mourning habiliments of the doomed Jews.[3]

Canadians continued their support and enthusiasm for *Esther* throughout much of the nineteenth century. Singers in Carleton, New Brunswick, performed Bradbury's score on April 3, 1872.[4] In the late 1880s, the *Acton Free Press* called attention to regional productions, referring to one staged extravaganza in particular as "a rare treat," the actors attired in "appropriate" and "elegant" costumes.[5] Copies of Seager's score worked their way westward, and the piece soon became a sensation in the province of British Columbia. Residents of Victoria, the province's capital, launched productions in 1884, 1903, and again in 1918 in the local Philharmonic Hall. The singers, conducted by German native and esteemed teacher Emil Pferdner, were accompanied by an organist. Local historian and newspaper columnist Herbert Kent fondly remembered playing Haman in these productions. The English-born Kent, highly respected as a "musical pioneer" in the region for decades, taught music, conducted church choirs, and sang in operas.[6] Among newspaper comments about the 1903 production, a *Daily Times* critic lauded the "great magnitude" of the stage set with "no expense spared" for its design and construction. In addition, the paper expressed amazement over the effect of the picturesque "tambourine and shepherdess drills."[7] The review concluded, "[F]rom a spectacular point of view, the greatest achievement in this production is reached when Mordecai . . . enters on horseback, led by Haman and the grand triumphal march is given, 200 people being on the stage at one time."[8]

A reviewer of a performance in Winnipeg, Manitoba, was generally supportive, although the critic expressed some reservation about Bradbury's music and the stage settings:

> Better amateur material could not have been found than the majority of the voices forming the cast of principals and chorus for the production last night [May 16, 1900] at the Winnipeg Theatre . . . . The main points of the story were most creditably brought out, the leading musical features being strongly emphasized, and much of the acting in accordance with the emotional themes of the librettist . . . . A pretty modern waltz formed a suitable accompaniment to a simple step ballet danced before the King and Queen, and another waltz gave four pretty children an opportunity in the same scene. These, together with Leon Keach's [piano] additions completely threw poor Bradbury's saccharine music in the shade, although some of his choruses were effective enough . . . . The *mise en scène* in the Banquet Hall fairly glowed with color, and light, the Queen resplendent with a peculiar beauty and, gorgeously attired, looked every inch of her to the manner born, a very royal presence indeed.

Regarding the stage settings, this critic recommended "Egyptian scenery" rather than the "modern library for Haman's sanctum" used in this production. The reviewer also found the opening set, described as a "Chicago street scene for the front of the king's palace," quite loathsome.[9]

The Caribbean

Not long after Bradbury's death, newspaper advertisements confirmed performances of *Esther* in the Caribbean islands. A substantial review, quoted below, provided details of a production in 1870 in Hamilton, Bermuda:

The performance of this piece of music took place last Thursday evening [October 13, 1870] in the Mechanics' Hall of this Town. The public had been apprized [sic] of the coming event by newspaper advertisements and street placards, and the sensation produced by the prospect of hearing a complete Oratorio shewed itself in the rapid sale of tickets and the gathering of expectant crowds who hung round the yet unopened doors an hour before the performance commenced, and filled the body of the hall as soon as the doors were opened. The Mechanics' Hall is not the best of concert rooms, but much had been done to render it bright and well-lighted. In addition to the bracket lamps on the walls, triple lights were suspended over the heads of the singers and the front seats, while the centre of the hall was illuminated by a bronze candelabra garnished with cedar-brush flowers. The acoustic defects of the room were slightly palliated by the elevation of the ample stage which had been erected at the east end of the building for the accommodation of the singers. The concert commenced with an overture, which exhibited to advantage the *organ* tones of the harmonium . . . . The Oratorio then opened, if Oratorio it can be called, verging as it does somewhere on the [opera] *buffo*. The music of "Esther, the Beautiful Queen" is pretty, but rather ordinary . . . . [W]hat one feels in *Esther* is the absence of . . . "haunting melodies." It is nevertheless a pleasing representation and it was well sung. The spirited dialogue closing with a lively chorus, the passionate lament, the expostulations of Esther, the gay summons to the banquet hall, were expressed in music somewhat different indeed from the long-drawn fugues which distinguish the great Oratorios; but *Esther* at the Mechanics' Hall on Thursday evening was clearly a success. It was impossible to resist encoring the thrilling song of Zeresh whose delicate voice well merited the thunder of applause and bouquets with which it was greeted [probably "Thy Galling Defeat," Part II, no. 9]. We regretted indeed the defects of the room as much as anything else for the sake of the tenor [Mordecai], whose first notes were beautiful, and we hope that the next time the piece is sung some room will be found better calculated to display the qualities of his voice.[10]

Residents of Hamilton staged *Esther* again in 1873 and 1880.[11] A critic posted this brief comment about the latter production: "Happily the music, simple and effective, is adapted, more than such compositions usually are, to the capacity of amateurs . . . . [E]verything moved on smoothly with wonderful unity, time, and harmony. If we must single out, we must pronounce the last quartette the gem of the evening, 'Do I Wake or am I Dreaming?'"[12] Connective readings were included in this performance and the singers were accompaniment by a "small organ."[13]

A newspaper mentioned performances in the late 1990s in the tiny Caribbean island nation of Antigua and Barbuda. In 1997, the government produced *Esther* at the Cathedral Cultural Centre, located in the capital city of St. John's. The following year, the singers traveled to St. Croix, a US territory, for a repeat performance. Choir director and music educator Isalyn Richards conducted members of the country's National Choir in these performances as part of a gala commemorative event celebrating the success of the ensemble, founded in 1982 by Minister of Culture Reginald Knight.[14]

England

Great Britain's music educators, entrepreneurs, and philanthropists recognized and appreciated the educational, spiritual, and charitable benefits of producing *Esther*. In 1879, London's *Musical Times* advertised *Esther* as a work of "simple, yet pure and melodious character. The aim of the composer has been to make it accessible to as many singers as possible; hence it is constantly being used as a first attempt at a connected [multimovement] work by choirs in all parts of the country."[15] Another writer noted of Bradbury's style that the work's "simpler music" enjoyed "a certain currency in England," especially among the musically "uneducated."[16] Historian H. Augustine Simcoe confirmed that "*Esther*, an unpretentious but beautiful cantata . . . enjoys a wide popularity in the West of England and South Wales, and is likely to do so in the future."[17] Of particular significance in this regard, the education reformer Rev. John Curwen (1816–1880) promoted Bradbury's work throughout the region. Bradbury and Curwen met sometime in 1847, during the former's residency in England. They shared common beliefs in the elevating effects of singing, especially in matters of morality and in the attendant imperative to teach the general public how to read and perform music. Both educators had in mind the improvement of singing in churches and viewed choral pieces, such as *Esther*, as most appropriate for the promotion of their educational philosophy.

Curwen saw great potential for *Esther* as a vehicle with which to fulfill his pedagogical goals. In 1870, Curwen published an edition of *Esther* containing all of the original music but without cues or notation for accompaniment and also without Josephus's essay. Not only did Curwen prominently credit Bradbury for the music and Cady for the text, but he also incorporated the former's autographed portrait as a frontispiece to his score (see figure 1.4). In format, Curwen followed Bradbury's organization of the score into two main parts with divisions into numbers, and he also included the scriptural passages for the Messenger to declaim. He indicated, on the title page of his edition, that he wrote instrumental parts for accompaniment and made known their availability for separate purchase or rental.

Aside from its overall organizational scheme, Curwen's score bears almost no resemblance to Bradbury's as he set the work in tonic sol-fa notation. The tonic sol-fa system does not employ notes, clefs, or most of the elements familiar to those accustomed to staff notation. Instead, tonic sol-fa uses a series of letters, symbols, and occasional numbers separated by vertical lines that correspond to bar lines in standard notation and also imply stress of certain beats or text syllables. From a purely economic standpoint, music notated in tonic sol-fa could be printed in a condensed format using far fewer symbols and ultimately, less space and paper. In fact, tonic sol-fa repertoire and imprints, famous as "people's music," reflected the system's motto: "easy, cheap and true."[18]

Proponents of tonic sol-fa claimed it actually enabled the uninitiated to learn to read music more quickly. Instruction in tonic sol-fa relied on solmization (solfège) syllables and movable *doh*. The system's syllables represent pitches in an octave, spelled *doh, ray, me, fah, soh, lah, te* (usually abbreviated as the letters "d," "r," "m," "f," "s," "l" and "t") with superscripted numbers affixed to the letters to designate octaves. Other notational elements, such as dynamics, fermata, and tempo indications, largely duplicate those found in staff notation. The use of tonic sol-fa in a classroom required two instructional aids: first, "Curwen's Modulator," a wall chart listing solmization syllables and their abbreviations; and second, a placard illustrating hand gestures used by a teacher to represent solmization syllables. By pointing to letters and simultaneously using hand signals, the teacher demonstrated to students the relationship between pitch and syllable. After sufficient repetition of this introductory exercise, the teacher then led the students in actual song literature. As students gained confidence, a song's lyrics could replace reliance on solfège. Curwen claimed that all vocal music could be notated and taught most efficiently using his system.[19]

Curwen promoted his system through the publication of instructional manuals beginning with the *Grammar of Vocal Music* issued in 1843. He also founded the Tonic Sol-fa Association in 1853, and from 1851 until 1880, he published a periodical, *The Tonic Sol-fa Reporter and Magazine of Vocal Music for the People*. His success in England and British colonies notwithstanding, Curwen lamented, "[I]n the United States our method has made but little progress."[20] Quite possibly, US students and teachers were unwilling to sift through his voluminous *Teacher's Manual of the Tonic Sol-fa Method*–nearly four hundred pages in length–and to decipher seemingly obtuse instructions and exercises. Nonetheless, Curwen expressed considerable esteem for his American colleagues and respect for their methods. He wrote:

> When the dear and noble Dr. Lowell Mason gave me [a copy of] the "Vocalist" [tunebook compiled by Mason and George James Webb], with its German part-songs, he put into my hands a power of winning the people by means of music within their reach, and since that time the names of Lowell Mason, [Thomas] Hastings, Webb, [Isaac Baker] Woodbury, [William B.] Bradbury, [George F.] Root, and [T. F.] Seward have become almost as well known in England as in America. The Tonic Sol-faists of England owe to America a great debt. Its sound and unpretending music has filled our house with song.[21]

The tonic sol-fa version of *Esther* spread rapidly overseas and not surprisingly, Curwen perpetuated Bradbury's instructional purpose for the score. By the mid-1870s, missionaries and teachers had adopted his method, claimed Curwen, "in all parts of the globe."[22] Hence, it was Curwen's edition of *Esther*, and not Seager's or Keach's, that first made its way to distant British territories.

When he set *Esther* in tonic sol-fa, Curwen retained all of Bradbury's vocal music but did not provide any accompaniments. He titled the waltz number (Part II, no. 11) as simply "Banquet Music" and instructed the keyboardist to improvise "forty-eight three-pulse measures" for its performance without the aid of any notation. Curwen also added metronome markings and indicated the key at the beginning of each number. Although he listed the Bible verses by chapter and verse to be read by the Messenger (as in Bradbury's version), he did not include the actual texts. For a comparison of Curwen's notation with Bradbury's score, figure 8.1 and musical example 8.1 illustrate the same passage in tonic sol-fa and in standard notation, respectively.

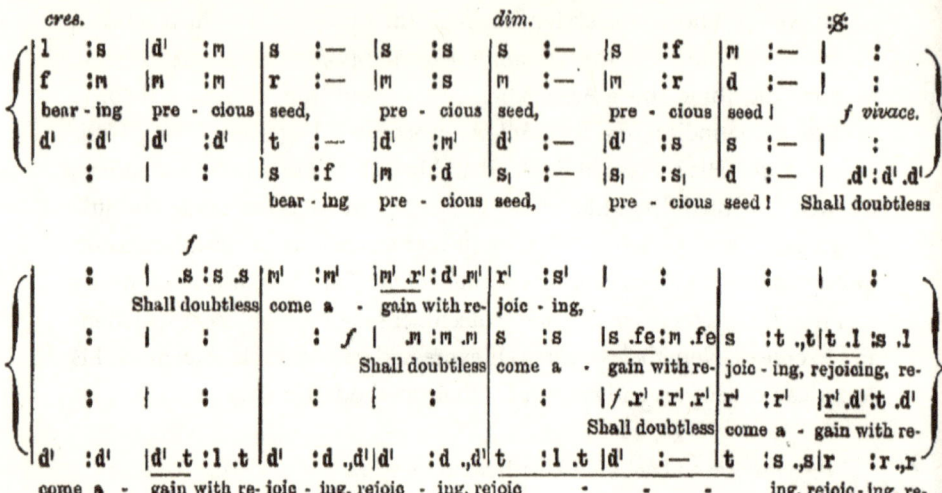

Figure 8.1. Bradbury, *Esther, the Beautiful Queen*, John Curwen, ed. (London: Bayley and Ferguson, 1870) notated in tonic sol-fa, Part I, no. 10, mm. 13–40.

Even though British audiences responded with considerable enthusiasm to *Esther*, a few English journalists nonetheless joined their American counterparts in voicing doubt as to whether or not Bradbury's score should be regarded as sacred music. One correspondent, clearly interrogating *Esther*'s genre identity, made equivocal reference to the work as a "so-called sacred cantata." The reviewer placed blame on Bradbury for the score's shortcomings, claiming his music "utterly fails from lack of ability on the part of the composer, resulting, in fact, in a parody, wherein in one place lines expressive of fervent supplication are set to a chorus, the subject of which is trivial, and the rhythm suggestive of a jig. The solos are either devoid of originality or else bald and meaningless."[23] Another British review offered tepid support for Bradbury's score and made an ill-advised comparison to revered classical composers, writing, "[T]he music shows little of the dignity, repose and devotional feeling which characterizes the works of our great composers."[24] Still another critic berated *Esther*'s music as a "mere *réchauffé* of the most familiar school songs and well-known Methodist hymn tunes" spiced with "a dash of Moody and Sankey" gospel melodies. This reviewer also detected a "strong flavor of the Christy Minstrels"—a reference to music associated with blackface entertainment.[25]

Musical Example 8.1. Bradbury, *Esther*, "He That Goeth Forth and Weepeth" (Part I, no. 10), mm. 13–21.

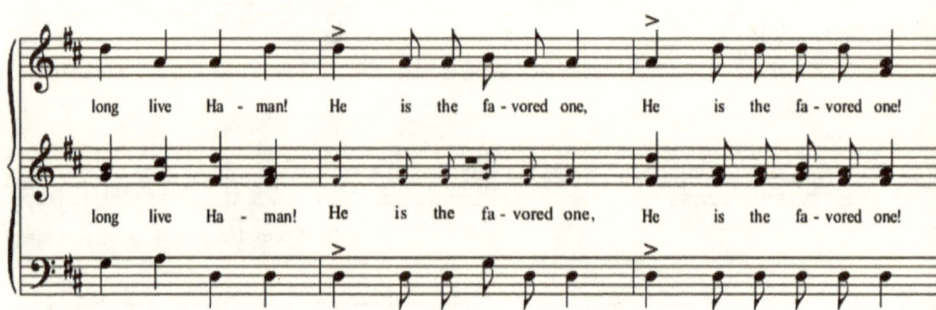

Musical Example 8.2. Bradbury, *Esther*, "Chorus of Haman's Friends" (Part I, no. 1), mm. 1–6. Note accompaniment cues

In 1878, English musician Henry Fisher (1845–1943) published yet another version of *Esther*. Although virtually forgotten today, Fisher earned accolades in his era as a respected keyboardist, educator, composer, and music critic. An author of several books and numerous articles, Fisher also arranged a number of opera selections for children's voices.[26] His edition of *Esther*, printed in standard notation, retains all of Bradbury's music and the original organizational scheme of an oratorio in two parts.[27] However, Fisher added a harmonium accompaniment throughout the work and appended an overture. His choice to write for harmonium reflected the preference in Europe for this instrument over the smaller and more portable melodeon, the latter being a popular instrument of choice in the United States for many *Esther* productions.[28] In brief introductory remarks to the harmonium player, Fisher offered these complicated directions about how to interpret his markings in Bradbury's score:

Figure 8.2. Bradbury, *Esther*, Henry Fisher, ed., Part I, no. 1, mm. 1–5, with registral indications for the harmonium player.

The figures 1, 2, 3, &c., denote the Stops of the Harmonium upon which, in addition to the names, these numbers will generally be found. When the figures are placed above the Treble stave, they indicate Stops on the right-hand side of the instrument, when below the Bass stave, the left-hand Stops are intended. The letter G [*Grand Jeu*] is always placed between the staves, as it belongs equally to both sets of Stops. The letter O means open, and the letter S, except when it refers to the Sourdine [mute] on the left-hand side of the instrument, means shut. The Stops indicated throughout this work must be looked upon as suggestions, as in many Harmoniums other combinations will be found quite as suitable; this, of course, arises from the different qualities of tone in instruments, no two being exactly alike. All Harmonium players are earnestly advised to master the Expression Stop and to use it whenever they play on the Instrument.[29]

Fisher also reorganized the choral parts in SATB order and provided metronome indications. For comparison, musical example 8.2 and figure 8.2 show the same passage with Fisher's harmonium markings clearly visible in latter image.

A fairly recent *Esther* performance in London merits mention. The director and singers, members of the Ghanaian Methodist Fellowship, a loose collective of Ghanaian immigrants, continue to gather for Sunday worship at the Methodist Central Hall in Westminster. According to the congregation's website, members produced *Esther* in June 2010 as part of their anniversary celebration. Proceeds raised at the event aided England's Methodist Home for the Aged and the Accra Psychiatric Hospital located in Ghana. Unfortunately, no other information has surfaced about this performance. Nevertheless, it holds the distinction of being arguably one of the most recent performances of *Esther* anywhere.[30]

WALES

The Welsh Band of Hope sponsored an *Esther* performance in March 1930 at the Jerusalem Chapel in Ton Pentre, a village in the Rhondda Valley, county borough of Rhondda Cynon Taf, located in southern Wales. Founded in 1847, the Band of Hope consisted of working-class citizens under the leadership of temperance activists Ann Jane Carlile (1775–1864) and Jabez Tunnicliff (1809–1865). The organization served as a faith-based initiative intended to impress upon its members the immorality of consuming alcoholic beverages. This initial organization provided the basis for an international movement that spread throughout Great Britain and subsequently overseas.[31] Each local Band of Hope branch formulated a constitution with a preamble that stated, "The object of this society shall be to induce the young to abstain from the use of intoxicating drink—including wine, beer and cider—as a beverage, tobacco, and profanity—and to advance the cause of Temperance by appropriate means."[32] Music served as a prominent activity for the Band of Hope, and the organization published song anthologies and produced musical events for fundraising and indoctrination purposes. Performances of works such as *Esther* helped financially sustain local Band of Hope chapters, support various publications, including children's periodicals, and solicit funds for the international maintenance and spread of the movement's philosophy. The Band of Hope considered Ahasuerus's debauchery as indictive of the dangers of intoxication. Additionally, adherents credited Queen Esther with a commitment to abstinence:

> [I]n a short time, from a humble Jewish captive, she was thus raised to the throne of Persia. Through this unexpected event, we also read that the destruction of the Jews, for which the king had been persuaded, when again

Figure 8.3. Photograph, cast, *Esther*, produced by the Band of Hope, Ton Pentre, Wales, 1930. Used with the permission of Aberdare Library, Aberdare, Wales.

under the influence of drink, to issue a decree, was averted, and the guilty parties to the conspiracy themselves brought to ruin instead. We insert these facts, in order to take the opportunity of mentioning that in an apocryphal writing this good and true Queen Esther . . . had not eaten at Haman's table, nor had pleasure at the king's feast, *nor had drunk the wine of the drink-offerings* [italics original].[33]

We should recall that R. W. Seager recommended stage action that underscored Esther's avoidance of alcoholic beverages. For the banquet scene (during Act 5, scene 2), Seager gave these instructions: "King gives one goblet to Haman and offers the other to the Queen, who declines [to accept a goblet of wine]."[34]

Only one photograph of the Band of Hope's production of *Esther* has been located (figure 8.3). Consistent with Seager's recommendations for costumes, the principal players wore the most elaborate attire with the chorus of Jews clad in dark-hued robes. In the very front row, center, the king, Esther, and Haman recline adjacent to a small banquet table. All are holding wine goblets including, unexpectedly, Esther. We should assume, given the Band of Hope's strict principals of abstinence, that the queen's goblet is empty. The conductor, clearly visible in the center of the photograph, clutches his score and baton; the accompanist stands to the far left.

Australia

Performances of *Esther* in Australia attracted newspaper coverage beginning in the early 1880s with notices published in the *Courier* of Brisbane.[35] In a Camperdown production in 1887, singers must have used Curwen's tonic sol-fa score as a review indicated the work's division into two parts. The writer credited Bradbury with doing "more for the cultivation of music among the people of the United States than any other person," and noted that *Esther* "has been a favourite in all parts of the English-speaking countries."[36] A review of a performance in the Theatre Royal, located in Broken Hill, New South Wales, confirmed that the entire cast of the "Scriptural cantata *Esther, the Beautiful Queen*" wore "picturesque and particolored garments appropriate to the period." This critic also mentioned "spirited dramatic action" and lively dancing.[37]

A critic in Euroa, Australia, offered "with much pleasure" the comments quoted below, concerning a production that took place in 1893:

> *Esther, the Beautiful Queen* is a sacred cantata . . . studiously free from any crucial tests of vocalization, the solos and concerted music being specially designed well within the range of ordinary musical training. None the less, however, it embraces some very beautiful harmonization and musical effects . . . . It is founded on the well-known scriptural history of Queen Esther's relations with King Ahasuerus and her noble acts on behalf of the Jewish people. The bulk of the solos fall upon some half-dozen voices and, given capable performers in these parts, the success of the cantata is assured. This is one of the principal reasons which make its rendition possible in provincial centres, where the number of really capable vocalists may usually be reckoned upon the fingers, while at the same time ample scope is allowed in the choruses for obtaining the best effects from singers of average ability . . . . The . . . becomingly attired . . . Beautiful Queen at once secured the favor of the audience . . . [and] the charms of her rich, mellow, well-modulated voice made her a prime favorite . . . . It was unfortunate that, owing to the limited stage accommodation, the organ, on which the accompaniments were played, was placed on a temporary staging projecting into the body of the hall, the result being that at times the instrument was too much in evidence, as against the tenors and basses, who, being far at the rear, had their voices shorn somewhat of penetrative power by the stage furnishings and the open space overhead. A screen sloping from the front to the rear of the platform [stage] would probably obviate or greatly modify this defect.[38]

A review of a performance in 1894 in Protestant Hall, Brisbane, Queensland, for the benefit of the city's Blind, Deaf, and Dumb Institute, indicates that the work "was given in a somewhat unique form, the soloists, as well as the chorus . . . being in character." The reviewer referred to this theatrical presentation as a "pleasing departure . . . thoroughly appreciated by the audience . . . . *Esther* is a cantata by no means new to lovers of this particular class of music here, and the beautiful and touching melodies which interpret the Hebrew story always insures for it a warm welcome."[39]

Residents of Sale, Australia, celebrated Christmas 1896 with an *Esther* performance in Victoria Hall. A reviewer for the local *Gippsland Times* noted:

> It is many years since the composition [*Esther*] was rendered in Sale, and people seemed to be under the impression that the text and the music were as solemn and, to the uninitiated, as dreary as a classical oratorio. As a matter of fact the "dry" parts of the Book of Esther are omitted, and only the touching, dramatic incidents are set to bright, spirited melodies, the connecting narrative being read . . . . The opening chorus of the cantata, "Long live Haman," at once showed that the conductor possessed the gift of inspiring his choir to put dramatic emphasis into their singing. Each one of the many succeeding choruses was rendered with the same excellent balance of parts and full toned harmony of the whole, no easy matter considering that the only accompaniment was the piano, a difficult instrument with which to lead a large chorus, as it affords no sustenance if the voices waver in the attack, and unlike the organ it gives no reed effects to smooth the piano passages if the sopranos over-balance the male voices. In each instance the choir had to depend upon themselves and they accomplished their task more than creditably–they were genuinely successful.[40]

Newspaper advertisements confirm *Esther*'s popularity in Australia into the 1940s.[41]

New Zealand

Esther became popular with New Zealanders beginning in the 1880s, and performances continued well into the 1930s. A performance sponsored by the Mosgiel Philharmonic Society took place in Volunteer Hall on May 18, 1883, and drew a substantial review in the *Otago Daily Times*. The director of this production credited "training on the Tonic Sol-fa system" for the singers' "very substantial results." With careful tutelage, a journalist wrote, "[T]he members of the choir appear to have attained a very fair degree of efficiency so far as reading [music] at sight [from a score] is concerned." As for *Esther* and the actual performance, the critic wrote guardedly:

> Mr. Bradbury is not remarkable in his generation for the depth or intrinsic value of his compositions, although a great deal of technical skill in arrangement is observable, in this work especially. The music of *Esther* is not very original, but it is pleasing, and is specially adapted for study by amateur musical organisations . . . . It is impossible to speak very highly of the manner which the first part of the cantata went. The mistakes, probably on account of nervousness, were rather frequent, but a marked improvement was noticeable after the interval [intermission]. The performers, without exception, entered thoroughly into the spirit of their work and they were assisted by the applause of a favourably-disposed audience who were not desirous of marking incidental shortcomings . . . . The audience was a large one, and signified its approval constantly in the course of the evening.[42]

In 1884, a production in Otago drew compliments from a local critic. The large number of participants mandated the construction of an additional "extensive platform [stage] . . . for the accommodation of the juvenile choral society (who mustered about 100 strong), the adult chorus-singers, and the soloists." The reviewer commented, "[I]t was a very pretty sight to watch the small sea of children's heads rising at a motion of the conductor's baton, and the little folk when upon their feet lent very effective assistance to the choruses." Evidently, this performance did not include staging, and instead, the singers stood or sat at the behest of the conductor—a practice typical of the oratorio tradition and one of which Bradbury would have voiced his approval.[43]

A lengthy review of a rehearsal of *Esther* that took place in Timaru in 1885 appeared in the community's local newspaper. The critic opened with a summary of Bradbury's significance as a music educator and then continued as follows:

> On Saturday night a full rehearsal [of *Esther*] was held in the Assembly Rooms by the Choir, and by request we had the pleasure of listening to it. We may remark before sketching the chief points of the cantata that the stage

has been specially arranged for this evening. The stage has been extended some five feet into the Hall, and this arrangement is a wise one, as it enables the audience to hear much better than if the Choir were placed on the stage proper. The orchestra is also arranged somewhat differently to what audiences at the Rooms have been used to, and this also is a great improvement . . . . After a short and pretty introduction by the orchestra, five verses of the Book of Esther are read, and the chorus of Haman's friends is then taken up by the whole company. The chorus is a fine and spirited one, creates a favorable impression at once, and is a sweet foretaste of what is to follow . . . . In the second part [of the score], the recitative by the King to Esther, "What Is Thy Petition," is perhaps the finest number, the downfall of the proud Haman being set forth very markedly in it; but the other numbers will be found almost equal in merit. The rehearsal was a splendid success, and we can most confidently state that lovers of music who find their way to the Assembly Rooms this evening will concur in our opinion that "Esther" is one of the most beautiful pieces of music they have ever listened to.

The performance, under the direction of James Rowles (1847–1933), included an accompanying ensemble comprised of organ, two violins, double bass, clarinet, cornet, euphonium, and piano.[44]

Many other performances of *Esther* occurred in New Zealand during the 1880s. In 1886, the Kaiapoi Choral and Orchestral Society performed *Esther* with accompaniment provided by an instrumental ensemble. A review lauded Bradbury's "music, which is of a light and sparkling character . . . [and] most attractive."[45] For another performance, residents of Devonport flocked to an *Esther* presentation at the city's Public Hall in November 1886. The *Auckland Star* covered the event and noted, "[T]his cantata has excited a great amount of enthusiasm in musical circles in England, America, and elsewhere."[46] An advertisement for a performance in Auckland, also in 1886, credited the popularity of *Esther* to "the music [that] is of a high class. The solos are exceedingly chaste and appropriate, the choruses most effective, and the whole composition has a good hearty swing about it which assists in rendering it so extremely popular."[47]

The *Taranaki Herald* reviewed a performance that took place on September 16, 1894, in Waitara's Alexandra Hall, the local opera house with seating for around 1,000. "Ornamental passages" provided by organ and piano accompanied the singers. Of the performance, a reviewer paid special attention to "the opening chorus [that] showed the attack of the choir to be excellent, and they were thoroughly under the control of their conductor." The critic continued, "The dramatic scene between the King and Esther was finely declaimed by both vocalists. The quartette [Part II, no. 13], unaccompanied, was the gem of the piece, and, being a fine effort of concerted singing, the audience highly appreciated its beauties. The final chorus [Part II, no. 15] was given with great energy, and during the intricate passages every word was distinct, the crucial test of part singing." Mention of the reading of "connecting texts" and the division of *Esther* into two parts suggests that the performers used Curwen's score.[48]

Fiji

In November 1946, students at the Seventh-Day Adventist Fulton Missionary School performed *Esther* in Tailevu, Fiji, and again the following year in the nearby Suva Town Hall. Residents of India and Fiji attended the school, located some thirty-two miles from Suva, now the nation's capital. Under the direction of sisters Louise and Adeline Whippy, this student production earned positive reviews. Rev. Henry McMahon lauded the event as "a wonderful demonstration of what Fijian talent, rightly trained, can do." He continued:

> The chorus work was particularly impressive and the dignity of the large choir enhanced the performance.... Hundreds waiting outside were unable to enter the hall, and requests were made for a repeat performance.... One of the striking features of the cantata *Esther*, presented by the Fijian choir (with a number of Indian students) of the Fulton School last evening, was the fact that the entire work had been memorized by the one hundred performers. As the work was sung in English, this constituted a remarkable feat.[49]

Another journalist, evidently familiar with *Esther*'s score, posted this review:

> History was in the making in Suva, Fiji . . . when for the first time a native choir attempted to sing in its entirety the sacred cantata *Esther*, by William Bradbury. The solos, duets, and choruses were sung entirely by natives. This is something new for them to sing solos in public, this being the first time it has

ever been attempted. The choir consisted of ninety-nine voices. The pianist was an Indian girl. The majority of the choir consisted of Fijians, with a few Tongans and Indians. The Suva Town Hall was filled to capacity, and everyone present was delighted with the performance . . . . The outstanding item of interest in the performance was the fact that the choir memorized every word and note in a language that was foreign to them. They sang in English, without a book [score] or a sheet of paper. They never missed a cue, sang in pure full tone, and never forgot a word.[50]

Singapore and the Philippines

There were apparently very few performances of *Esther* in Singapore prior to the 1950s. According to surviving newspaper accounts, the earliest performance of the piece took place in 1899, sung without costumes and staging by a Presbyterian church choir.[51] Mention of *Esther* does not appear again until 1928, when a performance by the Malaysian Union Seminary received notice. Also sung nontheatrically, this performance featured seminary faculty who assumed principal roles with students singing in the choruses.[52]

It was not until the early 1950s, however, that *Esther* became better known to the Singapore public. The person most responsible for inspiring greater interest in the work was an American, Minnie Iverson-Wood (figure 8.4). Born in Maine, Iverson-Wood completed studies in languages, vocal performance, piano, conducting, and music education before engaging in musically oriented missionary work in Asia. During her career, she taught in China, Hong Kong, Malaysia, the Philippines, and Singapore.[53] She produced *Esther* several times in Singapore and donated the proceeds to various charitable causes.[54] Singapore newspapers reported on one of her well-received performances that took place in November 1951 in the city's Victoria Theatre to benefit the Anti-Tuberculosis Association Fund.[55] According to journalist Hazel Pearl Wilcox, a packed house waited anxiously "as the curtain rolled up and revealed on the stage the choir of the Malayan Union Seminary colorfully gowned in Oriental dress . . . . The lovely blending of the many pastel shades of color in gown and headdress lent a pleasing sense of anticipation for what was to follow."[56] Helen Bond reported of this concert that "the audience gasped with delight when . . . they saw the gorgeously colored costumes and

Figure 8.4. Advertisement for an *Esther* performance conducted by Minnie Iverson-Wood (1908–2008) in Singapore, *The Straits Times*, November 3, 1951, 11. Image courtesy of *The Straits Times*, © SPH Media, Limited.

heard the singing of the eighty-five-voice choir." Asian natives of Singapore comprised much of the cast, supplemented with British residents.[57]

Iverson-Wood also introduced *Esther* to the Philippines. During her tenure as a music teacher, conductor, and soprano soloist in Manila, she mentored Rev. Dr. Ulysses M. Carbajal and influenced the direction his career eventually assumed. (I discussed Carbajal in the previous chapter.) Carbajal's fine bass voice impressed Iverson-Wood, and as a result, he sang the role of Ahasuerus many times under her direction. She also coached him in choral conducting. In 1961, various organizations in the Philippines sought Carbajal's expertise including his alma mater, Philippine Union College. Working with choruses from Union College, the Pasay City Academy, and staff members of the Manila Sanitarium and Hospital, he assembled a multiracial cast of over one hundred singers and presented *Esther* in many Philippine locations including Baguio City, Dagupan City, Lucena, Luzon, and Quezon City.[58]

South Africa

Tonic sol-fa made its way to South Africa largely through the work of John Curwen's protégés. The introduction and dissemination of tonic sol-fa in

Africa went through three distinct phases. The first phase occurred as a result of British colonial efforts to impose its own cultural expression in South Africa. Second, religious missionaries, some of them associated with Curwen, adopted tonic sol-fa for spreading the Christian faith and improving singing during church services. Third, the tonic sol-fa method eventually became established in schools for all children. Curwen's system continues to be an integral part of South African music education and the country's rich choral tradition.[59]

Documentation of one of the earliest performances of *Esther* in Africa appeared in London's *Musical Times*. The journal reported on a production in Cape Town, South Africa, on December 9, 1875, in Mutual Hall, under the patronage of Sir Henry Barkly (1815–1898), His Excellency the Governor. We might assume that this performance did not include costumes or staging as the work was "sung throughout with a painstaking care and due appreciation of the composer's intentions." Performed by members of the local Sacred Harmonic Society, directed by John Henry Ashley (1824–1898), the event earned press admiration for the conductor's "careful training" of the singers.[60] Ashley, an avid follower of Curwen's methods, promoted his mentor's tonic sol-fa system throughout the colony beginning in the early 1860s, especially in English and Dutch communities located in Cape Town. It seems reasonable to conclude that Ashley made use of John Curwen's edition of *Esther*.[61] In Durban, South Africa, a Methodist Episcopal choir comprised entirely of native Africans sang *Esther* in the local Town Hall in 1900. Their performance so amazed church officials that they subsequently took the choir on tour to some of the larger communities in the colony and to more distant outstations. American missionary initiatives funded these performances.[62]

Ghana

Teachers from England traveled to Ghana and worked to build schools and promote education and literacy. By the 1930s, a litany of English language plays and musical works had been performed in colonial Ghana. Among the most popular of these pieces, Bradbury's *Esther* held a respected place in the repertoire of the region. According to historian, poet, and novelist Kofi E. Agovi, works such as *Esther* rose in prominence owing to the efforts of Ghanaian teacher and headmaster of the Bishop's School, James Topp Nelson

Yankah (1890–1964), who advocated using only the English language in schools and in singing. In his survey of the newspaper *Gold Coast Spectator*, Agovi located documentation of productions of *Esther* sung in English in Accra, Ghana, beginning in the 1930s.[63]

Esther surfaced again, decades later, in Ghana. An obituary of respected leader Major Courage Emmanuel Kobla Quashigah (1947–2010) reports that Quashigah participated in a performance of *Esther* that took place in 1968 in Keta, a city in the Volta Region of Ghana. Quashigah earned national respect as a government official, especially through his accomplishments as Minister of Health and Minister of Agriculture. At the time of the performance in which he participated, Quashigah taught at the US-sponsored African Methodist Episcopal Zion School. Keta's residents "fondly remember" his portrayal of Mordecai in the school's production.[64]

Angola

Residents of Bailundo, Angola, and the surrounding area presented *Esther* in 1930 as part of a Jubilee celebration. Sponsored by missionaries, the production commemorated the fiftieth year of successful efforts to modernize medicine and introduce formal schooling in the region. Ovimbundu singers, members of the Bantu ethnic group, performed Cady's text in their native language, translated from English by Welsh missionary Rev. Joseph Arthur Steed (1883–1961). The celebration featured two performances of *Esther*, both conducted by Steed. According to missionary historian John T. Tucker (1883–1958), Steed's production ably fulfilled the objectives and spirit of the Jubilee as "surely nothing could be more appropriate to the present needs of the Ovimbunda."[65] American Congregationalist missionary Frank Knight Sanders (1861–1933) recorded his impression of the vast audience:

> The Jubilee was held at Bailundo ... [at a] natural amphitheatre, a gently sloping hill on which thousands could sit at ease .... The great throng of 12,000 or more made a colorful and impressive audience, intent, [and] quickly responsive .... To see it disperse, streaming up the hill after the meeting, was a never-failing attraction. To see it in a vast unity was thrilling. Its size, orderliness and unity impressed all .... Nothing quite like it had been seen before.

Finding the performances stirring and most remarkable, Sanders concluded, "Africans love to sing and take kindly to our [Western] harmonies."[66]

A Chicago writer and missionary nurse, Allegra Doyle Smith, in attendance at these performances, also expressed awe at the sight of the "vast assembled audience of natives, many of them having walked miles from far away distances." Smith then enthused about the

> musical intricacies and independent parts [performed] without reference to the score. It proved two things—the innate musical ability and aptitude of the Ovimbunda people and the masterful genius and musicianship of the leader, Mr. Arthur Steed. How amazing those wonderful solos of Mordecai! Carrying on his heart the cruel wrongs suffered by his people at the hands of Haman, how, with the true emotion, spiritual insight, and utter simplicity he rendered in rich, deep quality of voice those mournful strains of music.[67]

Another missionary, Marjorie Miller, offered succinct observations about the Jubilee Choir's rendition of *Esther*. She related her astonishment at the sight of the immense choir marching four abreast down the roadway on the Bailundo hillside just prior to their performances. The visual effect of the assembled choruses with all singers dressed in white presented a startling contrast to the colorful costumes of the principal players. Miller also complimented the clever resourcefulness of local craftspersons who constructed tall grass partitions and propped them on either side of the staging area. As players entered or exited, the grass structures effectively shielded their movements. Thoroughly impressed with what she witnessed, Miller observed, "The Africans are born actors and are noted for their wonderful gift in song, add to which the careful training they received and the beauty and grace of the costumes and you can understand how excellent was the presentation of the Cantata."[68]

The most substantial account of the Jubilee choir's rendition of *Esther* was written by Elizabeth Scattergood Chalmers, an American Quaker who attended the performances. Her detailed comments merit quotation at length:

> It is unfortunate that the [unnamed] German professor, who accuses missionaries of stultifying the African's creative power in the line of music, by teaching him the tunes of [W]estern civilization, was not present at the Jubilee of the West African Mission. Before we left Boston we had been warned of the

beauty of native Christian singing but, to use a hackneyed phrase for want of more adequate language, our actual experience has far surpassed our greatest hopes and our wildest dreams. Sitting on a Bailundo hillside, in view of the bluest of mountains, and surrounded by ten thousand Ovimbundu, we listened to the Jubilee choir for the first time.

About five hundred and twenty boys and girls, mostly between the ages of ten and thirty, selected from Means School, and the Currie Institute, with a representation from each of the six other mission stations, and under the extraordinary leadership of Mr. J. Arthur Steed, had been practicing and training to bring to pass the wonder that was ours that afternoon. They sang and acted to their huge audience the Cantata of "Esther, the Beautiful Queen" ... Nor can any of us forget [Henrique] Capiñala, the native music teacher at Dondi [Angola], who accompanied the choir on the organ and in musical ability is second to none.

This special Cantata was chosen by their director as particularly suited to their musical potentialities, partly on account of its antiphony, a very popular type of song with these people. But, indeed, the story of the suffering and oppressed Jews, rendered by those still subject to forces analogous to what [David] Livingstone termed "the open sore of the world," was very full of meaning and we felt the choice to be well merited. Whether the choir shared this feeling or not, they sang as if their hearts were in their voices. I do not pretend to have anything more than a keen appreciation of music, but I am confident that the most expert technician would have found beauty and something of eternal value in what was to my lay ears the voice of a nation's soul.

I find myself groping rather hopelessly to find words which will make that concert real to those who were not present. In its rich harmony, I was reminded of the Hampton [Institute] Quartette increased a hundred-fold in volume, yet in spite of such mass production just as perfect in enunciation, rhythm, and unity. But much more significant than the purely physical joy of hearing such heavenly sound issue from five hundred and twenty well-trained throats was the sense of spiritual victory over the baffling ignorance of a short fifty years ago. For, surely, if this many of a nation, who for centuries have lived unto themselves, scraping a miserable existence out of unfriendly plots of ground, eating and sleeping and worshipping in unthinkable poverty, treated by the equally squalid white settlers as no better than animals; if this many of a nation, with the loving cooperation of a man who believes in them can learn thus to sing together, a way is opened to them.[69]

Figure 8.5. *Esther* performance, Angola Jubilee, 1930. Lawrence W. Henderson Papers (Box 1, folder 4, "Angola Jubilee"), University of New Hampshire Archives. Handwritten text reads: "1) Coming down the hill on the Pageant ground led by Mr. Steed (Conductor) and Mrs. Steed (with veil), Miss Dibble (Dramatic Conductor), and Henrique Capiñala, ([Ghanaian] native [and] accompanist), then the actors in costume with the choir; 2) The choir marching down; and 3) The choir in position ready to begin."

Several photographs of the Angola Jubilee performances of *Esther* survive. A grouping of three images (figure 8.5) shows the enormous Jubilee Choir, Rev. Steed, and the players of major roles. In image one (top left), the soloists, accompanist, and conductor lead a procession through the huge throng of onlookers. The choruses of Jews, Persians, and Medians follow behind, shown in image two (top right), making their way to the performance area. Image three shows the assembled choruses with soloists standing immediately to the right.

Another photographer captured scenes of these performances from a vantage point that allows us to appreciate the individual actors and staging area in some detail. The small organ used for accompaniment appears to the right in figure 8.6. Regionally respected choir director Henrique Capiñala, a resident of Ghana, improvised organ accompaniments for these performances. He stands in readiness at the keyboard, a page turner at his side.

Figure 8.6. Mordecai sitting at the palace gate, Angola Jubilee, 1930. Image courtesy of the United Church of Canada Archives, Toronto.

Figure 8.7. Queen Esther and her courtiers, Angola Jubilee, 1930. Image courtesy of the United Church of Canada Archives, Toronto.

Two benches at the left of the photograph establish a minimalist set. One of these benches, draped with a blanket, serves as the king's throne. In this scene, Mordecai sits at the palace gate (Curwen, ed., Part I, no. 3, "Behold This Mordecai"). With guards facing the chorus, Ahasuerus stands before his throne. Notice, too, all the singers are barefoot.

In figure 8.7, Queen Esther, identifiable by her more elaborate costume, strolls in the company of her courtiers. One of Esther's attendants, immediately to the queen's left, clasps her hands prayerfully while the others gaze downward in reverence. This is, most likely, the moment when Esther asks her maidens to "fast ye and pray for me" (Curwen, ed., Part I, no. 8).

In figure 8.8, the king paces as he spends a sleepless night listening to a courtier who reads official edicts from a scroll. Thoroughly preoccupied with what he hears and seemingly, if only momentarily, unaware of his

Figure 8.8. King Ahasuerus listening to a courtier reading from the scroll of royal edicts, Angola Jubilee, 1930. Image courtesy of the United Church of Canada Archives, Toronto.

Figure 8.9. Mordecai awaits other cast members in preparation for the Finale, Angola Jubilee, 1930. Image courtesy of the United Church of Canada Archives, Toronto.

surroundings, the king has laid his scepter against the nearby throne. The readings from the scroll include a memorandum, contributed by Mordecai, alerting the king to a proposed deadly plot against him. This scene occurs just prior to the solo, "What Honor and Dignity?" sung by Ahasuerus. In this number, the king asks if anything has been done to honor Mordecai for revealing the traitorous plan.

In figure 8.9, Mordecai, to the far left, awaits the arrival of other principal players who approach from the right in preparation for *Esther*'s Finale.

Closing Thoughts

John Curwen became a most enthusiastic promoter of *Esther* as well as a producer of an edition of the work. His protégés used his edition to introduce *Esther* to innumerable communities and outlying areas not only in the British Commonwealth, but also on the continents of Africa and Asia. As we have seen, in foreign countries, *Esther* served some of the same functions the piece fulfilled in the United States: fundraising, spiritual engagement, music education, community *esprit des corps*, and just plain enjoyment. But in distant locations such as in Africa, *Esther* also served as teaching material for those learning to read music notation and striving to become fluent in English. The piece also became an overseas vehicle for missionary zeal and evangelical purpose—a role that would have pleased the devout Bradbury.

EPILOGUE

Not long after Bradbury returned from his European sojourn in 1849, he informed the press, "[S]ince hearing the best of German music I feel all the better prepared to appreciate that which is good of my own country's [musical] production."[1] Accordingly, he set out to make music accessible to the greater general public, and in pursuit of this goal, he called on US composers to produce more works designed to encourage competent amateur musicianship in communities: "Let us have more good music 'for the million'–music that all can understand, love and *afford* [italics original]," Bradbury proposed. He advised US composers to "write for the people and their children. Let the next be a music-loving and music-encouraging generation."[2] His vast catalogue of tunebooks and sheet music confirms the extraordinary effort he put forth to create a singularly American approach to music composition and to further the cause of musical accessibility.

Only three years after the initial publication of *Esther*, the *New York Musical Review and Gazette* lauded the score as "one of the few evidences we have of a distinct American school of music of decisive originality."[3] This style of music and approach to composition attracted the attention of Englishman John Curwen who praised the "wholesome middle ground in regard to both words and music in which you in America greatly excel."[4] T. F. Seward noted that Bradbury fortuitously created his vast compositional output at a crucial time he identified as "an important transitional period in the musical history of our country." Of the qualities of Bradbury's music that made it so appealing to the masses, Seward noted, "In the department of glees and light choral music, Mr. Bradbury was equally happy in striking the popular vein . . . . [H]is energy and enthusiasm have undoubtedly done much in shaping and modifying the popular taste." Citing some of the singular attributes of Bradbury's music that made it so popular, Seward singled out his compositions' "freshness . . . spirit and animation . . . that exactly met the average taste . . . throughout the country."[5] Writing decades later, music historian Edward E. Hipsher asserted that *Esther*, in particular, represented "a forward step from anything hitherto produced in its style, on our soil. It was *of* our soil [italics original]."[6]

The Possibilities of Community Music-Making

It is in the realm of community music-making and music education that Bradbury established another enduring component of his legacy. Throughout his career, he strove to democratize music and he remained steadfastly committed to universal music education for people of all ages and abilities. He optimistically stated, "I firmly believe that nine-tenths, yes, more even, of our adult population could be made [inspired and taught] to sing."[7] As we have seen, he also excelled in teaching children and composed numerous pieces for their more specialized needs. *Esther* served as an important vehicle with which he so heartily and successfully pursued his pedagogical goals. His confidence in the future of American music resonates to this day and many of his pedagogical innovations continue to sustain the philosophical and methodological underpinnings in the field of music education.

Of the significance of community music-making and music education, composer Arthur Farwell published insights that seem particularly applicable to Bradbury's career and to the *Esther* vogue. Farwell exclaimed in 1914: "Suppose the *community* becomes the artist! [italics original]." As he then explained:

> When the community becomes the artist, every individual becomes a *part of a mighty artist*. Each does that part of the art-work which he can, knowing that the whole can be perfect only by his doing his share, however little that may be. It may be only the making of a costume or a part of one . . . or something equally simple. Or it may be the taking of an acting part, unpretentious or prominent, [or] playing or conducting the music . . . . The little talents of individuals, bound together in one common effort, make the genius of the people . . . . [E]very community, no matter how remote or obscure, is rich in unsuspected ability and talent of innumerable sorts . . . . I have seen village blacksmiths, farmers, ministers, schoolteachers, students, not forgetting wives, mothers and sisters, blossom out into creditable and even very excellent actors with but the slightest coaching . . . . And I have not failed to

notice the happiness which it has given them to find that they could do so, and especially to find that they were forming an indispensable part of a great spectacle of dramatic art such as they had never before seen or dreamed of [italics original].[8]

Whether or not Farwell had in mind, specifically, performances of *Esther*, there can be no doubt that Bradbury's work and its storied reception history fulfill Farwell's conception of community-as-artist admirably. The sincerity and critical acclaim of *Esther* performances depended on participants' cooperation and a commitment to a common, wholesome goal. Innumerable rural and urban communities experienced a lasting sense of accomplishment and newfound pride after producing *Esther* no matter how excellent or mediocre their performance, or the success or lack thereof of an attendant fundraising campaign. Ultimately, *Esther* performances invited participants to exercise musical, aesthetic, and dramatic self-determination while they also profoundly influenced, and simultaneously responded to, public musical taste.

This level of commitment to community-based musical initiatives brings to mind Christopher Small's groundbreaking ideology of "musicking"—a latter-day vision, of sorts, of the "community-as-artist" concept with equal application to *Esther*. According to Small, "[M]usicking is an activity in which all those present are involved" and one that encompasses "all participation in a musical performance, whether it takes place actively or passively."[9] Thus it mattered not whether individuals at an *Esther* performance were in the audience, onstage, backstage, or in the lobby collecting tickets, as everyone connected with a production fulfilled an integral role. Musicking also accounts for the interchangeability and interactive essence of secular and sacred realms as associated, especially, with staged productions of *Esther*. As Small wrote, "Whether we call it sacred or secular, its function is fundamentally the same: to preserve the community and to enable the individual to affirm, to explore and to celebrate his or her place in the community. Between sacred and secular there is in fact not opposition at all, but continuity . . . . Sacred and secular musicking should interpenetrate and should feed back and forth, one to the other."[10] The rich mosaic of interconnected and inextricable sacred and secular elements in *Esther* exemplifies Small's ideology.

Ultimately, *Esther* was produced in more locations than any other musical theater piece of its era. Although the popularity of the work has faded, the memories of its significance, the sheer enjoyment of its performances, and the community *esprit de corps* its productions generated and nurtured continue to receive mention in the press. No other American musical theater piece of the mid-nineteenth century attracted so much newspaper attention as did *Esther*. Whether sung for evangelical purposes, charitable fundraising, community entertainment, or music instruction, the work won accolades for nearly all of its performances. Audiences and critics alike expressed enthusiast support, and communities often launched repeat presentations as a result. Many directors found in *Esther* unprecedented opportunities for experimental and innovative dramaturgy, and their work became famous for its spectacle, lavish staging, and resourceful costuming. The impressive and mammoth performances of *Esther* in Angola in 1930 surely must have been the largest assembly of singers and audiences for most any similar work. *Esther*'s astounding popularity endured more than a century—yet another milestone in the world of religious musical theater. In the end, *Esther, the Beautiful Queen* was, by any measure, an international megahit.

APPENDIX

LIST OF NUMBERS IN BRADBURY'S *ESTHER*

Part I

No. 1. Chorus of Haman's Friends: "Haman, Haman, Long Live Haman"
No. 2. Solo (Haman): "Behold This Mordecai"
No. 3. Solo (Haman): "There Is a Certain People"
No. 4. Solo (Ahasuerus): "The Silver Is Given"
No. 5. Duet and Chorus (Ahasuerus and Haman): "A Song of Joy"
No. 6. Solo (Prophet or Prophetess): "Lo! O'er the Wicked"
No. 7. Chorus of Jews: "Woe Is Me"
No. 8. Duet (Mordecai and Esther) with Chorus of Jews: "Go Thou unto the King" and "Fast Ye and Pray for Me"
No. 9. Solo (Mordecai) and Chorus of Jews: "To Thee O Lord We Raise Our Cries"
No. 10. Chorus: "He That Goeth Forth and Weepeth"
No. 11. Duet (Ahasuerus and Esther): "What Is It, Queen Esther?"
No. 12. Song and Duet (Ahasuerus and Esther): "Long Live Our Beauteous Queen"
No. 13. Chorus: "Haste to the Banquet Hall"
No. 14. Solo (Zeresh) and Chorus: "Why Should This Hebrew Vex My Lord?"

Part II

No. 1. Chorus of Jews with Solos (First Maid of Honor, Mordecai): "God Is the Refuge"
No. 2. Solo (Ahasuerus) and Chorus: "What Honor and Dignity"
No. 3. Duet (Ahasuerus and Haman): "Who Is in the Court?"
No. 4. Chorus: "A-ha, Proud Haman Begins to Fall"
No. 5. Quartet of Male Voices: "The King Has Given Commandment"
No. 6. Chorus: "Rejoice"
No. 7. Solos (High Priest or Maid of Honor and Hegai) with Chorus: "Thou Wilt Keep Him"
No. 8. Solo (Haman) and Chorus: "Thus Shall It Be Done"
No. 9. Solo (Zeresh or Maid of Honor): "Thy Galling Defeat"
No. 10. Duet (Ahasuerus and Haman) and Chorus: "Long Live Our Beauteous Queen" (reprise)
No. 11. At the Banquet (instrumental)
No. 12. Dialogue (Ahasuerus, Esther and Harbonah): "What Is Thy Petition"

No. 13. Quartet (First Maid of Honor, Zeresh, Mordecai, Hegai): "Do I Wake or Am I Dreaming?"
No. 14. Chorus: "When the Lord Turned Again the Captivity"
No. 15. Finale, Chorale: "Praise Ye the Lord"

NOTES

INTRODUCTION

1. Newspapers variously described Bradbury's piece as a cantata, oratorio, opera, or music drama. For the sake of brevity and convenience, I will usually refer to *Esther, the Beautiful Queen* as, simply, *Esther*.

2. Eugene Wood, "Drama in Our Town." Wood (1860-1923), a prominent journalist, author, and humorist, contributed numerous stories and articles to nationally circulating magazines and newspapers.

3. Lynn Zerschling, "Royal Performance." For a review of the event recalled by Zerschling, see "Cantata of 'Queen Esther,'" *Sioux City Journal*, June 17, 1894, 6.

4. Stoddard, quoted in Anna Howell Clarkson, *Beautiful Life*, 202. Drusilla Chapman Allen Stoddard (1821-1913) taught at Iowa Central University located in Fort Dodge, IA. Clarkson (1847-1922), a friend and former student of Stoddard's, was best known as a journalist.

5. Frederic Stanley Law, undated letter, quoted in Charles H. Leeds, ed., *Old Home Week Letters*, 195. A version of Law's letter also appeared as "Old Home Week Letter." Law (1849-1913) published books about music for a general readership, including: *Operatic Tales* (1903) and *Life Stories of Great Composers* (1910). Law's mother, Ann Celestia Southworth Law (1822-1905), sang the role of Queen Esther in Pennsylvania, where several productions took place over a period of many years beginning in 1857.

6. Bill Arp, "Bill Arp's Philosophy." "Bill Arp" was the pseudonym used by Georgia politician and author Charles Henry Smith (1826-1903). Arp's columns were reprinted in major newspapers throughout the United States for many years. An elementary school in Douglasville, Georgia, bears his name.

CHAPTER ONE: PRELUDE: BRADBURY, MUSICIAN AND ENTREPRENEUR

1. "William B. Bradbury," *Daily Inter Ocean* (Chicago), January 13, 1868, 3.

2. Some of the best known of Bradbury's hymns are "He Leadeth Me," "Jesus Loves Me, This I Know," "Just as I Am, without One Plea," "Savior, Like a Shepherd Lead Us," and "Sweet Hour of Prayer."

3. William Bradbury had four siblings: one sister, Elizabeth C. Bradbury (1813-1859); and three brothers: Cotton Chase Bradbury (1814-1896), Jotham Bradbury (1819-1905), and Edward Grow Bradbury (1820-1865). David Bradbury participated in local politics, and in addition to farming, also maintained a cobbler business at which his sons helped out; see "Death of Wm. B. Bradbury," *New York Evangelist*, January 16, 1868, 2; *Eastern Argus* (Portland, ME), March 23, 1830, 2; Alan Burl Wingard, *Life and Works*, 23-24.

4. *New York Tribune*, January 21, 1868, 8. Bradbury occasionally mentioned farming in his writings on music education. For example, he compared teaching to farming in this quote: "The faithful teacher, in commencing his labors, is in many respects like the farmer upon his spring works. He must consider the various soils, and the amount of cultivation that each field has secured before he can reasonably expect good crops. In one, he must commence and 'break up,' plow deep, and perhaps subsoil, trench and drain, and prepare it for good seed. Another field is already under a good degree of cultivation, and this secures a different course of treatment. In another there are trees to be leveled, stumps to be uprooted, and underbrush to be cleared away before the soil can be worked to advantage. Another is in first-rate condition, and from this he feels sure of a bountiful crop"; see William B. Bradbury, "Home Thoughts of the Musical Past, No. III."

5. Wingard, *Life and Works*, 24.

6. T[heodore] F[relinghuysen] Seward, "Sketches of American Composers: William B. Bradbury."

7. Ibid.

8. William and Adra Esther Bradbury had six children: Caroline S. (1839–?); Amanda F. (1843–1918); Emily "Lilla" Marie (1845–1910); May Jeannette "Netty" (1847–after 1923), born in Leipzig, Germany; Kate ("Kittie") Lizzie (1850–1855); and William Lowell (1856–1940). Bradbury published several items about the untimely death of his daughter, Kate, including "Death of a Child." Information about Bradbury's children can be found in William Lowell Bradbury, "Family Recollections," September 28, 1928, typewritten manuscript, William B. Bradbury Collection, Library of Congress, Washington, DC.

9. Simeon Pease Cheney, *American Singing Book*, 210. Cheney (1818–1890), a respected music teacher, performed as a member of the acclaimed Cheney Family Singers who toured the eastern United States in the 1840s.

10. Seward, "Sketches" (1867), 10–11.

11. The original Broadway Tabernacle was built in 1836. Renowned Tabernacle church officials included Rev. Charles Grandison Finney (1792–1875), later famous for his tenure at Oberlin College, where he eventually served as president. The Tabernacle's congregation advocated abolition, temperance, and women's suffrage. Several celebrated activists lectured at the Tabernacle and addressed these pressing issues, notably Frederick Douglass, Ralph Waldo Emerson, William Lloyd Garrison, and Sojourner Truth; see Susan Hayes Ward, *History of the Broadway Tabernacle*, xv, 28–29, 101, 107, 170.

12. Mention of Bradbury's classes at the Classical and English School and in the New York public schools appeared in local newspapers during the 1840s; see, for example, *New York Evangelist*, November 6, 1841, 180; *Evening Post* (New York), August 27, 1842, 3.

13. "Juvenile Singing," *New York Evangelist* November 27, 1841, 190.

14. "Musical Convention," *New York Observer and Chronicle*, October 11, 1845, 2.

15. [Walt Whitman], "An Evening at a Children's Concert." Whitman wrote for and edited the *Evening Star* and *Daily Eagle*, both published in Brooklyn. His articles in these newspapers were frequently unsigned. A most comprehensive collection of Whitman's journalistic writings during the years 1845–1848 is still Florence Bernstein Freedman, *Walt Whitman Looks at the Schools*. Freedman included many of Whitman's writings about Bradbury's concerts.

16. Bradbury, *Flora's Festival*. Hewitt added pieces by these composers to *Flora's Festival*: Daniel-François Auber (1782–1871), Giuseppe Mercadante (1795–1870), Gioachino Rossini

(1792–1868), Reginald Spofforth (1769–1827), Louis Spohr (1784–1859), Johann Strauss Jr. (1825–1899), and Carl Maria von Weber (1786–1826).

17. Jacklin Bolton Stopp, "James C. Johnson and the American Secular Cantata"; Howard E. Smither, *The Oratorio in the Nineteenth and Twentieth Centuries* 4:454–58, 465–66. James C. Johnson (1820–1895) and his brother, Artemas Nixon "A. N." Johnson (1817–1892), were initially members of Lowell Mason's circle but eventually charted their own paths in the music teaching and compositional realms.

18. Wm. Bradbury, "Juvenile Oratorio."

19. Bradbury, *Flora's Festival*, preface.

20. "Musical Reminiscences: Something about Wm. B. Bradbury, Thomas Hastings, and Lowell Mason," *Musical Visitor* (Boston) (January 1885): 9. The actual number of persons the Broadway Tabernacle could accommodate varied widely, especially if the building's substantial space for standing room was taken into account.

21. Michael Mark and Charles L. Gary estimate, in their *History of American Music Education*, that some 1,400 tunebooks were published during the nineteenth century (82); Judson Blair listed 567 tunebooks in his *"Tune-Books" in America*; and John Weeks Moore listed some 550 in his *Dictionary*, 187–211. The article "Tune-Books" listed 375 tunebooks by some 200 compilers, published up to 1860; see *Grove's Dictionary of Music and Musicians*, "American Supplement," ed. Waldo Selden Pratt (New York: Macmillan, 1942), 386–91. The best summary of tunebook history is still the article "Tune-Books" in *Grove's*. See also Mark and Gary, 82–91; James L. Fisher, "The Roots of Music Education in Baltimore"; Juanita Karpf, "'In an Easy and Familiar Style,'" 122–44.

22. "The Musical Concert" *Franklin Repository* (Chambersburg, PA), March 21, 1866, 2.

23. James M. Hewins, *Hints Concerning Church Music*, 20–21.

24. Richard Crawford, *American Musical Landscape*, 50–58.

25. Christopher W. Knauff, *Doctor Tucker, Priest Musician*, 249.

26. William B. Bradbury and Charles W. Sanders, *Young Choir*.

27. *New York Evangelist*, September 25, 1841, 2.

28. Charles W. Sanders, "Music Books for Schools," in *The School Reader, Fourth Book* (New York: Newman and Ivison, 1842), 312.

29. "First Concert of the United Juvenile Choir," *New York Evening Post*, April 19, 1843, 3. See also "Juvenile Music Festival," *New York Evening Post*, May 4, 1843, 2; "Mr. Bradbury's Last Juvenile Musical Festival," *New York Evening Post*, May 6, 1843, 2.

30. William B. Bradbury, *Social Singing Book*; William B. Bradbury, *Bradbury's Singing School for Ladies and Gentlemen*.

31. *Psalmodist*; *New York Choralist*; *Congregational Harmony*; *Mendelssohn Collection*; *Psalmista*.

32. Hastings and Bradbury, *New York Choralist*, preface. For more on the super abundance of tunebook publications in this era, see Peter Mercer-Taylor, *Gems of Exquisite Beauty*, especially 26–27.

33. William B. Bradbury, Private Journal, [2]. A photocopy of the original journal was kindly made available to me by J. Randolph Grymes III, a great-grandson of William Bradbury. The Bradburys left their youngest children in the care of relatives while they toured Europe. One of the first prominent US musicians to study in Europe, Bradbury was nonetheless preceded by three of his contemporaries: Lowell Mason traveled to Europe in 1837; Isaac Baker Woodbury (1819–1858) studied in London and Paris during the years

1838 to 1839; and Artemas Nixon "A. N." Johnson studied composition and music theory in Switzerland, 1842–1843.

34. William B. Bradbury, "Music and Musicians in Europe, No. 1."

35. For more on Bradbury's time in Europe, see Juanita Karpf, "'Would That It Were So in America!'" 5–38; Robert Stevenson, "William Batchelder Bradbury in Europe," 41–44.

36. Bradbury, "Music and Musicians in Europe, No. 3."

37. Bradbury included mountain songs in many of his tunebooks, most notably, *Metropolitan Glee Book*, *Musical Gems for School and Home*, and *Alpine Glee Singer*. See also Juanita Karpf, "'Wild and Soul-Stirring.'"

38. Bradbury, "Music and Musicians of Europe, No. 12. See also Wm. B. Bradbury, "Vocal Music in Germany"; this article was reprinted in various newspapers across the continent.

39. William B. Bradbury, "Mendelssohn"; see also William Lowell Bradbury, "Family Recollections"; William B. Bradbury, Private Journal, [3]; Peter Mercer-Taylor, "Mendelssohn in Nineteenth-Century American Hymnody," 235–38.

40. "William B. Bradbury," *Frank Leslie's Illustrated Newspaper* (New York), October 31, 1863, 84.

41. Peter Mercer-Taylor credits Bradbury and *The Mendelssohn Collection* with furthering Felix Mendelssohn's reputation and music in the United States; see Mercer-Taylor, "Mendelssohn in Nineteenth-Century American Hymnody," 335–39.

42. *New Hampshire Patriot* (Concord), August 30, 1849, 3.

43. Thomas Hastings, Letter to E. P. Hastings, November 17, 1849. Eurotas Parmelee Hastings Collection, Burton Collection, Detroit Public Library, Detroit, MI. Thomas Hastings wrote frequently to his brother, Eurotas Parmalee Hastings (1791–1866), the latter always referred to only as "E. P."; see Mary D. Teal, "Letters of Thomas Hastings," 308–18. E. P. Hastings, a prominent Detroit banker, held various elected political offices.

44. Thomas Hastings, Letter to E. P. Hastings, November 17, 1849; Thomas Hastings, Letter to E. P. Hastings, January 19, 1850. Burton Collection, Detroit Public Library, Detroit, MI.

45. *New York Observer*, June 9, 1849, 90.

46. Bradbury, "Vocal Music in Germany."

47. *New York Observer*, December 7, 1850, 195; "Flora's Festival," *Brooklyn Daily Eagle*, February 6, 1849, 3; "Flora's Festival," *Evening Post* (New York), February 8, 1849, 2.

48. William B. Bradbury, "Musical Conventions."

49. "Circular of the Normal Academy of Music at Geneseo, Livingston County, NY," *New York Musical Pioneer*, May 1, 1859, 120.

50. Originally intended to be a neighborhood church, the Tabernacle experienced a serious loss of attendance when a significant portion of the congregation moved to other locations. Tabernacle officials, soon faced with overwhelming financial challenges and considerable debt, decided in 1853 that the congregation needed to relocate to a smaller edifice. Members of the Tabernacle finalized their plans in 1855 and sold the property in 1856. The purchasers of the property razed the original church building the following year. The Bradburys were one of many families to relocate as they became disillusioned with the dramatic increase in businesses and manufacturing in their neighborhood and in the area around the Tabernacle; see Susan Hayes Ward, *History of the Broadway Tabernacle*, 98–102.

51. US Federal Census, 1860.

52. Nancy Groce, *Musical Instrument Makers*, 97–98; Daniel Spillane, *History of the American Piano-forte*, 198, 248.

53. Bradbury, Private Journal, [4].

54. *New York Musical Review and Choral Advocate*, January 19, 1854, 1.

55. William B. Bradbury, "Piano-forte Co-partnership."

56. "Lighte, Newton and Bradburys," *Musical World: A Weekly Record of Musical Science, Literature and Intelligence* (London), May 10, 1855, 35.

57. *Musical Review and World*, August 18, 1860, 264.

58. "William B. Bradbury," *Frank Leslie's Illustrated Newspaper*, October 31, 1863, 84; Groce, *Musical Instrument Makers*, 97.

59. Bradbury, Private Journal, [9]; Wingard, *Life and Works*, 140-44.

60. "Musical Memoranda," *New York Musical Pioneer*, January 2, 1860; *New York Times*, December 13, 1859, 5; "Destructive Fire," *New York Tribune*, December 10, 1859, 6; "Mr. William B. Bradbury," *New York Musical Pioneer and Choristers' Budget* 9, no. 4 (January 1864): 54.

61. George Washington Howard, *Monumental City*, 936.

62. Groce, *Musical Instrument Makers*, 6, 18, 144-45. See also Alfred Dolge, *Pianos and Their Makers*, 314-15.

63. Wingard, *Life and Works*, 211-17.

64. "Raising the Old Flag over Fort Sumter," *Brooklyn Daily Eagle*, April 3, 1865, 2; "The Excursion to Fort Sumter," *Evening Star* (Washington, DC) April 8, 1865, 4; "The Fort Sumter Excursion," *Brooklyn Daily Eagle*, April 8, 1865, 2; "Charleston," *New York Herald*, April 18, 1865, 4; Aaron M. Powell, "The Excursion to Charleston."

65. Beecher (1813-1887), a fiery Congregationalist clergyman, and Garrison (1805-1879), were the most famous antislavery leaders onboard the *Oceanus*. Howard (1830-1909), a Civil War hero and eventual leader of the Freedman's Bureau, served as the first president of Howard University, an institution that bears his name. The *Oceanus* passengers, a veritable who's who of influential civic, political, religious, and activist leaders, also included Henry Chandler Bowen (1813-1896), a close associate of Beecher, editor of the *Independent*, the Broadway Tabernacle's newspaper advocating abolition, suffrage, and temperance; Edward Cary (1840-1917), long associated with the *New York Times*; James Leonard Corning (1828-1903), a respected art historian and a friend of Abraham Lincoln and Ulysses S. Grant, who served as a US diplomat in Munich, Germany; Theodore Ledyard Cuyler (1822-1909), a Presbyterian clergyman and outspoken activist; Justus Clement French (1831-1899), a Congregationalist clergyman and activist; Octavious Brooks Frothingham (1822-1895), a radical Unitarian clergyman, Transcendentalist, and author; Edgar Ketchum (1840-1905), a New York tax collector and one of the original signatories of a national petition to end slavery; Joshua Leavitt (1794-1873), temperance and abolitionist lecturer and author, journalist, and editor; Aaron Macy Powell (1832-1899), Quaker antislavery activist; Alfred Porter Putnam (1827-1906), a Unitarian clergyman; and Alfred M. Wood (1825-1895), Civil War veteran and mayor of Brooklyn, 1864-1865. For additional information about these and other leaders, see "American Abolitionists and Antislavery Activists: Conscience of the Nation." http://www.americanabolitionists.com.

66. "Victory at Last" (New York: Wm. B. Bradbury, 1865).

67. Justus Clement French and Edward Cary, *Trip of the Steamer*, 5.

68. Charles F. Jordan, "Occupation of Fort Sumter," 406.

69. French and Cary, *Trip of the Steamer*, 37; William B. Bradbury, "Rally 'Round the Flag" (Boston: Oliver Ditson, 1862).

70. Aaron Macy Powell, *Personal Reminiscences*, 51.

71. "Personal," *New York Times*, July 7, 1866, 5.

72. This comment belatedly appeared as "Personal," *Milwaukee Sentinel*, July 2, 1866, 2.

73. "Wm. B. Bradbury," *Newark Daily Advertiser*, June 28, 1866, 2.

74. *Graham's Magazine* (Philadelphia) 36, no. 4 (April 1850): 288. See also Edwin B. Goodell, *Montclair*, 66; J. K. Hoyt, *Pen and Pencil Pictures*, 144. The Mountain House, built in 1838, was originally the Mount Prospect Institute, an elite private boarding school for boys.

75. Henry Whittemore, *History of Montclair*, 68. Philip Henry Doremus (1829–1897), a carpenter and builder by trade, also ran a livery stable; see "Philip Henry Doremus," *News* (Patterson, NJ), March 17, 1897, 1. See also "An Affecting Scene," *Vermont Christian Messenger* (Montpelier), July 5, 1866, 2.

76. "A Touching Scene—Wm. B. Bradbury," *Newark Daily Advertiser*, June 19, 1866, 2.

77. "Minnesota," *St. Cloud Democrat*, March 14, 1861, 1. See also "Health in Minnesota," *Goodhue Volunteer* (Red Wing, MN), April 2, 1862, 1; "Winter in Minnesota," *Minnesota Democrat* (St. Paul), November 16, 1853, 2.

78. *Cleveland Plain Dealer*, March 5, 1868, 2. Bradbury was not the first famous person to visit Minnesota for its climate and natural resources, as celebrated writer and transcendentalist Henry David Thoreau (1817–1862), also a tuberculosis patient, traveled to the state in 1861. Among the sources with information about the purported benefits of Minnesota's climate for tuberculosis sufferers consulted for this discussion, see Ledyard Bill, *Minnesota*, 85–104; David P. Steensma, Carol A. Roede, and Robert A. Kyle, "Henry David Thoreau's Final Journey"; and John T. Flanagan, "Thoreau in Minnesota," 35–46.

79. *St. Paul Daily Press*, November 2, 1866, 4.

80. "The Chapel Festival," *St. Paul Daily Press*, November 11, 1866, 4.

81. *St. Paul Daily Press*, December 25, 1866, 4.

82. "Personal: Mr. Wm. B. Bradbury," *New York Independent*, February 28, 1867, 4.

83. *New York Musical Pioneer and Choristers' Budget*, 12, no. 4 (April 1867): 4; *Rutland* [VT] *Daily Herald*, May 29, 1867, 2.

84. *Goodhue County Republican* (Red Wing, MN), January 24, 1868, 1.

85. "Bradbury," *Lake City* [MN] *Leader*, January 24, 1868, 1. This item was reprinted in several newspapers coast to coast. See also "Mr. Bradbury's New Sunday-School Music Book, *Fresh Laurels*," *New York Musical Pioneer and Choristers' Budget* 12, no. 9 (September 1867): 6.

86. Bradbury, Preface, *Fresh Laurels*, [1].

87. Edwin M. Long, "William B. Bradbury," *Illustrated History of Hymns*, 35.

88. T. F. Seward, "Sketches of American Composers: William B. Bradbury (concluded)," 57.

89. Ibid.

90. For example: "Obituary: Wm. B. Bradbury," *Milwaukee Daily Sentinel*, January 14, 1868, 2; "Obituary: W. B. Bradbury," *New York Tribune*, January 9, 1868, 8; *New York Times*, January 9, 1868, 4; J. H. C., "Death of Wm. B. Bradbury"; "Professor Bradbury," *New York Observer and Chronicle*, January 16, 1868, 22; *Montana Post* (Virginia City, MT), January 11, 1868, 4; *Boston Daily Advertiser*, January 9, 1868, 1; *Salt Lake* [City, UT] *Daily Telegraph*, January 9, 1868, 2; *Cheyenne* [WY] *Leader*, January 9, 1868, 2; *Bangor* [ME] *Whig and Courier*, January 11, 1868, 3.

91. "Musical Reminiscences: Something about Wm. B. Bradbury, Thomas Hastings, and Lowell Mason," 9.

92. Cheney, *American Singing Book*, 210–11.

93. "A New York State Music Teacher Abroad," *Evening Post* (NY), November 10, 1858, 1.

94. Thomas Hastings, quoted in "Death of Wm. B. Bradbury," *New York Evangelist*, January 16, 1868, 2.
95. [John Sullivan Dwight], "Native Oratorios," 84.

Chapter Two: *Esther*: The Early Years

1. *Esther* was the only large-scale work for which Bradbury wrote the entire score. Bradbury and Cady also collaborated with George F. Root in the composition of the oratorio *Daniel, or the Captivity and Restoration*, with Cady providing the text. Root wrote nearly all of the music for *Daniel* with Bradbury contributing only two numbers.
2. Chauncey Marvin Cady, "Reminiscences of Wm. B. Bradbury."
3. Ibid.
4. Bankruptcy and dissolution of the firm soon followed; see Polly H. Carder, *George F. Root*, 181; Dena J. Epstein, "Music Publishing in Chicago before 1871."
5. "Chauncey M. Cady," *Chicago Tribune* June 18, 1889, 3; "Chauncey M. Cady," *Music Trade Review* (New York), December 23, 1889, 424; "De Alumnis," *Oberlin Review* 19, no. 11 (December 1, 1891): 155.
6. Flavius Josephus, "Concerning Esther, and Mordecai, and Haman."
7. William B. Bradbury, *Esther*, 83.
8. For a list of *Esther*'s numbers, see the Appendix.
9. To view Bradbury's score online, visit https://Hathitrust.org.
10. The announcement belatedly appeared in the *New York Musical Review and Gazette* 7, no. 25 (December 13, 1856): 296.
11. A reprint of *Esther* appeared in 1857 as part of Bradbury's tunebook, *The Jubilee*, 333–72. However, subsequent reprints of *The Jubilee* did not include *Esther*. Bradbury's score also appeared in *The Book of Cantatas*, published by Mason Brothers in 1858.
12. For a modern critical edition of *Esther* recast in SATB notation, see Juanita Karpf, ed., *William B. Bradbury: "Esther, the Beautiful Queen."* For more on TASB scoring, see Juanita Karpf, "'In an Easy and Familiar Style'"; Peter Mercer-Taylor, *Gems of Exquisite Beauty*, 30–31.
13. Bradbury, *Alpine Glee Singer*, 3.
14. [Thomas Hastings], "What Constitutes Melody?" 238. I attribute this article to Hastings as he edited *Musical Magazine* and wrote most of the periodical's editorials.
15. Lowell Mason, "Figured Base," 123–24. By the 1850s, Mason had abandoned the use of figured bass—denoted by him as "a miserable system"—in favor of the more pragmatic arrangement of TASB scoring (Mason, "Thorough Base," 81).
16. "The Cantata of Esther," *New National Era* (Washington, DC), March 23, 1871, 3.
17. *New Orleans Picayune*, May 28, 1859, 6.
18. *New York Musical Review and Gazette* 7, no. 26 (December 27, 1856): 406.
19. Richard Crawford, "Musical Learning," 2–7; Richard Crawford, *American Musical Landscape*, 58–59.
20. "The Musical Concert" *Franklin Repository* (Chambersburg, PA), March 21, 1866, 2.
21. Bradbury, *Bradbury's Singing School for Ladies and Gentlemen*, 2; Bradbury, *Social Singing Book*, 2.
22. William B. Bradbury, "Lecture to Musical Students," 165; William B. Bradbury, "The Singing School of Twenty Lessons: First Article," 23.

23. Bradbury, *Bradbury's Singing School for Ladies and Gentlemen*, 2; Bradbury, *Social Singing Book*, 2.

24. Bradbury, "Singing School of Twenty Lessons: First Article"; William B. Bradbury, "Introductory Chat," *Singing Bird*, 2.

25. William B. Bradbury, *Musical Gems for School and Home*, 2.

26. "Death of Wm. B. Bradbury," *New York Evangelist*, January 16, 1868, 2.

27. Bradbury called specifically for treble (children's) voices in Part II, no. 6, and Part II, no. 10.

28. For Bradbury's justification for the use of vocables as a legitimate instructional exercise, see William B. Bradbury, "Note from Mr. Bradbury," in Thomas Hastings and William B. Bradbury, eds., *Psalmista*, 32.

29. The exception to Bradbury's careful balancing of voices occurs in the work's Finale, Part II, no. 15, where overly dense choral writing threatens to overwhelm the melody and text.

30. Bradbury's skillful instruction in harmony and composition inspired this comment from one of his students: "This [lesson in harmony and composition] is . . . the most interesting exercise we have, and that chiefly on account of the astonishing progress we are making. As a matter of course, the majority of us came here entirely ignorant of the laws of harmony and composition, and from the voluminous works written upon the subject, naturally supposed it required many years of study; but to our astonishment, under the valuable instruction of Professor Bradbury, we are already able to compose and harmonize common melodies tolerably correct. This is certainly encouraging. And no other living teacher could, we believe, present the subject of harmony and composition in a clearer and simpler manner than Professor Bradbury does. All seem to comprehend every step taken, and to take a delight in it, which is not generally the case, as the subject of harmony is supposed to be very dry and tedious" ("The Normal Academy," *New York Musical Pioneer and Choristers' Budget* 4, no. 12 [September 1, 1859]: 177–78).

31. *Ohio Observer* (Hudson), October 5, 1853, n.p.; reprint, *Lewisburg* [PA] *Chronicle*, October 28, 1853, 1.

32. Most of the tunebooks published by Bradbury and his contemporaries contained lessons in singing and music fundamentals, usually positioned as a preface section at the beginning of the book before the actual song literature.

33. See, for example, *New York Musical Review and Gazette* 7, no. 25 (December 13, 1856): 392.

34. "Letter from the People, River Head, LI [Long Island], May 21, 1859," *New York Musical Pioneer* 9, no. 9 (June 1, 1859): 133.

35. "Musical Convention," *Cincinnati Commercial Tribune*, November 8, 1858, 1.

36. William B. Bradbury, "Western Conventions," 296; Bradbury, quoted in Mary Elizabeth, "Mr. Bradbury's Conventions," 360.

37. C[hauncey] M[arvin] C[ady], "Orient, LI [Long Island]," 263.

38. "Greenport, LI [Long Island]," *New York Musical Review and Gazette* 7, no. 21 (October 16, 1856): 328.

39. *New York Musical Review and Gazette* 7, no. 23 (November 15, 1856): 354.

40. Unsigned review, quoted in Newton Bateman, Paul Selby, and David McCulloch, eds., *Historical Encyclopedia of Illinois* 2:436.

41. Jane Martin Johns, *Personal Recollections of Early Decatur*, 172–73.

42. "Musical Convention," *Weekly Hawk-Eye and Telegraph* (Burlington, IA), November 19, 1856, 1; "Burlington, Iowa," *New York Musical Review and Gazette* 7, no. 25 (December 13, 1856): 392.

43. Ibid., "Burlington, Iowa."
44. *New York Musical Review and Gazette* 8, no. 24 (November 28, 1857): 370.
45. *Emery's Journal of Agriculture and Prairie Farmer* (Chicago) 2, no. 1 (July 1, 1858): 8.
46. C. A. S., "Franklin, Mass.," 198.
47. "Commencement at Oberlin," *Cleveland Plain Dealer*, August 26, 1858, 3.
48. Bradbury, quoted in Sadie E. Martin, *Life and Professional Career of Emma Abbott*, 17–18.

Chapter Three: *Esther*, Revised

1. For newspaper accounts of some of the earliest staged productions of *Esther*, see, for example: "Musical," *St. Johnsbury* [VT] *Caledonian*, February 10, 1860, 2; "Concert in Gardner," *Barre* [MA] *Gazette*, March 1, 1861, 2; "Sing and Shout Aloud," *Daily Milwaukee News*, September 6, 1861, 1; *Berkshire County Eagle* (Pittsfield, MA), January 9, 1862, 3; "The Concert," *Appleton* [WI] *Post*, March 24, 1864, 1.
2. William B. Bradbury, "Cantata of Esther," 181.
3. Many newspapers mentioned Seager's affiliation with the St. Paul Academy of Music, including these items: "Oratorio of Esther," *Indianapolis News*, October 17, 1870, 3; *Cincinnati Daily Gazette*, June 2, 1871, 2; *Springfield* [MA] *Republican*, December 8, 1873, 3. Other mention of Seager's activities in Minneapolis include these sources: "Music," *Stillwater* [MN] *Messenger*, September 4, 1860, 3; "Attractive Concert," *Stillwater Messenger*, November 6, 1860, 2. During the mid-1860s, Seager also toured Ohio and Illinois, as confirmed by the following press notices (and many others): "Cleveland City Normal Institute," *Plain Dealer*, March 13, 1867, 4; "Concert by Professor Seager's Convention," *Plain Dealer*, April 13, 1867, 4; "Sunday Schools," *Rockford* [IL] *Weekly Register-Gazette*, May 18, 1867, 1.
4. *Stillwater Messenger*, September 25, 1860, 2.
5. R. W. Seager, letter to Charles Francis Hall, February 7, 1863, Charles Francis Hall Papers, Smithsonian Institution, Washington, DC. In 1863, Seager consulted Hall (ca. 1821–1871), the famous Artic explorer, regarding a possible business collaboration. No documentation has been located to confirm that such relationship between Seager and Hall ever materialized.
6. *Jamestown* [NY] *Journal*, August 25, 1865, 3.
7. R. W. Seager, quoted in "Musical," *Cleveland* [OH] *Daily Leader*, July 25, 1866, 3.
8. "Queen Esther," *Daily Globe* (St. Paul), March 10, 1879, 4.
9. To view Seager's version of *Esther* online, visit https://Hathitrust.org.
10. Seager, quoted in "The Reigning Triumph," *Atlanta Constitution*, September 2, 1894, 5.
11. The Mendelssohn anthem was taken from his oratorio, *St. Paul* (1836); the source for the Emerson work was most likely his compilation, *The Choral Tribute* (1869).
12. "Reigning Triumph."
13. Announcements of Seager's death appeared in newspapers throughout the continent. Here is a small sampling of those items mentioning Seager as the composer of *Esther*: "Composer of *Queen Esther* Dies Here," *Santa Ana* [CA] *Register*, January 8, 1913, 3; "Composer of *Queen Esther* Dies on Coast," *El Paso Herald*, January 9, 1913, 2; "Composer of *Queen Esther* Dead," *Atlanta Constitution*, January 9, 1913, 3; "Richard W. Seager Dead, Was Composer of the Cantata of *Queen Esther*," *Bennington* [VT] *Banner*, January 9, 1913, 1.
14. "Reigning Triumph."
15. Ibid.

16. R. W. Seager, "Directions for Organization, Costuming, and Etc.," in Seager, ed., *Esther, the Beautiful Queen*, 1–2.

17. Ibid.

18. Seager, "Directions."

19. Ibid. In his prefatory recommendations, Seager mentions the possibility of an encore in response to the pages' dance. In the nineteenth century especially, audience enthusiasm sometimes signaled a request for the repetition of a number just performed. Encores could occur at any point during a performance rather than just at the conclusion, as is common today.

20. Newspapers mention R. W. Seager playing the roles of Ahasuerus or Haman, and Ella Knapp Seager in various *Esther* roles. One critic welcomed Ella Knapp Seager as a "new candidate for popular favor" and lauded her "fresh soprano" voice and "purity of execution" ("Cantata of Esther," *Sherman and Hyde's Musical Review* 4, no. 6 [June 1877]: 22). See also "Esther," Utica [NY] *Daily Observer*, January 31, 1872, n.p.; *Indiana* [PA] *Democrat*, May 16, 1872, 7; "Community Journal," Oneida [NY] *Circular* 10, no. 13 (March 24, 1873): 101; "Oratorio of Esther," Clinton [NY] *Courier*, April 3, 1873, 1. The well-known soprano Inez Fabbri (1831–1909) sang as Queen Esther with Ella Knapp Seager playing Mordecai's sister in 1877; see "Grand Opera House," *Daily Alta California*, June 21, 1877, 1; "Grand Opera House," *Daily Evening Bulletin* (San Francisco), June 23, 1877, 1. For mention of Frank Seager as the Herald, see "Oratorio of Esther," *Indiana* [PA] *Democrat*, May 23, 1877, 3.

21. R. W. Seager, letter to the editor, 2. Seager occasionally ran afoul with communities over contractual matters. Tempers flared in 1874 when Seager sparred with local officials in Springfield, MA; see "*Esther* to Be Repeated," *Springfield Republican*, January 2, 1874, 6. A year later, a Newark, NJ, resident accused Seager of absconding with more than his fair share of fees. The dispute resulted in a jury trial; see *New York Herald*, January 15, 1875, 8. For detailed accounts of Seager's apparent financial malfeasance in Plymouth, PA, see Hughes Bros., "Letters from the People: *Queen Esther*"; R. W. Seager, "Letter No. 1"; and Seager, "Letter No. 2," all found in *Weekly Star* (Wilmington, NC), February 23, 1876, 4; and in John W. Leyson, "Queen Esther," 4. Seager's most protracted and heated dispute with singers and local residents occurred in Denver in 1883; see *Denver Republican*, December 16, 1883; "Row in the Camp: Prof. Seager Relates His Side of the Story in the *Queen Esther* Muss," *Denver Republican*, December 17, 1883, 1; *Denver Rocky Mountain News*, December 20, 1883, 4; *Denver Rocky Mountain News*, December 21, 1883, 4; "Queen Esther at the Academy," *Denver Rocky Mountain News*, December 22, 1883, 1. A St. Paul newspaper took serious issue with Seager's business dealings and referred to him as a "hustler" (*St. Paul Daily Globe*, March 27, 1886, 3).

22. "Reigning Triumph."

23. Ibid.

24. "Music in the Air: Prof. Seager Is Smoked Out by the Denver Papers," *Daily Bee* (Omaha, NE), December 26, 1883, 6, a reprint of an item from an unidentified Denver newspaper.

25. "Queen Esther at the Academy," *Denver Rocky Mountain News*, December 22, 1883, 1; "Music in the Air," 6.

26. "Esther," *Waterbury Daily American*, June 15, 1874, 2; "The Musical Drama of *Esther*," *Waterbury Daily American*, June 17, 1874, 3.

27. "Queen Esther—Third Night," *New Port* [RI] *Daily News*, April 7, 1877, 2.

28. "*Esther*: The Cantata as Presented at the Grand Opera House Last Night," *Daily Alta California* (San Francisco), June 22, 1877, 1.

29. "Grand Opera House," *Daily Alta California*, June 21, 1877, 1.

30. "Edmund C. Hill," *New York Times*, April 17, 1936, 22.

31. All quotations taken from Edmund C. Hill's diary, Trentoniana Collection, Trenton Historical Society, https://trentonhistory.org. Hill (1855–1936) oversaw the design of several public recreational facilities in Trenton and is credited with pioneering the park movement in the region. In addition to singing in his church choir and in local stage productions, Hill performed on flute and organ. He ran his family's baking and catering business, held various local offices, and became a successful real estate developer; see "Edmund C. Hill," *New York Times*, April 17, 1936, 22; "Edmund C. Hill Dies, Trenton Civic Leader," *Morning Post* (Camden, NJ), April 17, 1936, 2.

32. Margaret Gordon, "Women of the Old Testament," 72.

33. "The Cantata," *Hammonton [NJ] Item*, May 27, 1876, 5.

34. "*Esther!*" *Sentinel Democrat* (Mt. Sterling, KY), April 16, 1880, n.p.

35. "The Cantata Is a Success," *Leadville [CO] Daily and Evening*, February 16, 1895, 4.

36. "Cantata of *Esther*," *Morning Oregonian* (Portland), April 4, 1900, 8.

37. *Utica [NY] Morning Herald and Daily Gazette*, December 5, 1876, 1.

38. *Vermont Watchman*, (Montpelier) February 10, 1886, 1.

39. "Musical Entertainment at the Highlands," *Boston Daily Globe*, April 9, 1893, 18.

40. Newspaper reviews of Keach's operas include "Leon Keach's Comic Opera," *Boston Globe*, July 28, 1887, 10 (comments about *The Corsair*); and "The Mermaid," *Boston Globe*, April 28, 1888, 2.

41. Information about Keach was culled from these sources: Frank W. Kirk, "Mr. Leon Keach," *Music Trades* (New York); reprint, *Musical Record*, 11; "Death of Leon Keach," *Music Trade Review* (New York), August 22, 1896, 9. Advertisements for and reviews of Keach's operas, along with his performances as an accompanist and opera conductor, can be found in numerous periodicals.

42. Leon Keach, Preface, *Esther, the Beautiful Queen*.

43. At least one newspaper columnist stated that Keach's changes to the *Esther* score "much improved" the piece; see *Rockland [ME] Courier-Gazette* September 14, 1897, 3. See also advertisement for an *Esther* performance, *Eureka [KS] Herald and Greenwood County Republican*, May 30, 1901, 5.

Chapter Four: Genre Intrigue

1. Eugene Wood, *Our Town*, 116–17. The archaic spelling and pronunciation of "theater" as "the-ay-ter" was a fairly common colloquial use of the word in Wood's day. Such usage referenced any staged, secular, dramatic event that incorporated little, if any, singing.

2. George F. Root, "Our Musical Correspondence, North-Reading, Mass.," 5–6.

3. William B. Bradbury, *Jubilee*, 2–3.

4. Bradbury, preface, *Alpine Glee Singer*. *Ranz des vaches* are traditional melodies performed by Alpine shepherds, usually sung or played on an alphorn. These melodies fascinated a handful of European composers, and Bradbury surely knew of their use in the following works: Ludwig van Beethoven, Symphony No. 6, "Pastoral" (1808), Gioachino Rossini, *William Tell Overture* (1829), and Hector Berlioz, *Symphonie Fantastique* (1836), to name but a few.

5. Nicholas E. Tawa, *Sweet Songs for Gentle Americans*, 159–60.

6. Peter Mercer-Taylor, *Gems of Exquisite Beauty*, 13.

7. Tawa, *Sweet Songs for Gentle Americans*, 159–60.

8. Mercer-Taylor, *Gems of Exquisite Beauty*, 195–96.

9. Michael Broyles, *Music of the Highest Class*, 90–91; Richard Crawford, *American Musical Landscape*, 179–83.

10. *New York Observer*, December 18, 1847, 1.

11. Mercer-Taylor, *Gems of Exquisite Beauty*, 172–76.

12. Richard Crawford, *America's Musical Life*, 135–36, 140–41; Mercer-Taylor, *Gems of Exquisite Beauty*, 92–95, 190–91; Nicholas E. Tawa, "Serious Songs," 274–75.

13. To be sure, the study of a "tune family" and attendant correspondences of its melodic members to one another is most often associated with the analysis of folk songs. I apply the term here as a method of illustrating the contents of Bradbury's musical "reservoir" and his propensity for borrowing melodic material from his own compositions as well as from those by other composers. For useful discussions of tune families, see James R. Cowdery, "A Fresh Look," 495–504 and Anne Dhu Shapiro, "Black Sacred Song," 110–17.

14. "The Music World," *Pittsburgh Dispatch*, January 27, 1889, 6.

15. "The Musical Concert" *Franklin Repository* (Chambersburg, PA), March 21, 1866, 2.

16. *New Orleans Picayune*, May 25, 1859, 6. Nicolas Slonimsky defines an *olla podrida* (literally a "rotten pot" in Spanish) as a "miscellany or medley of musical or comic dialogues and 'exotic' dances at a burlesque show" (*Lectionary of Music*, 333).

17. The lyrics of Buckley's "Kiss Me Quick and Go" first appeared in James Buckley's *Buckley's Ethiopian Melodies*, 18. A note on the title page of this song's score indicates that it was "sung with great applause at the concerts by Buckley's [Ethiopian Minstrelsy] Opera Troupe at their new Opera House [in] Brooklyn, NY" prior to its publication (Frederick Buckley, "Kiss Me Quick and Go," 1856). James Buckley (1803–1882), along with his three sons, R. Bishop Buckley (1826–1867), George Swain Buckley (1829–1879), and Frederick Buckley (1833–1864), toured extensively as "Buckley's Serenaders" and became one of the most famous US minstrelsy ensembles during the nineteenth century. Bradbury, acutely conscious of audience taste and preferences, would surely have known of Buckley's song.

18. *New Monthly Magazine and Literary Journal* (London), July 1831, 485. See also *National Gazette* (Philadelphia), February 10, 1832, 2, for comments about a performance of "Laughing Trio" during which "a serious face among the audience was not to be seen." Popular throughout the United States and British Commonwealth in the 1830s to 1860s, "Laughing Trio" elicited unstinting applause and spontaneous outbursts of hilarity.

19. For example, the well-known Hutchinson Family Singers popularized George Kingsley's arrangement of "Laughing Trio," originally written by J. P. E. Martini (1741–1816); see George Kingsley, ed., *Social Choir*, 154–56. J. P. E. Martini was often confused with Giovanni Battista Martini (1706–1784), and the "Laughing Trio" has sometimes been incorrectly attributed to the latter composer. Another example, "Laughing Finale," written by the African American bandmaster Francis Johnson (1792–1844), served as the closing movement of his celebrated *Voice Quadrilles*. Directions in Johnson's score called for musicians to put down their instruments and vocalize "ha-ha" repeatedly, much to the delight of dancers at glittery upper-class events in major cities throughout the eastern United States. And finally, two minstrelsy troupes included laughing songs as part of their standard repertoire in Bradbury's day: the first, "The Laughing Chorus" composed by E. Renzlus and sung by Buckley's Serenaders; and the second, "Laughing Darkies: Comic Ethiopian Song," also composed by Renzlus, was sung by Fellow's Minstrels.

20. *New Orleans Picayune*, May 28, 1859, 6. Bradbury undoubtedly saw this review, most likely written by John Sullivan Dwight, a portion of which appeared in Boston's *Dwight's Journal of Music* as "Native Oratorios," 84.

21. Elizabeth Aldrich, *From the Ballroom to Hell*, 18–20; Mark A. Knowles, *Wicked Waltz*, 26–58.

22. Bradbury, *Esther*, Finale, Part II, no. 15.

23. "Oswego, NY," *New York Musical Review and Gazette* 13, no. 1 (January 10, 1857): 7.

24. Quoted in Lawrence, *Resonances*, 6. Strong's diary entry is dated May 21, 1848.

25. The Ditson firm used Bradbury's printing plates for Seager's edition and retained the original title page. Leon Keach referred to *Esther* as a "sacred cantata" on the title page of his edition (see figure 3.2).

26. *Lake Geneva* [WI] *Herald*, May 6, 1910, 5. Singer Henry Clark Buell (1832–1928), lauded by the press as "a man of unusual musical sensitivity," served as a church organist in Beloit, WI, for decades; see "H.C. Buell, 95, Dies at Home in Linn Township," *Lake Geneva Regional News*, September 20, 1928, 1; "Early Lake Geneva Organist, 95, Dies," *Capital Times* (Madison, WI), September 16, 1928, 5.

27. Bradbury, "Cantata of *Esther*."

28. Bradbury was undoubtedly familiar with Felix Mendelssohn's *Elijah*, Op. 70 (1846), divided into two main parts, as he admired Mendelssohn's music. Other examples of oratorios written in two parts include George Frideric Handel, *La Resurrezione* (*The Resurrection*, 1708); Alessandro Scarlatti, *La Vergine Addolorata* (*The Virgin of Sorrows*, 1717); Antonio Vivaldi, *Juditha Triumphans* (*The Triumph of Judith*, 1717); and Georg Philipp Telemann, *Die Donnerode* (*The Ode of Thunder*, 1760).

29. *Chariton* [IA] *Leader*, May 15, 1875, 4.

30. *New York Musical World*, 16 (December 3, 1856): 675.

31. *New Orleans Picayune*, May 28, 1859, 6.

32. "*Esther*: Scheme of a New Cantata," *Chicago Tribune*, April 17, 1870, 2.

33. "*Esther*," *Waterbury* [CT] *Daily American*, June 15, 1874, 2; "The Musical Drama of *Esther*," *Waterbury Daily American*, June 17, 1874, 3.

34. "Cantata of *Esther*—the Drama," *Coldwater* [MI] *Sentinel*, January 11, 1867, 3.

35. Edward Ellsworth Hipsher, *American Opera*, 79–80. Hipsher (1871–1948), a graduate of London's Royal Academy of Music, published numerous articles and books and served as editor of *Etude Magazine*.

36. "Domestic Musical Report," *American Musical Journal* (New York) 1, no. 5 (April 1835): 115–16; "Theatrical and Musical," *New York Herald*, October 18, 1842, 1. Examples of biblical operas, performed to critical acclaim, included Étienne Méhul's *Joseph* (1807), Gioachino Rossini's *Mosé in Egitto* (*Moses in Egypt*), and Giuseppe Verdi's *Nabucco* (1841). Rossini revised his *Mosé in Egitto* (1818) as *Moses and Pharaoh, or The Crossing of the Red Sea* (1827). The score of *The Israelites in Egypt* (New York: J. C. House, 1842), referred, on its title page, to the work as "the first sacred drama performed in America, consisting of sacred music, scenery and personation. The music composed by Handel and Rossini. The drama written and the music adapted by M[ichael] Rophino Lacy [1795–1867]. Performed for the first time in this country at the Park Theatre, New York, on Monday, Oct. 31, 1842."

37. *Denison* [IA] *Review*, August 2, 1893, n.p.

38. "The Cantata," *Sacramento Daily Union*, February 1, 1895, 4; "*Esther* Cantata," *Sacramento Daily Union*, February 6, 1895, 3.

39. "Last Evening's Cantata," *Emporia* [IL] *Daily Gazette*, January 20, 1892.

40. *Ferndale* [CA] *Enterprise*, January 8, 1897, 5.

41. Noteworthy appearances of horses in nineteenth-century opera productions included these works: Verdi's *Falstaff* and *Aida*, Mascagni's *Cavalleria Rusticana*, Bizet's *Carmen*, Puccini's *La Fanciulla del West*, and Wagner's *Götterdämmerung*.

42. "Grand Opera House," *Daily Alta California* (San Francisco), June 17, 1877, 1; "Cantata of *Esther*," *Sherman and Hyde's Musical Review* (San Francisco) 4, no. 7 (July 1877): 195.

43. *Chicago Tribune*, March 3, 1878, 16. DeWitt, the owner of a Springfield, Illinois, music store, sometimes sang the role of Ahasuerus.

44. "The Cantata *Esther*," *Inter Ocean* (Chicago) March 8, 1878, 8.

45. "Music," *Los Angeles Evening Express*, June 30, 1894, 4.

46. "The Cantata Queen *Esther*," Butler [MO] *Weekly Times*, April 9, 1914, 5.

47. Sue Ruple Watson, "Local Historian Gives Story," 8.

48. "Madame de Turczynowicz," *La Jolla Light*, May 22, 1922, 1. See also Turczynowicz, "La Jolla Woman's Club," 8. A Canadian native (née Blackwell, 1878–1953), Turczynowicz acquired her title upon marriage in 1907 to Polish-born Count Stanislaw de Turczynowicz (1873–1957). The Countess, who claimed Cosima Wagner as a mentor, trained for an opera career in Bayreuth, working with conductor Felix Josef von Mottl (1856–1911). She studied voice with renowned pedagogues including soprano Lilli Lehmann (1848–1929) in Berlin and in Paris with tenor Ange Albert Pattou (1833–1911) and Polish native and opera star Jean de Reszka (1850–1925). Turczynowicz sang with the Berlin Opera before marrying. She fled occupied Poland around 1910 with her three children. Subsequently, she became an activist for the cause of aiding the beleaguered Polish people and war-torn Poland. For a firsthand account of her ordeal, see Turczynowicz, *When the Russians Came to Poland*. After leaving Europe, she resided for a time in Canada. She then moved to the United States, became a US citizen, performed with the Metropolitan Opera in New York, and eventually moved to California.

49. "First Pageant Performance Today," *Evening Tribune* (San Diego, CA), April 22, 1922, 26.

50. "Many Dances to be Presented in *Esther, the Beautiful Queen* at Auditorium Next Saturday," *San Diego Union*, June 8, 1922, 9. Born in Poland, Wanda Jolanda de Turczynowicz (1908–2001) studied dance under the tutelage of her mother and eventually, with European teachers. She later abandoned her professional prospects as a dancer and became a painter. A few of her works can be viewed online; see, for example, https://www.askart.com/artist/Wanda_de_Turczynowicz/129802/Wanda_de_Turczynowicz.aspx.

51. "*Esther* Comes into Light," *La Jolla Journal*, April 14, 1922, 2. A church organist and popular singer in the La Jolla region, Delano Cadman (1894–1954) performed in many California productions including works by Gilbert and Sullivan.

52. "*Esther* Comes into Light." For more photographs from this production, see Turczynowicz, "La Jolla Woman's Club."

53. "*Esther*: Scheme of a New Cantata."

54. Jake Johnson, *Lying in the Middle*, 25. For more on the religious and sacred connections between musicals and theological or spiritual engagement consulted for this discussion, see Ian C. Bradley, *You've Got to Have a Dream*, 25–35; Henry Bial, *Playing God*, 11–16.

Chapter Five: Religious Controversy

1. "*Esther*," *Chicago Tribune*, May 13, 1870, 3.

2. *Cincinnati Commercial Tribune*, February 26, 1876, 5; reprinted as "Out in Iowa," *Evening Star* (Washington, DC), February 28, 1876, 1. An Iowa newspaper source for this quote has not been located.

3. For an excellent overview of moral controversy and the theater consulted for this chapter, see Henry Bial, *Playing God*, particularly 11–16. See also R. Laurence Moore, "Religion, Secularization," 216–42.

4. *Kansas State Journal* (Lawrence, KS), March 21, 1861, 3.

5. Rev. J[ames] D[emarest] Eaton, "*Esther*," 1.

6. Adams, quoted in "Slanders Refuted: It Was Not an Opera, but an Oratorio," *Chicago Tribune*, December 7, 1879, 10.

7. Seager, "Directions for Organization, Costuming," 5.

8. Rev. L. L. Hobbs, quoted in "'Thinks He Was Duped: Pastor Hobbs Thought 'Twas a Service of Song; Low Necks and Abbreviated Skirts Not Just the Proper Thing, He Thinks," *Boston Daily Globe*, January 21, 1891, 2. Rev. Lacassard Lazarus Hobbs (1859–1951) avoided using his first or middle name, preferring to be addressed as "L. L. Hobbs." In diary entries written in 1876 (discussed in chapter three), Edmund C. Hill remarked that the woman playing the Queen's Maid of Honor in the production in which he sang wore a dress of unacceptably short length—that is, "abbreviated"—"that came down just below her knees."

9. Taylor, quoted in "A Chicopee Pastor's Objection to the Performance of *Queen Esther*," *Springfield* [MA] *Republican*, May 19, 1891, 8.

10. "Skirts Not So Very Short," *Boston Herald*, May 20, 1891, 12.

11. *Times-Picayune*, May 28, 1891, 4.

12. *Placer Herald* (Rockland, CA), July 13, 1895, 5.

13. "Prayer and Dancing," *Sacramento Bee*, March 17, 1877, 2.

14. Many midwestern newspapers printed this editorial, including *Cincinnati Daily Gazette*, December 12, 1879, 8; "Religious Reading," *New Albany* [IN] *Daily Ledger Standard* December 13, 1879, 2; *Belmont Chronicle* (Saint Clairsville, OH), December 18, 1879, 1; *Sterling* [IL] *Gazette*, December 20, 1879, 3; *Cleveland Leader*, December 24, 1879, 4; *Kalamazoo* [MI] *Gazette*, December 24, 1879, 2; and *Jackson Sentinel* (Maquoketa, IA), January 1, 1880, 7.

15. *Lebanon* [IN] *Boone County Pioneer*, January 24, 1873, 1. The original source of this comment has not been located.

16. "The Cantata," *Peninsular Courier and Family Visitant* (Ann Arbor, MI), November 22, 1866, 5.

17. "Cantata of *Esther*—the Drama," *Coldwater* [MI] *Sentinel*, January 11, 1867, 3.

18. "The C[entral] C[hristian] Advocate [St. Louis, MO] Once Again," *Weekly Rescue* (Sacramento, CA), April 12, 1877, 4.

19. "Cantata of *Esther*—The Drama," *Coldwater* [MI] *Sentinel*, January 11, 1867, 3.

20. H[enry] B[ixby] Hemenway, "Sacredness of Churches," 4.

21. George A. Maston, "Religious Failings," 4. Born into slavery in Virginia, Maston (1849–1930) escaped and later attended Oberlin College. He worked as a barber, taught school, joined the ministry, and eventually settled in Nebraska; see Lila Gravatt Scrimsher, ed., "Diaries and Writings," 133–68.

22. *R.I. Schoolmaster* (Providence, RI) 4, no. 1 (March 1858): 14.

23. "Cantata of *Esther*—The Drama."

24. Lawrence W. Levine, *Highbrow, Lowbrow*, 178–92; "Theatrical and Musical," *New York Herald*, October 18, 1842, 1.

25. *Twi-weekly Herald* (Marshall, TX), February 12, 1880, 4. "Cut it fat" means to exaggerate, show off, or make a vulgar display; a "duffer" is an incompetent or foolish person. See Jonathan Green, *Green's Dictionary of Slang*. https://greensdictofslang.com.

26. "The Theatrical World," *New World: A Weekly Family Journal of Popular Literature, Science, Art and News* (New York), November 12, 1842, 320.

27. William Weston Patton, "Defense of Theater and Opera," 4. Patton (1821–1889), an abolitionist, conservative clergyman, one-time faculty member at the Oberlin College School of Theology, and editor of Chicago's religious newspaper, *Advance*, served as president of Washington, DC's Howard University from 1877 until his death.

28. Robert Laird Collier, "Theatre, the Opera, and the Church," 28. Collier (1832–1890) initially delivered this sermon in 1868. In addition to his duties as a clergyman, Collier served as a correspondent for the *New York Herald*.

29. Robert Laird Collier, "Preacher's Defense of the Drama and the Opera," 3.

30. Collier, "Theatre, the Opera, and the Church," 34.

31. Patton, "Defense of Theater and Opera."

32. Israel Edson Dwinell, "Church and the Stage," 2.

33. "Praying and Dancing," *Sacramento Bee*, March 17, 1877, 2.

34. J[ames] D[emarest] Eaton, "*Esther*," 1. Eaton (1848–1928) delivered this sermon on June 15, 1873 at the First Congregational Church, Portland.

35. "*Esther*: The Cantata as Presented at the Grand Opera House Last Night," *Daily Alta California* (San Francisco), June 22, 1879, 1.

36. I discuss Abbott's performance as Queen Esther in chapter two.

37. "Reforming a Bad Opera [from the *Chicago News*]," *Weekly Democratic Statesman* (Austin, TX) August 7, 1884, 3; reprinted as "Abbott as Semiramide," *Salt Lake* [City] *Daily Herald*, August 10, 1884, 5; "Abbott," *Watertown* [NY] *Daily Times*, July 12, 1884, 3. For more about Abbott, including her choice of operatic roles, see Katherine K. Preston, *Opera for the People*, 311–409.

38. "The Passion Play," *Madisonian* (Virginia City, MT), June 24, 1882, 1.

39. For consideration of authenticity and accuracy in the use of biblical texts for dramatic or musical purposes, see Henry Bial, *Playing God*, 18–31, 82.

40. Thomas Lamb Eliot, quoted in "Sermon on the Book of Esther," *New Northwest*, July 14, 1871, 3. Eliot (1841–1936) supported universal suffrage, worked ceaselessly for the betterment of the lives of the impoverished and mentally ill, and advocated universal access to free public education. For more on discomfort with Vashti and her absence in some interpretations and adaptations of the Book of Esther, see Tzvi Sinensky, "Vashti Comes to America," in Stuart W. Halpern, ed. *Esther in America*, 108–15.

41. Abigail Scott Duniway, untitled article, *New Northwest*, June 27, 1873, 3. Duniway (1834–1915), a noted women's rights advocate, author, and feminist, edited the *New Northwest* and wrote many of the paper's editorials.

42. Ibid.

43. "Church Theatricals," *Trenton* [NJ] *Evening Times*, April 30, 1900, 4.

44. Charles Dudley Warner, "Editor's Study," 801. Among his myriad publications, Warner (1829–1900) coauthored, with his friend Mark Twain, the novel *The Gilded Age* (1873).

45. Debates regarding the biblical canonicity of the Book of Esther extend far beyond the present discussion. For excellent summaries of salient arguments, see Frederic W. Bush, "Book of Esther: *Opus non gratum*," 39–54; Stephen Curto, "Should She Stay or Should She Go?" http://mygiveonthings.com/should-she-stay-or-should-she-go-the-canonicity-of-esther/; David J. Zucker, "The Importance of Being Esther," 102–8.

46. Henry Bial, *Playing God*, 18–31, 82.

47. For more on the nuances and intricacies of musical exoticism/Orientalism that extend beyond the scope of the present discussion, see Ralph P. Locke, *Musical Exoticism*, 43–50, 177–78; Locke, *Music and the Exotic*, 187–95. See also Naomi Rosenblatt, "Orientalism in American Popular Culture." https://repository.upenn.edu/cgi/viewcontent.cgi?article=1005&context=phr.

48. Seager, quoted in "The Reigning Triumph," *Atlanta Constitution*, September 2, 1894, 5.

49. [Washington Irving], "Orientalism," 478–80. Biblical historian and cultural critic David D. Grafton confidently cites Washington Irving (1783–1859) as this article's author even though it is unsigned (email communication, April 23, 2021). The practice of publishing unsigned articles was fairly commonplace in this era, especially among editors of periodicals and newspapers. It should be added that Irving edited the *Knickerbocker* at the time this article appeared. He amassed considerable knowledge about culture and life among Oriental peoples during the years he resided in Spain. He published four books about his experiences with particular attention paid to the Moors and Spanish Orientalism.

50. In my discussion, I consider Orientalism as a broadly defined cultural response to all things Eastern. Ralph Locke also takes a similar stance in his consideration of musical exoticism; see his *Musical Exoticism*, 43–50, 177–78; and his *Music and the Exotic*, 187–95. For more on Irving's conceptualization of "spiritual orientalism," see David D. Grafton, *American Biblical Orientalism*, 9–20.

51. For example, the Book of Esther profoundly influenced Abraham Lincoln as he struggled with the possibility of issuing the Emancipation Proclamation. Accordingly, Lincoln consulted with Rev. William Weston Patton, a prominent abolitionist, regarding the advisability and efficacy of releasing this pivotal and volatile edict. The two discussed the Book of Esther and its themes as they related to the president's proposed executive decision. As a result of their meeting, Lincoln proceeded with his plan; see Meir Y. Soloveichik, "Lincoln, Esther, and the Rav," in Stuart W. Halpern, ed. *Esther in America*, 91–101; Ari Lamm, "'The Secret Political History of Queen Esther." https://www.tabletmag.com/sections/holidays/articles/political-history-of-queen-esther.

52. Stuart W. Halpern, "Editor's Introduction," in Halpern, ed., ix–xii.

53. John Kuo Wei Tchen, *New York before Chinatown*, xvi, xxi–xxii.

54. Ralph P. Locke, "A Broader View of Musical Exoticism," 477–85; Locke, *Musical Exoticism*, 20, 22, 45, 65, 196–202.

55. For more on these issues, see Ralph P. Locke, "Cutthroats and Casbah Dancers," 105, 130.

56. Locke, "Broader View," 483–84.

57. Locke, "Cutthroats and Casbah Dancers," 105.

58. "Cantata of *Esther*," *Morning Oregonian* (Portland), April 4, 1900, 8.

59. "*Esther!*" *Sentinel Democrat* (Mt. Sterling, KY), April 16, 1880, n.p.

60. *Ferndale* [CA] *Enterprise*, January 8, 1897, 5.

61. "Last Evening's Cantata," *Emporia* [IL] *Daily Gazette*, January 20, 1892, n.p.

62. "Played *Queen Esther*," *Spokesman-Review* (Spokane, WA), April 10, 1903, 3.

63. "Sacred Queen Esther: Large Audience Greets Its Rendition at Opera House Last Evening," *Daily Capital Journal* (Salem, OR), June 18, 1904, 5.

64. H[enry] W. Marden, "Old-Time Recollections," 3.

65. Eugene Field, quoted in Slason Thompson, *Life of Eugene Field*, 34. The original source of this quote has not been found. Knox College is located in Galesburg, IL. Field

(1850–1895) is best remembered for his children's poetry, especially "Wynken, Blynken, and Nod" (1889).

66. Among the widely read travel memoirs that included descriptions of harems and their occupants' attire must be listed Sarah Rogers Haight, *Letters from the Old World* and Julia Sophia Pardoe, *City of the Sultan*. See also Billie Melman, *Women's Orients*, especially 59–164; Joan DelPlato, *Multiple Wives, Multiple Pleasures*.

67. *Luther League Review* 33, no. 8 (November 1920): 22.

68. Sarah Smith Pratt, *Old Crop*, 172.

69. "The Oratorio of *Esther* Last Night," *Milwaukee Daily Sentinel*, February 8, 1867, 1.

70. *New Hampshire Statesman* (Concord) March 8, 1867, 3.

71. "*Esther* Shaping Up for Presentation in April," *La Jolla Journal*, March 31, 1922, 3.

72. Among the illustrated Bibles and reference works available in the United States in the nineteenth century were *Bible Illustrations* (New York: F. W. Bradley, 1830); Robert Sears, *Two Hundred Pictorial Illustrations*; *The Pictorial Bible* (New York: J. S. Redfield, 1843); John Kitto, *A Cyclopaedia of Biblical Literature*; *Cassell's Illustrated Family Bible*, 4 vols. (London: Cassell, Petter & Galpin, 1860); and Gustave Doré, *Holy Bible with Illustrations*. Beyond these sources, missionary and artist William McClure Thomson's two-volume bestseller, *Land and the Book*, featured not only the author's descriptive prose, but also his drawings of the sights and people he encountered; see David D. Grafton, *American Biblical Orientalism*, 147–80. For more on illustrations of scenes from the Book of Esther specifically, see Steven W. Holloway, "Assur [Ahasuerus] Is King of Persia," 2–7.

73. "Attend Esther," *Eureka* [KS] *Herald and Greenwood County Republican*, May 30, 1901, 5; "Cantata of *Esther*," *Eureka Herald and Greenwood County Republican*, June 13, 1901, 1.

74. "Harper's Illuminated Bible," *New York Evangelist*, January 18, 1844, 10.

75. Mary Roberts, *Intimate Outsiders*, 103.

76. Henry J. Van-Lennep, *Bible Lands*, 654. Van-Lennep (1815–1889), a missionary, traveled extensively in the Middle East and left behind a treasure trove of writings along with marvelous watercolor paintings of the places he visited.

77. Shimon Levy, "Book of Esther," 158; Shimon Levy, *The Bible as Theatre*, 108–9.

78. For more on the multiple intricacies, nuances, and interplay of gender, power, hierarchy, and race in US Orientalist representation that extends outside my analysis of *Esther* reception, see these informative sources: Reina Lewis, *Gendering Orientalism*, 1–52; Reina Lewis, *Rethinking Orientalism*, 96–141; Douglas Little, *American Orientalism*, 9–42; and Mari Yoshihara, *Embracing the East*, 6–10, 191–98.

79. For more on humor in the Book of Esther, see Michael LeFebvre, "Story of Esther." https://hebraicthought.org/esther-redemptive-humor-in-the-bible/. Debbie Blue, "Biblical Farce." https://www.christiancentury.org/article/2015-12/biblical-farce.

80. *New York Musical World* 16 (December 3, 1856): 675.

81. William B. Bradbury, "Cantata of *Esther*," 181.

82. Blue, "Biblical Farce."

83. Susan Nance, *How the Arabian Nights Inspired the American Dream*, 2, 10–12.

84. Richard Crawford, "Musical Learning," 2–7.

Chapter Six: Interlude: *Esther* Images

1. "Groupings of *Esther*," *Seattle Post-Intelligencer* April 9, 1896, 3. These photographs have not been located. For a review of this performance, see "*Queen Esther*: The Beautiful Cantata at the Seattle Theater Last Night," *Seattle Post-Intelligencer*, April 17, 1896, 8.
2. "Cantata of *Esther*," *Cambridge* [MA] *Chronicle*, April 29, 1893, 6.
3. Local newspapers mentioned these performances many times; see, for example: "Minneapolis Music," *St. Paul Press*, January 28, 1865, 7; "Minneapolis," *St. Paul Daily Press*, February 2, 1865, 4; "Oratorio of Queen Esther," *Anoka* [MN] *Star*, February 4, 1865, 2; "Queen Esther," *St. Paul Press*, February 21, 1865, 4; "Queen Esther," *St. Paul Press*, February 22, 1865, 4; "Ingersoll's Hall, To-Night," *St. Paul Press*, February 24, 1865, 4; "Queen Esther," *St. Paul Press*, February 25, 1865, 4; "Our Musical Society among the Minneapolitans," *St. Paul Press*, March 12, 1865, 8; "Queen Esther Again," *St. Paul Press*, March 14, 1865, 4; "Queen Esther," *St. Paul Press*, March 16, 1865, 4; and "Musical," *Winona* [MN] *Daily Republican*, February 22, 1867, 2.
4. Shuey, quoted in Nell S. Overpeck, "Minneapolis," 15; A[lfred] M. Shuey, "Veteran Musician Recalls," 25, 31. For more information about Shuey, see "Captain A. M. Shuey, Father of All Shrine Uniform Units, Dies," *Star Tribune* (Minneapolis), April 30, 1930, 1–2. Both these articles draw attention to the significance of *Esther* for Minneapolis's musicians and theater audiences. Alfred Mayhew Shuey (1847–1930), composer, singer, and multi-instrumentalist, was a founding member of the Minneapolis Orchestral Union, the precursor of the Minnesota Orchestra. Beginning in 1866, Shuey played violin in Minneapolis's earliest productions of *Esther*, and in later years, he fondly recalled his participation in those events.
5. "Musical," *St. Paul Daily Press*, October 24, 1866, 4; "Musical," *St. Paul Daily Press*, December 16, 1866, 4.
6. "Musical," *Winona Daily Republican* (Minneapolis), February 22, 1867, 3.
7. "Pence Opera House," *Star Tribune* (Minneapolis), June 14, 1867, 4; "Pence Opera House," *Minneapolis Daily Tribune*, June 25, 1867, 4.
8. "Pence Opera House," *Star Tribune* (Minneapolis), June 14, 1867, 4.
9. James Benjamin "J. B." McGibney (1835–1905), a relative newcomer to Minneapolis, arrived in the city around 1864. He, his wife, and their many children (thirteen total), all singers and multi-instrumentalists, began touring as a performing family troupe sometime after 1870. They earned glowing reviews coast to coast, in Canada and overseas, and continued touring for over two decades. Their astounding success and proceeds from their concerts enabled them to purchase a custom-designed Pullman Palace train car for their travels. The coach eventually became their home on the road, and reputedly could accommodate the entire family ("Description of the McGibney Family Car," *Burlington* [VT] *Free Press*, July 8, 1891, 5). See also Bart J. Kowallis, "Magnificent McGibneys." http://urthgen.blogspot.com/2011/07/magnificent-mcgibneys.html.
10. Larger and more robust than its cousin, the melodeon, a pump organ still required the player to operate a system of bellows by continually and rhythmically depressing foot pedals. Burdett pump organs were manufactured in Chicago.
11. Louise Chapman, "First Fifty Years," 25.
12. *Star Tribune* (Minneapolis), November 15, 1868, 4. See also advertisement, *Star Tribune* (Minneapolis), November 10, 1868, 4.
13. For an excellent essay on the history of Pence Opera House and a diagram of the theater's floor space, see Donald Z. Woods, "Playhouse for Pioneers," 169–78.

14. For information about Beal (1833–ca. 1906), see Peter E. Palmquist and Thomas R. Kailbourn, *Pioneer Photographers*, 97–99; and an autobiographical passage contributed by Beal to the article "Minneapolitans Hold Reunion," *Star Tribune* (Minneapolis), April 10, 1904, 27.

15. *Star Tribune*, November 15, 1868, 4. See also "Beal's Photographic Studio," Minnesota Historical Society. http://www.placeography.org/index.php/Beal%27s_Photographic _Studio,_34_Washington_Avenue,_Minneapolis,_Minnesota_(Razed).

16. *Star Tribune* (Minneapolis), November 14, 1868, 4. "Bearded like pards" recalls William Shakespeare's phrase "bearded like a pard" from the monologue "All the world's a stage," *As You Like It*, Act II, Scene 7. The *Tribune*'s critic likened the excessive faux facial hair of the king's guards to a pard's fur. A pard was a terrifying, mythological, leopard-like feline known for its aggressive temperament and (oftentimes) shaggy coat.

17. *Daily Rocky Mountain News* (Denver), February 1, 1874, 4. See also Paul Porchea, *Musical History of Colorado*, 28.

18. R. W., "Correspondent's Opinion," 4.

19. "The Oratorio of *Esther*," *Daily Rocky Mountain News*, April 11, 1874, 4. French natives Constant Benjamin Louis Duhem (1840–1933) and Victor Marie Duhem (1843–1931) ran a successful photography studio in the Denver region for many years. See the photograph of the Duhem Brothers' "Photo Art Gallery," Denver Public Library Digital Collections. https:// digital.denverlibrary.org/digital/collection/p15330coll22/id/26682.

20. "City and Vicinity: Local Briefs," *Daily Rocky Mountain News*, April 21, 1874, 4.

21. A regional newspaper advertised this production; see "Oakham," *Worcester* [MA] *Daily Spy*, August 26, 1891, 2.

22. The astrology and alchemy symbols on the Prophetess's gown include Infinity (or possibly Bismuth or Arsenic), Jupiter (or Tin), Aries (or Oxidation), Venus (or Copper), Sublimation, and Salt Armoniack.

23. "A Grand Affair," *Lake County Independent* (Libertyville, IL), April 3, 1896, 1. Review courtesy of the Liberty-Mundelein Historical Society, Libertyville, IL. In addition to its principle function as a place of worship, the ecumenical Union Church provided the community with an assembly space for local nonreligious gatherings; see Jenny Barry, "Stitches in Time." https://shelflife.cooklib.org/2018/08/24/stitches-in-time-discovering-libertyville-history -through-the-1889-union-church-signature-quilt-part-3/.

24. Mary Hays Marable and Alberta W. Constant, "When O.U. Was Very Young," 54.

25. *State Democrat* (Norman), April 15, 1897, 1.

26. *Peoples Voice* (Norman), April 16, 1897, 5.

27. *Territorial Topic* (Norman), March 5, 1897, 8.

28. Ibid.

29. "*Queen Esther*: The Greatest Cantata of the Ages," *Democrat-Topic* (Norman) April 30, 1897, 1. For a useful summary of events connected with the influx of thousands of settlers into Oklahoma, see Stan Hoig, "Land Run of 1889." https://www.okhistory.org/publications /enc/entry.php?entry=LA014.

30. *Peoples Voice* (Norman), April 16, 1897, 5.

31. "Queen Esther: The Greatest Cantata of the Ages," *Democrat-Topic*, April 30, 1897, 1.

32. C[arlton] Ross Hume [1878–1960], "Messages and Memories," 44–45. As Hume stated, this photograph appeared in a local newspaper in 1897; it was reprinted in the *Daily Oklahoman*, February 18, 1990 (special retrospective issue), 217.

33. In his directions for staging, Seager recommended casting "a bright child of five or six years for the part of 'Ida,' child of Haman and Zeresh." Keach had Seager's directions reprinted in his edition.

34. Information about Thorne found in Doris Karren Burton, *Leo Thorne's Story*. Thorne (1883-1969) operated a photography studio in Vernal and left behind thousands of images. An avid collector of Native American artifacts, Thorne bequeathed the bulk of his collection to Vernal's Western Heritage Museum where it is still on permanent exhibit.

35. Sue Ruple Watson, "How Vernal's Library Began," unpublished memoir, Uintah [UT] Public Library; Sue Ruple Watson, "Local Historian Gives Story," 8. Watson (1892-1992) sang as a chorister in this production; at the time she was fourteen or fifteen years old.

36. Watson, "Local Historian Gives Story," 8.

37. Watson, Ibid.

38. Watson, Ibid.

39. Watson, Ibid.

40. Watson, Ibid.

41. *Vernal Express*, October 27, 1906, 4.

42. Watson, "Local Historian Gives Story," 8. For anecdotes about Jacob R. Workman (1838-1912), see "'Uncle' Jake Workman Dead," *Vernal Express*, March 12, 1912, 1, 4; Thelma Chidester Anderson, *Workman Family History*, 245-46.

43. "Queen Esther Cantata a Great Success," *Valley City* [ND] *Times-Record*, February 11, 1911. A copy of this clipping was made available to me courtesy of the Barnes County Historical Society, Valley City, ND. The printed program for this performance, also held by the Barnes County Historical Society, indicates that Keach's edition of *Esther* was used as the cast included a Beggar, a Persian Princess, and a Median Princess.

44. "Gave Good Performance," *Times Dispatch* (Richmond, VA), June 17, 1911, 7. German-born violinist John H. Borjes (d. 1933) studied at Leipzig Conservatory prior to emigrating to the United States. Frank Richard Hufty (1870-1944) studied voice in London and was at one time affiliated with the San Carlo Opera Company.

45. Foster (1857-1935), a prolific photographer, left behind some 30,000 glass negatives depicting scenes in Virginia, including the photographs shown here. For information on Foster, see Sara B. Bears and Patricia D. Thompson, "Eye of a Master," 641-66.

46. [Washington, DC] *Herald*, October 15, 1911, 5.

47. Quotes in this paragraph taken from these sources: *Los Angeles Herald*, October 14, 1911, Part II, 3; "Elaborate Production of Queen Esther," *Monrovia* [CA] *Daily News*, October 21, 1911, 1; "Cantata *Esther, the Beautiful Queen* Is Presented to Aid Parent-Teachers," *Los Angeles Herald*, October 27, 1911, 12; "Children Sing, Win Plaudits: Cantata of Queen Esther," *Los Angeles Times*, October 27, 1911, 16; "Several Hundred Pupils of Los Angeles Public Schools Make Up Harmonious Chorus in Big Production at Auditorium," *Los Angeles Herald*, October 27, 1911, 12.

48. Program and *Playbill*, 1912, Clarence Stevenson Photograph Collection, J. Willard Marriott Library, University of Utah, Salt Lake City, UT, P0718 os#2.

49. *Carbon County News* (Price, UT), February 9, 1912, 3. John Anthon Hendrickson (1860-1940), born in Norway, ran a successful knitting and weaving business.

50. "Dramatic Cantata Excellently Presented," *Reedley* [CA] *Exponent*, February 8, 1917; clipping made available to me by the Reedley Historical Society.

51. In addition to teaching music in the Reedley area schools, Lewis William Harvey (1862-1929) was a church choir director, organist, pianist, and occasional composer; see "Harvey Funeral Is Conducted at Redlands Cortner Chapel," *San Bernardino Valley Sun*, March 30, 1929, 14.

52. "New City Park Named 'C. F. Mueller Park,'" *Reedley Exponent*, December 18, 1963, 1. For more on Mueller, see Gus Reimer, "Armchair Ramblings," 4. Christian Frederick

Mueller (1881–1972), a German native, studied at Leipzig Conservatory before immigrating to the United States.

53. Publicity about performances of *Esther* by the Battle Creek Academy Players can be found in these sources: *Battle Creek* [MI] *Moon Journal*, July 8, 1922, 3; *Battle Creek Moon Journal*, November 10, 1922, 8; *Battle Creek Enquirer*, November 13, 1922, 6; *Battle Creek Enquirer and the Evening News*, December 27, 1922, 5; *Battle Creek Enquirer and the Evening News*, January 1, 1923, 69; *Adventist Heritage* 15, no. 3 (Winter 1993): 45. For more about the career of Serns, see "Mahlon Serns Dies," *Battle Creek Enquirer and News*, July 8, 1957, 4.

54. For more on Dr. John H. Kellogg (1852–1943) and his Battle Creek Sanitarium, consulted for this discussion, see Brian C. Wilson, *Dr. John Kellogg*; John H. Kellogg, *Battle Creek Sanitarium System*.

55. "The Advent of a New American Graphic Satirist: Hill's Pictorial Revelation of New York," *Current Opinion* 61, no. 6 (December 1916): 414–15; Helen M. Staunton, "Average Joe, Jane Satirized by Hill," 16.

56. "W. E. Hill Retires after 40 Years of Cartooning Just Plain Folks for the Sunday Papers," *Daily News* (New York), August 21, 1960, 703.

57. Bill Griffith, "W. E. Hill," 69.

58. Accessorized for comfort rather than strict adherence to sitting decorum, "Turkish cozy corners" featured such Orientalist furniture designs as the divan and ottoman. Their overstuffed upholstery and puffy pillows lent themselves to more casual lounging, conversation, and entertainment. Other accouterments might include exotic vases, oversized floral arrangements, luxurious fringes, and prints of Oriental scenes adorning the walls; see Gülen Çevik, "American Style," 367–85.

Chapter Seven: *Esther and Minorities*

1. Lawrence W. Levine, *Black Culture*, 23, 32–33, 37, 50–52, 158.

2. Albert J. Raboteau, *Fire in the Bones*, 42–44; Charles B. Copher, "Black Presence," 146–64.

3. "Address to the Colored People of North Carolina," December 19, 1870. https://docsouth.unc.edu/nc/address/address.html. For a comprehensive analysis of this address consulted for this discussion, see Matthew Harper, *End of Days*, 45–64.

4. Francis James Grimké, *Gideon Bands*, 17–18.

5. Sidnie Ann White, "Esther: A Feminine Model," 166.

6. Evelyn Brooks Higginbotham, *Righteous Discontent*, 143. Also consulted for this discussion: Erica Brown, "Finding Her Voice," 75–89 and Ariel Clark Silver, "Palace of Shushan," 63–74.

7. Sources of information about African trickster figures consulted for this discussion include Henry Louis Gates Jr., *Signifying Monkey*, 5–6, 20–22; Levine, *Black Culture*, 102–33; John W. Roberts, *Trickster to Badman*, 44–45; Jon Michael Spencer, *Theological Music*, 120–23.

8. Kevin Young, *Gray Album*, 25.

9. For examples of Stewart's and Truth's Esther-inspired rhetoric, see, Marilyn Richardson, ed., *Maria W. Stewart*, 68–70; Nell Irvin Painter, *Sojourner Truth*, 135–36; *Proceedings of the Woman's Rights Convention Held at the Broadway Tabernacle* (New York: Fowles and Wells, 1853), 76–77. https://documents.alexanderstreet.com/d/1004734278.

For other useful references to the Book of Esther as an inspiration for African American women's activism and rhetoric and as a source of empowering imagery, see Susan Zaeske, "Unveiling Esther," 193–220; Jacquelyn Grant, "Faithful Resistance," 204–8.

10. E. Azalia Hackley, *Colored Girl Beautiful*, 11, 30–31.

11. Henri Bergson, *Laughter*, 197, 202.

12. Kenneth M. Craig Jr., *Reading Esther*, 150–55.

13. Jacqueline Bussie, *Laughter of the Oppressed*, 183–93.

14. Bradbury did not supply music for these passages from the Book of Esther: 2:16–18, 3:1–2, 3:12–15, 5:1–3, 6:1–2, 6:14, and 7:1.

15. Raboteau, *Fire in the Bones*, 141–51; Geneva Smitherman, *Talkin' and Testifyin'*, 134–41; Jon Michael Spencer, *Sacred Symphony*, 12–16; Cleophus James LaRue, *Heart of Black Preaching*, 9–13.

16. Raboteau, *Fire in the Bones*, 143–47.

17. Wilson's comments about African American performance practices were culled from these sources, all published by him: "Black American Composer," 33–36; "Black Music," 1–22; "Composition," 43–51; "Heterogeneous Sound," 327–40; "'It Don't Mean a Thing,'" 153–68; and "Significance," 3–22.

18. Smitherman, *Talkin' and Testifyin'*, 134–41.

19. However, the earliest known performance of *Esther* by Black singers occurred in New York City at the fashionable City Assembly Rooms. On June 9, 1862, students at the city's Colored Grammar School No. 2 sang with local soloists in a production to benefit the Colored Orphan Asylum. Regional singers "of considerable merit" assumed most of the principal roles, with accompaniment provided by a pianist and a violinist. The success of this performance prompted repeated presentations later in June 1862 to raise funds for sick and wounded Civil War soldiers. Unfortunately, these performances attracted very little publicity; see *New York Times*, June 7, 1862, 7; "Grand Oratorio," *New York Times*, June 30, 1862, 7; "A Colored Concert for the Wounded," *Evening Post* (New York), July 1, 1862, 2; "A Concert for the Wounded," *National Anti-Slavery Standard* (New York), July 19, 1862, 3. The Colored Orphan Asylum burned to the ground only a year after these *Esther* performances, the victim of a horrific racially motivated riot; see Leslie M. Harris, *Shadows of Slavery*, 279–88; Sarah Mulhall Adelman, "'Permitted to Proceed Unmolested.'" http://commonplace.online/article/permitted-to-proceed-unmolested-childhood-and-race-in-the-burning-of-the-colored-orphan-asylum/.

20. Porter left Fisk in 1868 to begin teaching in a rural school some twenty-five miles away in Murfreesboro, Tennessee. With the exception of Porter, the original Jubilee Singers were all students at Fisk University in 1871.

21. Porter, quoted in W. Barton Beatty, "Maggie Porter-Cole," 5.

22. Randall C. Bailey, "Beyond Identification," 165–84; Cain Hope Felder, *Troubling Biblical Waters*, 12, 32–36.

23. Beatty, "Maggie Porter-Cole," 5.

24. "Tennessee: Status of Colored Citizens," *New York Tribune*, March 3, 1871, 5.

25. "The Cantata of Esther," *New National Era* (Washington, DC), March 23, 1871, 3.

26. Adam Knight Spence (1831–1900), letter to Elizabeth Spence, March 13, 1871. American Missionary Association Archives, Amistad Research Center, Tulane University, New Orleans, LA.

27. "Second Concert of the Fisk University Pupils," *Memphis Daily Avalanche*, June 19, 1871, n.p.

28. Toni P. Anderson, *Tell Them We Are Singing for Jesus*, 100, 184; Andrew Ward, *Dark Midnight*, 118–19.

29. "How One Thing Brings on Another," *People's Advocate*, December 2, 1881, 2. See also *People's Advocate*, February 5, 1881, 2.

30. For more about Tilghman, see Juanita Karpf, "Early Years," 143–68; Juanita Karpf, "'As with Words of Fire,'" 603–32.

31. "Musical Progress of the Colored People," *Commercial Appeal* (Memphis, TN), May 29, 1881, 2.

32. *Evening Star* (Washington, DC), November 22, 23, and 25, 1881.

33. "Queen Esther," *Cincinnati Enquirer*, May 6, 1881, 1; "*Esther*: Brilliant Production of the Cantata by the Queen City Choral Society," *Cincinnati Commercial Tribune*, May 7, 1881, 2.

34. Jno (John) B. Jeffery, *Jno. [John] B. Jeffery's Guide and Directory*, 21.

35. *People's Advocate*, December 3, 1881, 3.

36. *People's Advocate*, December 3, 1881, 2. We should recall that Bradbury scored the number "Do I Wake, or Am I Dreaming?" as a quartet sung by Mordecai, Zeresh, Hegai, and the Queen's First Maid of Honor. In Tilghman's production, however, this number was performed as a duet. In 1873, Washington, DC, barber William T. Benjamin (1846–1907) helped establish Washington's Colored American Opera Company. Richard W. Tompkins (1846–1916), a social activist and member of the Fifteenth Street Presbyterian Church, worked at DC's Freedmen's Bank and sang tenor roles with the Colored American Opera Company.

37. Juanita Karpf, "Music in Montgomery's African-American Community," 112–39.

38. *Montgomery Advertiser*, May 16, 1886, 2.

39. John B. Jeffrey, *Jno. [John] B. Jeffery's Guide and Directory*, 3.

40. Quoted in Irvine Garland Penn, *Afro-American Press*, 402. The original newspaper source for this quote has not been located.

41. *Montgomery Advertiser*, May 19, 1886, 5.

42. *Huntsville Gazette*, May 29, 1886, 3.

43. "The Cantata of Queen Esther," *Southern Workman* 28, no. 6 (June 1889): 1.

44. "To Aid Hampton Institute: The Cantata of *Esther* to Be Sung at Daly's Theatre," *New York Daily Tribune*, January 16, 1893, 2; "The Fund for Hampton," *New York Times*, January 16, 1893, 4; "The Hampton Institute: An Effort Is Being Made to Raise a Fund for Scholarships," *New York Times*, January 11, 1893, 10; "The Hampton Meetings," *Southern Workman* (February 1893): 26; Francis Greenwood Peabody, *Education for Life*, 215; and Edith Armstrong Talbot, *Samuel Chapman Armstrong*, 291–95. Unfortunately, no review of the Singers' performance of *Esther* in Commonwealth Hall, East Orange, NJ, on January 20, 1893, has been located.

45. "Hampton Meetings."

46. Washington (1856–1915), a graduate of Hampton Institute, began his tenure as founding principal of Tuskegee Institute in 1881.

47. Quotations in this paragraph taken from "Cantata by the Hampton Singers," *New York Sun*, January 20, 1893, 7.

48. Joseph Francis Daly, *Life of Augustin Daly*, 88. Information about Augustin Daly in the present discussion was culled from this biography.

49. Box office journal, Daly's Theatre, 1893. Rare Book and Manuscript Library, Columbia University, New York.

50. Emily Putnam shared common philanthropic interests with her husband, George Havan Putnam (1844–1930), president of the New York publishing giant Putnam and Sons.

51. "An Appeal for Hampton: The Ladies Committee at Work to Raise Funds," *New York Times*, March 22, 1892, 9. In the early twentieth century, Fanny Villard perpetuated her family's legacy of commitment to racial justice by becoming a founding member of W. E. B. Du Bois's National Association for the Advancement of Colored People.

52. "A Cantata by the Hampton Singers"; "Hampton Meetings." For Charles Dudley Warner's evaluation of Booker T. Washington and his philosophy, see Warner, "Education of the Negro," 1–14.

53. Edith Armstrong, "Inside View of the Cantata," 36. The stage Armstrong described was left in place after performances of Augustin Daly's revival of Richard Brinsley Sheridan's *School for Scandal* (1777); see Daly, *Life of Augustin Daly*, 564.

54. Box office journal, Daly's Theatre, 1893. Information about Daly's Theatre culled from Edward Augustus Dithmar, *Memories of Daly's Theatres*. According to email communication with Jennifer B. Lee (Rare Book and Manuscript Library, Columbia University, New York), the box office receipts for plays at Daly's Theatre around this time period usually ranged from $400 to $1,000 per event (personal email correspondence). The Hampton performance was listed in "To-Day's Doings," *New York Times*, January 19, 1893, 4.

55. Like the Fisk Jubilee Singers, the Hampton Singers augmented their touring ensemble with additional students who sang in the choruses.

56. "A Cantata by the Hampton Students," *Sun*.

57. All quotations in the foregoing discussion from Charles Dudley Warner, "Editor's Study" (1893), 800–803. Warner commented on this performance again the following year; see "Editor's Study," 800–803.

58. Ronald Radano remarks on the frequent reluctance, or inability, of white critics to write informed reviews of African American performers during the nineteenth century; see Radano, *Lying Up a Nation*, 186–89, 261–62.

59. "Building Our Legacy," Beth Eden Baptist Church. https://www.betheden.com/general-1.

60. For information about the history of Oakwood College generally and the institution's fundraising campaigns and accreditation initiatives more specifically, see Holly Fisher, "Oakwood College," 110–25; "Oakwood College Special," *The North American Informant* (Washington, DC) 14, no. 76 (August 1960), entire issue; Lela Gooding, "Pierre-Louis, Joni Mae." https://encyclopedia.adventist.org/article?id=9FW3.

61. Moran Hall, an instructional and office facility and for a time, the campus chapel, was largely built by student labor. In 1940, construction on the building began with students gathering rocks from nearby slopes for the structure's striking exterior walls. For their efforts, they received tuition waivers; see Leslie N. Pollard, Samuel London, Mervyn A. Warren et al., "Oakwood University." https://encyclopedia.adventist.org/article?id=AFWD.

62. Su Zheng, *Claiming Diaspora*, 89–90.

63. Ibid., 660.

64. Fenggang Yang, *Chinese Christians in America*, 90–91, 95–100, 106–16, 132–34, 163–200.

65. "Opera in Martinez—Strong Tradition for 123 Years." https://patch.com/california/martinez/bp--opera-in-martinez-strong-tradition-for-123-years.

66. Appreciation is extended to Menglin Gao, who provided this translation.

67. Sources regarding Chinese male actresses and gender roles more generally, consulted for this discussion, include Will Irwin, "Drama in Chinatown," 857–58, 862–63; Louis Joseph Beck, *New York's Chinatown*, 94; Siu Lueng Li, *Cross-Dressing in Chinese Opera*, 29–36; Zheng, *Claiming Diaspora*, 84–90; and Nancy Yunhwa Rao, *Chinatown Opera Theater*, 236–39.

68. Gary Y. Okihiro, *Margins and Mainstreams*, 66–92. By "staged gender roles," I refer here specifically to male portrayals of females in Chinese opera and not to "travesti" or "trouser" roles found in some classical European operas. One of the most famous of these is the role of Cherubino (Mozart, *Marriage of Figaro*), with a young male played by a female singer.

69. "Chinese Singers to Give *Cantata Esther*," *Oakland Tribune*, April 24, 1932, 20; "Chinese Cast Giving Benefit Opera Tonight," *San Francisco Call Bulletin*, April 30, 1932, 14; "Chinese Will Sing in Opera," *Oakland Tribune*, May 17, 1932, 18.

70. A full-length version of this photograph appeared in the *San Francisco Chronicle*, April 26, 1932, 4. However, the image shown here is of better quality than the newspaper illustration, albeit cropped toward the bottom.

71. "The Opera *Queen Esther*," *San Francisco Police and Peace Officers' Journal of the State of California* 10, no. 3 (March 1932): 22.

72. *Republic of China Report of the National Flood Relief Commission* (Shanghai: N.p., 1933): i–iii, 2–3; George G. Stroebe, "Great Central China Flood," 667–79.

73. Donald A. Jordan, *China's Trial by Fire*, 192–200.

74. Ulysses Mejia Carbajal, "Music's Role," 7. https://www.feu-alumni.com/attachment/EM12012.pdf. "Combined Choir to Sing Cantata," *Los Angeles Times*, November 5, 1959, B10.

75. "Choir to Sing at Loma Linda," *Redlands* [CA] *Daily Facts*, November 12, 1959, 4.

76. Carbajal, 5–7. Another Seventh-Day Adventist performance of *Esther*, directed by Singapore native Robert Cheng-Hai Tan (1936–2014) took place in Fortuna, California, in 1969. In this production, Tan, respected regionally as a pianist and choir director, sang the role of Haman. No other information about this performance has been located; see "Tan's Final Musical Production Next Sunday Evening [in] Fortuna," *Times Standard* (Eureka, California), May 15, 1969, 15. See also "Robert Cheng-Hai Tan." http://www.iamaonline.com/Bio/Robert_Tan.htm.

77. Bill V. Mullen, *Afro-Orientalism*, xi–xliv.

78. Frederick Douglass, "Our Composite Nationality," 4:253–54.

Chapter Eight: An International Megahit

1. *New York Musical Pioneer and Choristers' Budget* 4, no. 7 (April 1, 1859): 103.

2. Mel Robertson, "A Burford Landmark–What Next?" *Burford* [Ontario, Canada] *Advance*, July 14, 1982, 7; "Burford," *Brantford* [Ontario] *Weekly Expositor*, June 24, 1870, 2; "Burford Musical Convention," *Brantford Weekly Expositor*, July 8, 1870, 2.

3. "Burford," *Brantford Weekly Expositor*, July 8, 1870, 2.

4. "Concert in City Hall, the Cantata of *Esther, the Beautiful Queen*," program, April 3, 1872, Carleton, New Brunswick, Canada. https://HathiTrust.org.

5. "The Oratorio of Esther," *Acton* [Ontario, Canada] *Free Press*, June 18, 1889, 3.

6. Herbert Kent, "Music Chronicles of Early Times," *Victoria* [British Columbia, Canada] *Daily Times*, December 7, 1918, 13; Herbert Kent, "Musical Chronicles of Early Times," *Victoria Daily Times*, December 28, 1918, 8; "Noted Musical Figure Passes," *Victoria Daily Times*, August 1, 1923, 7 (article about Emil Pferdner [1856–1923]); "City Musical Pioneer Dies," *Times Colonist* (Victoria, British Columbia), December 6, 1958, 11 (article about Herbert Kent [1862–1958]).

7. "Cantata of Queen Esther," *Victoria Daily Colonist*, March 15, 1903, 5.

8. *Victoria Daily Times*, March 21, 1903, 7.

9. *Winnipeg Tribune*, May 17, 1900, 6, 7.

10. "The Oratorio of *Esther, the Beautiful Queen*," *Royal Gazette* (Hamilton, Bermuda), October 18, 1870, 2.

11. "Concert," *Royal Gazette*, February 4, 1873, 2.

12. "Sacred Concert at the Mechanics Hall, Hamilton," *Royal Gazette* (Hamilton), July 27, 1880, 2.

13. Ibid.

14. "National Choir of Antigua & Barbuda Celebrates 21 Years of Singing," *Antigua Daily Observer* (St. Johns), July 7, 2006, n.p.; email correspondence with Paul Cort, a choral director in Antigua and Barbuda and past conductor of the National Choir, March 21, 2021.

15. "Popular Cantatas," *Musical Times and Singing-Class Circular*, 20 (March 1, 1879): 170.

16. "American Composers of the Front Rank," *Music* 2 (September 1892): 491.

17. H. Augustine Simcoe, *Sullivan vs. Critic*, 117.

18. Sarah Kaufmann, "'Easy, Cheap and True': Tonic Sol-fa in Print." 8–23.

19. The information on the tonic sol-fa system presented here was culled from these sources: Charles E. McGuire, *Music and Victorian Philanthropy*, 1–29; Bernarr Rainbow, "Tonic Sol-fa," *Grove Music Online*. https://doi-org.ezproxy.oberlin.edu/10.1093/gmo/9781561592630.article.28124. H. Watkins Shaw, "The Musical Teaching of John Curwen"; John Curwen, *Teacher's Manual*, 377–86.

20. Curwen, *Teacher's Manual*, 374.

21. Curwen, *Teacher's Manual*, 376; Lowell Mason and George James Webb, eds. *Vocalist*. In addition to listing Mason, Hastings, Bradbury, Root, and Seward, Curwen also mentions these respected educators and members of Mason's circle: George James Webb (1803–1887) and Isaac Baker Woodbury (1818–1858).

22. Curwen, *Teacher's Manual*, 386.

23. "Tonic Sol-Fa Choral Society," *Staffordshire Advertiser*, October 1, 1870, 4.

24. "Nicolson Street Church Musical Association," *Scotsman* (Edinburgh, Scotland), June 4, 1875, 4.

25. "Concert at the Philharmonic Hall," *Hampshire* [England] *Advertiser*, December 15, 1877, 5–6. Ira D. Sankey (1840–1908) and Dwight L. Moody (1837–1899) pioneered the subgenre of gospel hymns. The French word "réchauffé" translates approximately to "a rehash, or a dish of warmed-up food left over from a previous meal." In the early 1840s, Edwin Pearce Christy organized his blackface troupe, the Christy Minstrels, a group that helped popularize the songs of Stephen Foster.

26. James Duff Brown, *British Musical Biography*, 145–46. Other than these few facts, Fisher remains quite obscure.

27. Henry Fisher, ed., *Esther, the Beautiful Queen* (London: Tonic Sol-fa Agency, 1878).

28. Barbara Owen, "Reed Organ," *Grove Music Online*. https://doi-org.ezproxy.oberlin.edu/10.1093/gmo/9781561592630.article.A2252280. Barbara Owen and Alistair Dick. "Harmonium," *Grove Music Online*. https://doi-org.ezproxy.oberlin.edu/10.1093/gmo/9781561592630.article.12395. Although the harmonium and the melodeon produce sound by means of vibrating reeds set into motion by air currents, there were two main differences between them. First, the harmonium used a bellows system that forced air to be blown over the reeds, whereas the melodeon's mechanism made use of a vacuum system that drew in air to vibrate the reeds. Second, the harmonium, capable of more expression and tone color than US cabinet organs, included a tremolo stop and a pulsating vibrato-like sound in its pallet of registers and timbral possibilities.

29. H[enry] F[isher], "Notice to the Player," in *Esther, the Beautiful Queen*, ed. Henry Fisher, 4. *Grand Jeu* is the loudest volume most harmoniums are capable of producing.

30. Ghanaian Methodist Fellowship UK. https://gmfuk.org.

31. Dawson Burns, "Bands of Hope," 43–62; Lillian Lewis Shiman, "The Band of Hope Movement: Respectable Recreation for Working-Class Children," *Victorian Studies*, 17, no. 1 (September 1973): 49–74. Other useful sources about the Band of Hope include James B. Dunn, *Band of Hope Manual*; George Henry Graham, *Origin of the Band of Hope Movement*; Frederick Sherlock, *Ann Jane Carlile*.

32. Dunn, *Band of Hope Manual*, 6.

33. John William Kirton, *Water Drinkers of the Bible*, 107.

34. R. W. Seager, "Directions for Organization, Costuming, and Etc.," *Esther, the Beautiful Queen*.

35. *Brisbane* [Australia] *Courier*, November 22, 1882, 5.

36. "Esther," *Camperdown* [New South Wales] *Chronicle*, July 2, 1887, 3.

37. "Hospital Benefit," *Barrier Miner* (Broken Hill, New South Wales), March 3, 1892, 2.

38. "Esther, the Beautiful Queen," *Euroa Advertiser*, October 27, 1893, 2.

39. "Cantata in Character," *Brisbane Courier*, May 16, 1894, 6.

40. "The Cantata Esther," *Gippsland Times*, December 31, 1896, 3.

41. For example, *Albany* [Australia] *Advertiser*, April 25, 1940, 6; *West Australian* (Perth), November 22, 1941, 1.

42. "Entertainment at Mosgiel," *Otago Daily Times* May 19, 1883, 2. See also Robin S. Stevens, "Missionaries, Music and Method," 1–19.

43. *Otago Daily Times* August 23, 1884, 2.

44. "Sacred Cantata, *Esther, the Beautiful Queen*," *Timaru Herald*, July 27, 1885, 3. See also *Timaru Herald*, July 29, 1885, 3.

45. "Local and General," *Star* (Canterbury), November 27, 1885, 3.

46. *Auckland* [New Zealand] *Star*, November 10, 1886, 2.

47. *Auckland Star*, November 16, 1886, 1.

48. "The Cantata of Esther," *Taranaki Herald*, September 17, 1894, 2.

49. "Life at Fulton School," *Australasian Record* 50, no. 18 (May 6, 1946): 5; Henry E. McMahon, "Fulton Missionary School," 3; Henry E. McMahon, "High Praise for *Esther*," 5, 8.

50. Reuben E. Hare, "Fijian Choir," 17.

51. "Esther," *Singapore Free Press and Mercantile Advertiser*, May 5, 1899, 3; "Esther," *Singapore Free Press and Mercantile Advertiser*, May 6, 1899, 2; "Presbyterian Church Esther," *Singapore Free Press and Mercantile Advertiser*, May 11, 1899, 8; "A Sacred Cantata," *Straits Budget* (Singapore), May 12, 1899, 8.

52. *Straits Times* (Singapore), July 31, 1928, 10; "Queen Esther: Famous Cantata at the Malaysian Union Seminary," *Malaya Tribune* (Singapore), July 30, 1928, 7.

53. Hon. Jerry Lewis, "Tribute to Minnie Iverson-Wood," E1009. https://www.govinfo.gov/content/pkg/CRECB-2003-pt9/html/CRECB-2003-pt9-Pg12718.htm. "Wood Taught Music around the World," *Redlands* [CA] *Daily Facts*, March 15, 2008, 1; "Minnie Iverson-Wood," *San Bernardino Sun*, March 13, 2008, n.p.

54. For example, see "Choir to Sing *Esther* Cantata," *Singapore Standard*, November 3, 1951, 10.

55. "Cantata for TB Fund," *Straits Times*, November 29, 1951, 7.

56. (Mrs.) Lyle C. Wilcox (Hazel Pearl Wilcox), "Malayan Union Seminary," 6.

57. "85-Voice Choir," *Straits Times*, October 31, 1951, 4. See also "Crowds Hear Cantata," *Straits Times*, November 5, 1951, 7; Helen Bond, "Repeat Performance of Cantata," 3.

58. Ulysses M. Carbajal, "Music's Role," 5. https://www.feu-alumni.com/attachment/EM12012.pdf.

59. Charles McGuire, *Music and Victorian Philanthropy*, 61–67, 81–97; Robin S. Stevens, "Tonic Sol-fa: An Exogenous Aspect," 39. See also Robin S. Stevens, "'Easy, cheap and true'"; Robin S. Stevens, "Tonic Sol-fa in Asian," 52–76; Robin S. Stevens, "A System." https://music-ed.net/music-in-action/index_htm_files/MiA_2008_6-1.pdf. Sarah E. Taylor, "'Easy, cheap and true': Tonic Sol-fa in Print," 8–23.

60. "Cape Town [South Africa]," *Musical Times and Singing-Class Circular* 16 (February 1, 1875): 788.

61. Stevens, "Tonic Sol-fa: An Exogenous Aspect," 40.

62. Erwin H. Richards, "Africa," 20–23.

63. Kofi Ermeleh Agovi, "Origin of Literary Theatre," 32, 61, 63.

64. "Life History of the Late Major Courage Quashigah," March 6, 2010. https://www.myjoyonline.com/the-life-history-of-the-late-major-courage-quashigah/.

65. John T. Tucker, *Old Ways*, 84.

66. Frank Knight Sanders, "Impressions of the Angola Jubilee," 331–33.

67. Mrs. Douglas Smith (Allegra Doyle Smith), untitled article, 333–34.

68. Marjorie Miller, "The Angola Jubilee," typewritten essay, box 3, folder 18, Lawrence Henderson Papers, Milne Special Collections and Archives Division, University System of New Hampshire, Durham, NH.

69. Elizabeth Scattergood Chalmers, "Music at the Jubilee," 335–38. Missionary, explorer, and physician Dr. David Livingstone (1813–1873) referenced the Atlantic slave trade and its horrific effects on Africans in his remark about the "open sore of the world"; see Tim Zeal, *Livingstone*, 356. The Livingstone quote first appeared in his article, "Doctor Livingstone: The Explorer's Story of the Slave Trade in Eastern Africa," *New York Herald*, July 27, 1872, 7.

Epilogue

1. William B. Bradbury, "Tune Authorship," 100.
2. William B. Bradbury, "Music for the People," 3.
3. "Musical Gossip," *New York Musical Review and Gazette* 10, no. 3 (February 5, 1859): 49.
4. John Curwen, quoted in George F. Root, *Story of a Musical Life*, 122.
5. Theodore F. Seward, "Sketches of American Composers: William B. Bradbury (concluded)," 57–58.
6. Edward Ellsworth Hipsher, *American Opera*, 79–80.
7. William B. Bradbury, "Learning to Sing," 20.
8. Arthur Farwell, "Community Music-Drama," 418. To be sure, when Farwell (1872–1952) made this pronouncement, he was reflecting on the rising popularity of pageantry in the United States, a movement in which he exerted considerable influence and leadership. In addition to his contributions to the American Pageantry Movement, Farwell composed instrumental and vocal music, published numerous essays, supported universal music education, and championed the music of Native Americans.
9. Christopher Small, *Musicking*, 8–10.
10. Christopher Small, *Music of the Common Tongue*, 102.

BIBLIOGRAPHY

Adelman, Sarah Mulhall. "'Permitted to Proceed Unmolested': Childhood and Race in the Burning of the Colored Orphan Asylum," *Common Place: The Journal of Early American Life*. http://commonplace.online/article/permitted-to-proceed-unmolested-childhood-and-race-in-the-burning-of-the-colored-orphan-asylum/.

Agovi, Kofi Ermeleh. "The Origin of Literary Theatre in Colonial Ghana, 1920–57," *Research Review* 6, no. 1 (1990): 1–23.

Aldrich, Elizabeth. *From the Ballroom to Hell: Grace and Folly in Nineteenth-Century Dance*. Evanston, IL: Northwestern University Press, 1991.

Anderson, Thelma Chidester. *Workman Family History*. Salt Lake City: By the author, 1962.

Anderson, Toni P. *Tell Them We Are Singing for Jesus: The Original Fisk Jubilee Singers and Christian Reconstruction, 1871–78*. Macon, GA: Mercer University Press, 2009.

Arp, Bill (pseud. of Charles Henry Smith). "Bill Arp's Philosophy," *Intelligencer* (Anderson, SC) April 3, 1890, 1.

Bailey, Randall C. "Beyond Identification: The Use of Africans in Old Testament Poetry and Narratives." In *Stony the Road We Trod: African American Biblical Interpretation*, Cain Hope Felder, ed. Minneapolis: Fortress Press, 1991, 165–84.

Barry, Jenny. "Stitches in Time: Discovering Libertyville History through the 1889 Union Church Signature Quilt," June 30, 2018. https://shelflife.cooklib.org/2018/08/24/stitches-in-time-discovering-libertyville-history-through-the-1889-union-church-signature-quilt-part-3/.

Bateman, Newton, Paul Selby, and David McCulloch, eds., *Historical Encyclopedia of Illinois and History of Peoria County*. Chicago and Peoria: Munsell, 1902.

Bears, Sara B., and Patricia D. Thompson. "The Eye of a Master: Foster's View of Richmond, 1900–1925," *Virginia Magazine of History and Biography* 98, no. 4 (October 1990): 641–66.

Beatty, W. Barton. "Maggie Porter-Cole," *Fisk University News* 5 (December 1939): 5, 8.

Beck, Louis Joseph. *New York's Chinatown*. New York: Bohemia, 1898.

Bergson, Henri. *Laughter: An Essay on the Meaning of the Comic*. Trans. Cloudesley Brereton and Fred Rothwell. New York: Macmillan, 1912.

Bial, Henry. *Playing God: The Bible on the Broadway Stage*. Ann Arbor: University of Michigan Press, 2015.

Bill, Ledyard. *Minnesota, Its Character and Climate*. New York: Wood and Holbrook, 1871.

Blair, Judson. *"Tune-Books" in America, 1712–1865*. Fort Worth: N.p., 1963.

Blue, Debbie. "Biblical Farce," *The Christian Century*, January 12, 2016. https://www.christiancentury.org/article/2015-12/biblical-farce.

Bond, Helen. "Repeat Performance of Cantata," *Far East Division Outlook* 38, no. 1 (January 1952): 3.

Bradbury, William B. *The Alpine Glee Singer: A Complete Collection of Secular and Social Music, Arranged in Four Vocal Parts for Choirs, Singing Classes and Musical Societies with a Full Course of Exercises for the Cultivation of the Voice and for Improvement in Musical Notation.* New York: Newman and Ivison, 1850.

Bradbury, William B. *Bradbury's Singing School for Ladies and Gentlemen.* New York: Mark H. Newman, 1844.

Bradbury, William B. "The Cantata of Esther," *New York Musical Review and Gazette* 11, no. 12 (April 9, 1860): 181.

Bradbury, William B. "Death of a Child," *New York Evangelist.* January 10, 1856, 4.

Bradbury, William B. *Esther, the Beautiful Queen.* Boston: Oliver Ditson, 1856.

Bradbury, William B. *Flora's Festival.* New York: Mark H. Newman, 1847.

Bradbury, William B. *Fresh Laurels.* New York: Biglow and Main, 1867.

Bradbury, William B. "Home Thoughts of the Musical Past, No. III," *New York Musical Review and Gazette* 10, no. 10 (May 15, 1858): 150.

Bradbury, William B. *The Jubilee.* New York: Mason Brothers, 1857.

Bradbury, William B. "Juvenile Oratorio," *New York Evangelist.* February 4, 1847, 4.

Bradbury, William B. "Learning to Sing," *New York Evangelist.* January 31, 1850, 20.

Bradbury, William B. "Lecture to Musical Students," *New York Musical Pioneer and Choristers' Budget* 4 (August 1, 1859): 165.

Bradbury, William B. "Mendelssohn," *Boston Evening Transcript.* December 14, 1847, 2.

Bradbury, William B. *The Metropolitan Glee Book.* New York: Newman and Ivison, 1849.

Bradbury, William B. "Musical Conventions—What Are They?" *New York Evangelist.* July 19, 1855, 116.

Bradbury, William B. *Musical Gems for School and Home.* New York: Newman and Ivison, 1852.

Bradbury, William B. "Music and Musicians in Europe, No. 1," *New York Evangelist.* November 25, 1847, 1.

Bradbury, William B. "Music and Musicians in Europe, No. 3: Mr. John Hullah and His Classes," *New York Evangelist.* May 11, 1848, 1.

Bradbury, William B. "Music and Musicians of Europe, No. 12: Music in the Schools," *New York Evangelist.* September 14, 1848, 1.

Bradbury, William B. "Music for the People," *Home Journal.* August 12, 1848: 3.

Bradbury, William B. "Note from Mr. Bradbury," in Thomas Hastings and William B. Bradbury, eds., *Psalmista.* New York: Mark H. Newman, 1851, 32.

Bradbury, William B. "Piano-forte Co-partnership," *New York Evangelist.* January 19, 1854, 12.

Bradbury, William B. "Rally 'Round the Flag." Boston: Oliver Ditson, 1862.

Bradbury, William B. *Singing Bird, or Progressive Music Reader.* New York: Ivison and Phinney, 1852.

Bradbury, William B. "The Singing School of Twenty Lessons: First Article," *New York Musical Pioneer and Choristers' Budget* 5 (October 1, 1859): 23.

Bradbury, William B. *The Social Singing Book.* New York: Mark H. Newman, 1844.

Bradbury, William B. "Tune Authorship," *Independent* (New York) June 23, 1853, 100.

Bradbury, William B. "Victory at Last." New York: Wm. B. Bradbury, 1865.

Bradbury, William B. "Vocal Music in Germany—How Taught," *Commercial Advertiser* (New York), January 18, 1850, 2.

Bradbury, William B. "Western Conventions," *New York Musical Review and Gazette* 7, no. 25 (December 13, 1856): 296.

Bradbury, William B., and Charles W. Sanders. *The Young Choir*. New York: Mark H. Newman, 1841.

Bradley, Ian C. *You've Got to Have a Dream: The Message of the Musical*. Louisville, KY: Westminster John Knox Press, 2004.

Brown, Erica. "Finding Her Voice: Black Female Empowerment and the Book of Esther," in Stuart W. Halpern, ed. *Esther in America: The Scroll's Interpretation in and Impact on America*. Jerusalem and New Milford, CT: Maggid Books, 2020, 75–89.

Brown, James Duff. *British Musical Biography: A Dictionary of Musical Artists, Authors and Composers, Born in Britain and Its Colonies*. Birmingham, England: S.S. Stratton, 1897.

Broyles, Michael. *Music of the Highest Class: Elitism and Populism in Antebellum Boston*. New Haven: Yale University Press, 1992.

Buckley, Frederick. "Kiss Me Quick and Go." New York: Firth, Pond & Co., 1856.

Buckley, James. *Buckley's Ethiopian Melodies*. New York: Philip J. Cozans, 1853.

Buckley, James Monroe. *Christians and the Theater*. New York: Nelson and Phillips, 1875.

Bumstead, Horace. "The Baccalaureate Sermon," *Bulletin of Atlanta University* (June 1902): 2–4.

Burns, Dawson. "Bands of Hope from Their Origin in 1847 to the Formation of the United Kingdom Band of Hope Union in 1855," *The Jubilee of the Band of Hope Movement*, Frederic Smith, ed. London: United Kingdom Band of Hope Union, 1897, 43–62.

Burton, Doris Karren. *Leo Thorne's Story*. Vernal, UT: Uintah County [UT] Library, 2005.

Bush, Frederic W. "The Book of Esther: *Opus non gratum* in the Christian Canon," *Bulletin for Biblical Research* 8 (1998): 39–54.

Bussie, Jacqueline. *The Laughter of the Oppressed: Ethical and Theological Resistance in Wiesel, Morrison, and Endo*. New York: T and T Clark International, 2007.

Cady, Chauncey Marvin. "Reminiscences of Wm. B. Bradbury," *Advance* (Chicago). January 23, 1868, 1.

C[ady], C[hauncey] M[arvin]. "Orient, LI [Long Island]," *New York Musical Review and Gazette* 7, no. 17 (August 23, 1856): 263.

Carbajal, Ulysses Mejia. "Music's Role in My Life through the Years," *Ectopic Murmurs* 23, no. 1 (January 2012): 4–13. https://feu-alumni.com/attachment/EM12012.pdf.

Carder, Polly H. *George F. Root, Civil War Songwriter*. Jefferson, NC: McFarland, 2008.

C.A.S. "Franklin, Mass.," *New York Musical Review and Gazette* 9, no. 13 (June 26, 1858): 198.

Çevik, Gülen. "American Style or Turkish Chair: The Triumph of Bodily Comfort," *Journal of Design History* 23, no. 4 (2010): 367–85.

Chalmers, Elizabeth Scattergood. "The Music at the Jubilee," *Missionary Herald* 126, no. 9 (September 1930): 335–38.

Chapman, Louise. "The First Fifty Years of Music in Minneapolis," *Star Tribune*. January 27, 1935, 25.

Cheney, Simeon Pease. *The American Singing Book*. Boston: White, Smith and Co., 1879.

Clarkson, Anna Howell. *A Beautiful Life and Its Associations*. New York: J. J. Little and Co., 1899.

Collier, Robert Laird. "A Preacher's Defense of the Drama and the Opera," *Daily Journal* (Wilmington, NC), May 18, 1870, 3.

Collier, Robert Laird. "The Theatre, the Opera, and the Church," in *Every-day Subjects in Sunday Sermons*. Boston: American Unitarian Association, 1872, 27–49.

Copher, Charles B. "The Black Presence in the Old Testament," in Cain Hope Felder, ed., *Stony the Road We Trod: African American Biblical Interpretation*. Minneapolis: Fortress Press, 1991, 146–64.

Cowdery, James R. "A Fresh Look at the Concept of Tune Family," *Ethnomusicology* 28, no. 3 (September 1984): 495–504.
Craig, Kenneth M. Jr. *Reading Esther: A Case for the Literary Carnivalesque*. Louisville, KY: Westminster John Knox Press, 1995.
Crawford, Richard. *The American Musical Landscape*. Los Angeles: University of California Press, 2000.
Crawford, Richard. *America's Musical Life*. New York: W. W. Norton, 2001.
Crawford, Richard. "Musical Learning in Nineteenth-Century America," *American Music* 1, no. 1 (Spring 1983): 2–7.
Curto, Stephen. "Should She Stay or Should She Go?: The Canonicity of Esther" (March 13, 2015). http://mygiveonthings.com/should-she-stay-or-should-she-go-the-canonicity-of-esther/.
Curwen, John. *Standard Course of Lessons and Exercises in the Tonic Sol-fa Method of Teaching Music*. London: J. Curwen, 1872.
Curwen, John. *The Teacher's Manual of the Tonic Sol-fa Method*, 10th ed. (1875). Reprint, Clarabricken, Ireland: Boethius Press, 1986.
Curwen, John, ed. *Esther, the Beautiful Queen*. London: Bayley & Ferguson, 1870.
Daly, Joseph Francis. *The Life of Augustin Daly*. New York: MacMillan, 1917.
DelPlato, Joan. *Multiple Wives, Multiple Pleasures: Representing the Harem, 1800–1875*. Madison, NJ: Fairleigh Dickinson University Press, 2002.
Dithmar, Edward Augustus. *Memories of Daly's Theatres with Passing Recollection of Others Including a Record of Plays and Actors at the Fifth Avenue Theatre and Daly's Theatre, 1869–95*. New York: Dithmar, 1897.
Dolge, Alfred. *Pianos and Their Makers*. Covina, CA: Covina Publishing, 1911.
Doré, Gustave. *The Holy Bible with Illustrations*. New York: Cassell, Petter & Galpin, 1870.
Douglass, Frederick. "Our Composite Nationality: An Address Delivered in Boston, Massachusetts on December 7, 1869," *The Frederick Douglass Papers*, vol. 4. New Haven, CT: Yale University Press, 1991, 253–54.
Duniway, Abigail Scott. Untitled article, *New Northwest* (Portland, OR) June 27, 1873, 3.
Dunn, James B. *Band of Hope Manual*. New York: National Temperance Society and Publishing House, 1867.
[Dwight, John Sullivan]. "Native Oratorios," *Dwight's Journal of Music* (Boston) 15, no. 11 (June 11, 1859): 84.
Dwinell, Israel Edson. "The Church and the Stage," *Sacramento Daily Union*, March 16, 1877, 2.
Eaton, J[ames] D[emarest]. "Esther," *New Northwest* (Portland, OR) July 4, 1873, 1.
Elizabeth, Mary. "Mr. Bradbury's Conventions," *New York Musical Review and Gazette* 8, no. 23 (November 14, 1857): 360.
Emerson, Luther Orlando. *The Choral Tribute: A Collection of New Church Music for Choirs, Singing Schools, Conventions, &c*. Boston: Oliver Ditson, 1869.
Epstein, Dena J. "Music Publishing in Chicago before 1871: The Firm of Root and Cady, 1858–1871," *Notes: Journal of the Music Library Association*, second series 1, no. 4 (September 1944): 43–59.
Farwell, Arthur. "Community Music-Drama: Will Our Country's People in Time Help Us to Develop the Real American Theater?" *Craftsman* (Eastwood, NY) 26, no. 4 (July 1, 1914): 418.
Felder, Cain Hope. *Troubling Biblical Waters: Race, Class, and Family*. Maryknoll, NY: Orbis Books, 1989.
Fisher, Henry, ed. *Esther, the Beautiful Queen*. London: Tonic Sol-fa Agency, 1878.

Fisher, Holly. "Oakwood College Students' Quest for Social Justice Before and During the Civil Rights Era," *Journal of African American History* 88 (Winter 2003): 110–25.
Fisher, James L. "The Roots of Music Education in Baltimore," *Journal of Research in Music Education* 21, no. 3 (Autumn 1973): 214–24.
Flanagan, John T. "Thoreau in Minnesota," *Minnesota History* 16 (March 1935): 35–46.
Freedman, Florence Bernstein, ed. *Walt Whitman Looks at the Schools*. New York: King's Crown, 1950.
French, Justus Clement, and Edward Cary. *The Trip of the Steamer* Oceanus *to Fort Sumter and Charleston, S.C.* Brooklyn, NY: Union Steam Printing House, 1865.
Gates, Henry Louis Jr. *The Signifying Monkey: A Theory of Afro-American Literary Criticism*. New York: Oxford University Press, 1988.
Goodell, Edwin B. *Montclair: Evolution of a Suburban Town*. Montclair, NJ: Madison, 1934.
Gooding, Lela. "Pierre-Louis, Joni Mae," *Encyclopedia of Seventh-Day Adventists*, 2020. https://encyclopedia.adventist.org/article?id=9FW3.
Gordon, Margaret. "Women of the Old Testament," *Ladies Home Journal* 28 (November 1911): 72.
Grafton, David D. *An American Biblical Orientalism: The Construction of Jews, Christians, and Muslims in Nineteenth-Century American Evangelical Piety*. New York: Lexington Books/Fortress Academic, 2019.
Graham, George Henry. *Origin of the Band of Hope Movement*. London: Temperance Depot, ca. 1866.
Grant, Jacquelyn. "Faithful Resistance Risking It All: From Expedience to Radical Obedience," in *My Soul Is Witness: African-American Women's Spirituality*, ed. Gloria Wade-Gayles. Boston: Beacon Press, 1994, 204–8.
Green, Jonathan. *Green's Dictionary of Slang*, 2023. https://greensdictofslang.com.
Griffith, Bill. "W. E. Hill: An Appreciation," *Cartoonists on Music: The Comics Journal Special Edition* 2 (Summer 2002): 67–75.
Grimké, Francis James. *Gideon Bands for Work within the Race and for Work without the Race: A Message to the Colored People of the United States*. Washington, DC: R. L. Pendleton, 1913.
Groce, Nancy. *Musical Instrument Makers of New York: A Directory of Eighteenth and Nineteenth-Century Urban Craftsmen*. Stuyvesant, NY: Pendragon Press, 1991.
Hackley, E. Azalia. *The Colored Girl Beautiful*. Kansas City, MO: Burton, 1916.
Haight, Sarah Rogers. *Letters from the Old World by a Lady of New York*, 2 vols. New York: Harper, 1840.
Halpern, Stuart W., ed. *Esther in America: The Scroll's Interpretation in and Impact on America*. Jerusalem and New Milford, CT: Maggid Books, 2020.
Hare, Reuben E. "Fijian Choir Renders Cantata," *General Church Paper of the Seventh-Day Adventists* 124, no. 17 (April 24, 1947): 17.
Harper, Matthew. *The End of Days: African American Religion and Politics in the Age of Emancipation*. Chapel Hill: University of North Carolina Press, 2016.
Harris, Leslie M. *In the Shadows of Slavery: African Americans in New York City, 1826–1863*. Chicago: University of Chicago Press, 2003.
[Hastings, Thomas]. "What Constitutes Melody?" *Musical Magazine* 1, no. 9 (January 1836): 238.
Hastings, Thomas, and William B. Bradbury. *The Mendelssohn Collection*. Ivison and Phinney, 1849.

Hastings, Thomas, and William B. Bradbury. *New York Choralist*. New York: Mark H. Newman, 1847.
Hastings, Thomas, and William B. Bradbury. *Psalmista*. New York: Mark H. Newman, 1852.
Hastings, Thomas, and William B. Bradbury. *The Psalmodist*. New York: Mark H. Newman, 1844.
Hemenway, H[enry] B[ixby]. "The Sacredness of Churches," *Christian Advocate* (New York) April 19, 1885, 4.
Hewins, James M. *Hints Concerning Church Music, the Liturgy and Kindred Subjects*. Boston: Ide and Dutton, 1856.
Higginbotham, Evelyn Brooks. *Righteous Discontent: The Women's Movement in the Black Baptist Church, 1880–1920*. Cambridge: Harvard University Press, 1993.
Hipsher, Edward Ellsworth. *American Opera and Its Composers*. Philadelphia: Theodore Presser, 1927.
Hoig, Stan. "Land Run of 1889," *Encyclopedia of Oklahoma History and Culture*. https://okhistory.org/publications/enc/entry.php?entry=LA014.
Holloway, Steven W. "Assur [Ahasuerus] Is King of Persia: Illustrations of the Book of Esther in Some Nineteenth-Century Sources," *Journal of Religion and Society* 11 (2009): 2–7.
Howard, George Washington. *The Monumental City: Its Past History and Present Resources*. Baltimore: J. D. Ehlers, 1873.
Hoyt, J. K. *Pen and Pencil Pictures on the Delaware, Lackawanna, and Western Railroad*. New York: W. H. Caldwell, 1874.
Hughes Bros. "Letters from the People: Queen Esther," *Weekly Star* (Plymouth, PA) February 23, 1876, 4.
Hume, C[arlton] Ross. "Messages and Memories for Homecoming," *Sooner Magazine* (November 1933): 44–46.
[Irving, Washington]. "Orientalism," *Knickerbocker Magazine* (New York) 41, no. 6 (June 1853): 479–96.
Irwin, Will. "The Drama in Chinatown," *Everybody's Magazine* 20, no. 6 (June 1909): 857–69.
Jeffery, Jno. B. *Jno B. Jeffery's Guide and Directory to the Opera Houses, Theatres, Public Halls, Bill Posters, etc., of the Cities and Towns of America*, 5th ed. Chicago: John B. Jeffery, 1882.
J. H. C. "Death of Wm. B. Bradbury," *New York Evangelist* January 16, 1868, 2.
Johns, Jane Martin. *Personal Recollections of Early Decatur*. Decatur, IL: Decatur Chapter, Daughters of the American Revolution, 1912.
Johnson, Francis. *Voice Quadrilles*. Philadelphia: Geo. W. Hewitt, 1840.
Johnson, Jake. *Lying in the Middle: Musical Theater and Belief at the Heart of America*. Champaign: University of Illinois Press, 2021.
Jordan, Charles Francis. "The Occupation of Fort Sumter, and Hoisting the Old Flag Thereon, April 14, 1865," *United Service: A Quarterly Review of Military and Naval Affairs* (Philadelphia) 14, no. 5 (November 1895): 406–25.
Jordan, Donald A. *China's Trial by Fire: The Shanghai War of 1932*. Ann Arbor: University of Michigan Press, 2001.
Josephus, Flavius. "Concerning Esther, and Mordecai, and Haman, and How, in the Reign of Artaxerxes [Ahasuerus], the Whole Nation of the Jews Was in Danger of Perishing," *The Works of Flavius Josephus, the Learned and Authentic Jewish Historian and Celebrated Warrior*, trans. William Whiston. Cincinnati: Applegate, 1854: 303–9.
Karpf, Juanita. "'As with Words of Fire': Art Music and Nineteenth-Century African-American Feminist Discourse," *Signs: Journal of Women in Culture and Society* 24, no. 3 (Spring 1999): 603–32.

Karpf, Juanita. "The Early Years of African American Music Periodicals, 1886–1922: History, Ideology, Context," *International Review of the Aesthetics and Sociology of Music* 28, no. 2 (December 1997): 143–68.

Karpf, Juanita. "'In an Easy and Familiar Style': Music Education and Improvised Accompaniment Practices in the US, 1820–80," *Journal of Historical Research in Music Education* 32, no. 2 (April 2011): 122–44.

Karpf, Juanita. "Music in Montgomery's African-American Community, 1886–87: Amelia Tilghman as Performer, Journalist, and Teacher," *Alabama Review* 53, no. 2 (April 2000): 112–39.

Karpf, Juanita. "'Wild and Soul-Stirring': William Bradbury's Mountain Songs, 1847–52," *Popular Music and Society* 25 nos. 1–2 (Spring/Summer 2001): 101–20.

Karpf, Juanita. "'Would That it Were So in America!': William Bradbury's Observations of European Music Educators, 1847–49," *Journal of Historical Research in Music Education* 24, no. 1 (October 2002): 5–38.

Karpf, Juanita, ed., *William B. Bradbury: "Esther, the Beautiful Queen."* Madison, WI: A-R Editions, 2000.

Kaufmann, Sarah. "'Easy, Cheap and True': Tonic Sol-fa in Print and in the Concert Hall," *Brio* 40 (2003): 8–23.

Keach, Leon, ed. *Esther, the Beautiful Queen*. Boston: Oliver Ditson, 1896.

Kellogg, John H. *The Battle Creek Sanitarium System: History, Organization, Methods*. Battle Creek: N.p., 1913.

Kent, Herbert. "Music Chronicles of Early Times," *Victoria* [British Columbia, Canada] *Daily Times* December 7, 1918, 13.

Kent, Herbert. "Musical Chronicles of Early Times," *Victoria Daily Times* December 28, 1918, 8.

Kingsley, George, ed. *The Social Choir*. Boston: Crocker & Brewster, 1847.

Kirk, Frank W. "Mr. Leon Keach," *Music Trades*; reprint, *Musical Record* (November 1896): 11.

Kirton, John William. *The Water Drinkers of the Bible*. London: National Temperance Publication Depot, 1885.

Kitto, John. *A Cyclopaedia of Biblical Literature*. New York: Mark H. Newman, 1845.

Knauff, Christopher W. *Doctor Tucker, Priest Musician*. New York: A. D. F. Randolph, 1897.

Knowles, Mark A. *The Wicked Waltz and Other Scandalous Dances: Outrage at Couple Dancing in the Nineteenth and Early Twentieth Centuries*. Jefferson, NC: McFarland, 2009.

Kowallis, Bart J. "The Magnificent McGibneys," July 24, 2011. http://urthgen.blogspot.com/2011/07/magnificent-mcgibneys.html.

Labode, Modupe G. "'A native knows a native': African American Missionaries' Writings about Angola, 1919–1940," *North Star: A Journal of African American Religious History* 4, no. 1 (Fall 2000). https://princeton.edu/~jweisenf/northstar/volume4/labode.html.

Lamm, Ari. "The Secret Political History of Queen Esther," *Tablet Magazine* March 21, 2019. https://tabletmag.com/sections/holidays/articles/political-history-of-queen-esther.

LaRue, Cleophus James. *The Heart of Black Preaching*. Louisville, KY: Westminster John Knox Press, 2000.

Law, Frederic Stanley. "Old Home Week Letter," *Sentinel* (Carlisle, PA) July 15, 1909, 5.

Lawrence, Vera Brodsky. *Resonances, 1836–50*, vol. 1 of *Strong on Music: The New York Music Scene in the Days of George Templeton Strong, 1836–70*, 3 vols. New York: Oxford University Press, 1995.

Leeds, Charles H., ed. *Old Home Week Letters*. Carlisle, PA: Carlisle Evening Sentinel, 1909.

LeFebvre, Michael. "The Story of Esther as Redemptive Humor in the Bible," *The Biblical Mind Magazine*, 2021. https://hebraicthought.org/esther-redemptive-humor-in-the-bible/.

Levine, Lawrence W. *Black Culture and Black Consciousness: Afro-American Folk Thought from Slavery to Freedom*. New York: Oxford University Press, 1977.

Levine, Lawrence W. *Highbrow / Lowbrow: The Emergence of Cultural Hierarchy in America*. Cambridge: Harvard University Press, 1988.

Levy, Shimon. *The Bible as Theatre*. Portland, OR: Sussex Academic Press, 2000.

Levy, Shimon. "The Book of Esther," in *Biblical, Rabbinical, and Medieval Studies*, vol. 1 of *Jewish Studies at the Turn of the Twentieth Century*, 2 vols. Judit Targarona Borrás and Angel Sáenz-Badillos, eds. Leiden, The Netherlands: Brill, 1999, 154–63.

Lewis, Hon. Jerry. "A Tribute to Minnie Iverson-Wood, Still Teaching Music on Her 95th Birthday," speech of the Hon. Jerry Lewis before the US House of Representatives, *Congressional Record* 149, no. 76 (May 21, 2003): E1009. https://www.congress.gov/crec/2003/05/21/CREC-2003-05-21-pt1-PgE1009.pdf.

Lewis, Reina. *Gendering Orientalism: Race, Femininity and Representation*. New York: Routledge, 1996.

Lewis, Reina. *Rethinking Orientalism: Women, Travel and the Ottoman Harem*. London: I. B. Tauris, 2004.

Leyson, John W. "Queen Esther," *Weekly Star* (Plymouth, PA) March 1, 1876, 4.

Li, Siu Lueng. *Cross-Dressing in Chinese Opera*. Hong Kong: Hong Kong University Press, 2006.

Little, Douglas. *American Orientalism: The United States and the Middle East Since 1945*. Chapel Hill: University of North Carolina Press, 2008.

Livingstone, David. "Doctor Livingstone: The Explorer's Story of the Slave Trade in Eastern Africa," *New York Herald* July 27, 1872, 7.

Locke, Ralph P. "A Broader View of Musical Exoticism," *Journal of Musicology* 24, no. 4 (Fall 2007): 477–85.

Locke, Ralph P. "Cutthroats and Casbah Dancers, Muezzins and Timeless Sands: Musical Images of the Middle East," in *The Exotic in Western Music*, ed. Jonathan Bellman. Boston: Northeastern University Press, 1998, 104–27.

Locke, Ralph P. *Musical Exoticism: Images and Reflections*. Cambridge: Cambridge University Press, 2009.

Locke, Ralph P. *Music and the Exotic from the Renaissance to Mozart*. Cambridge: Cambridge University Press, 2015.

Long, Edwin M. "William B. Bradbury," *Illustrated History of Hymns and Their Authors*, 2nd ed. Philadelphia: P.W. Ziegler, 1876, 35.

Marable, Mary Hays, and Alberta W. Constant. "When O.U. Was Very Young," *Daily Oklahoman* (Oklahoma City) May 9, 1943, 54.

Marden, H[enry] W. "Old-Time Recollections," *Warren* [PA] *Mail*, February 11, 1897, 3.

Mark, Michael L., and Charles L. Gary, *A History of American Music Education*, 3rd ed. Lanham, MD: Rowman and Littlefield, 2007.

Martin, Sadie E. *The Life and Professional Career of Emma Abbott*. Minneapolis: L. Kimball, 1891.

Mason, Lowell. "Figured Base," *New York Music Review and Choral Advocate* 6, no. 8 (April 12, 1855): 123–24.

Mason, Lowell. "Thorough Base," *New York Music Review and Choral Advocate* 6, no. 12 (June 2, 1855): 81.

Mason, Lowell, and George James Webb. *The Vocalist: Consisting of Short and Easy Glees, or Songs, in Parts*. Boston: Wilkins and Carter, 1847.

Maston, George A. "Religious Failings: The Departure of the Protestant Church from the Old Paths," *New York Globe*, November 10, 1883, 4.

McGuire, Charles E. *Music and Victorian Philanthropy: The Tonic Sol-fa Movement*. Cambridge: Cambridge University Press, 2009.

McMahon, Henry E. "Fulton Missionary School," *Australasian Record* 50, no. 49 (December 9, 1946): 3.

McMahon, Henry E. "High Praise for 'Esther,'" *Australasian Record* 50, no. 49 (December 9, 1946): 5, 8.

Melman, Billie. *Women's Orients: English Women and the Middle East, 1718–1918*. Ann Arbor: University of Michigan Press, 1992.

Mercer-Taylor, Peter. *Gems of Exquisite Beauty: How Hymnody Carried Classical Music to America*. New York: Oxford University Press, 2020.

Mercer-Taylor, Peter. "Mendelssohn in Nineteenth-Century American Hymnody," *19th-Century Music* 32, no. 2 (Spring 2009): 235–83.

Moore, John Weeks. *Dictionary of Musical Information Containing Also a Vocabulary of Musical Terms and a List of Modern Musical Works Published in the United States, 1640–1875* (1876). Reprint, New York: B. Franklin, 1971.

Moore, R. Laurence. "Religion, Secularization, and the Shaping of the Culture Industry in Antebellum America," *American Quarterly* 41, no. 2 (June 1989): 216–42.

Mullen, Bill V. *Afro-Orientalism*. Minneapolis: University of Minnesota Press, 2004.

Nance, Susan. *How the Arabian Nights Inspired the American Dream, 1790–1935*. Chapel Hill: University of North Carolina Press, 2009.

Okihiro, Gary Y. *Margins and Mainstreams: Asians in American History and Culture*. Seattle: University of Washington Press, 1994.

Overpeck, Nell S. "Minneapolis a Music Loving Center Back in '70s," *Star Tribune* August 1, 1915, 15.

Owen, Barbara. "Reed Organ," *Grove Music Online*. https://doi-org.ezproxy.oberlin.edu/10.1093/gmo/9781561592630.article.A2252280.

Owen, Barbara, and Alistair Dick. "Harmonium." *Grove Music Online*. https://doi-org.ezproxy.oberlin.edu/10.1093/gmo/9781561592630.article.12395.

Painter, Nell Irvin. *Sojourner Truth: A Life, a Symbol*. New York: W. W. Norton, 1996.

Palmquist, Peter E., and Thomas R. Kailbourn. *Pioneer Photographers from the Mississippi to the Continental Divide: A Biographical Dictionary, 1839–1865*. Stanford: Stanford University Press, 2005.

Pardoe, Julia Sophia. *The City of the Sultan and the Domestic Manners of the Turks*. Philadelphia: Adam Waldie, 1837.

Patton, William Weston. "Defense of Theater and Opera," *Advance* (Chicago), November 19, 1868, 4.

Peabody, Francis Greenwood. *Education for Life: The Story of Hampton Institute*. New York: Doubleday, 1918.

Penn, Irvine Garland. *The Afro-American Press and Its Editors*. Springfield, MA: Willey and Co., 1891.

Pollard, Leslie N., Samuel London et al. "Oakwood University," *Encyclopedia of Seventh-Day Adventists*. https://encyclopedia.adventist.org/article?id=AFWD.

Porchea, Paul. *Musical History of Colorado*. Denver: Charles Westley, 1889.

Powell, Aaron Macy. "The Excursion to Charleston," *National Anti-Slavery Standard*, May 6, 1865, 2.

Powell, Aaron Macy. *Personal Reminiscences of the Anti-Slavery and other Reforms and Reformers*. New York: Caulon Press, 1899.

Pratt, Sarah Smith. *The Old Crop in Indiana*. Indianapolis: Pratt Poster, 1928.

Preston, Katherine K. *Opera for the People: English-Language Opera and Women Managers in Late 19th-Century America*. New York: Oxford University Press, 2017.

Raboteau, Albert J. *A Fire in the Bones: Reflections on African-American Religious History*. Boston: Beacon Press, 1995.

Radano, Ronald. *Lying Up a Nation: Race and Black Music*. Chicago: University of Chicago Press, 2003.

Rainbow, Bernarr. "Tonic Sol-fa," *Oxford Music Online*. https://doi-org.ezproxy.oberlin.edu/10.1093/gmo/9781561592630.article.28124.

Rao, Nancy Yunhwa. *Chinatown Opera Theater in North America*. Urbana: University of Illinois Press, 2017.

Reimer, Gus. "Armchair Ramblings," *Reedley Exponent*, January 27, 1972, 4.

Renzlus, E. *The Laughing Chorus*. New York: Horace Waters, 1853.

Renzlus, E. *Laughing Darkies: Comic Ethiopian Song*. New York: Firth, Pond & Co., 1851.

Richards, Erwin H. "Africa," in *The African, European and Latin American Fields*. New York: Eaton and Mains, 1904, 20–23.

Richardson, Marilyn, ed. *Maria W. Stewart: America's First Black Woman Political Writer*. Bloomington: Indiana University Press, 1987.

Roberts, John W. *From Trickster to Badman: The Black Folk Hero in Slavery and Freedom*. Philadelphia: University of Pennsylvania Press, 1989.

Roberts, Mary. *Intimate Outsiders: The Harem in Ottoman and Orientalist Art and Travel Literature*. Durham, NC: Duke University Press, 2007.

Robertson, Mel. "A Burford Landmark—What Next?" *Burford* [Ontario, Canada] *Advance*, July 14, 1982, 7.

Root, George F. "Our Musical Correspondence, North-Reading, Mass.," *New York Musical Review and Gazette* 8, no. 1 (January 10, 1857): 5–6.

Root, George F. *Story of a Musical Life*. Cincinnati: John Church, 1891.

Root, George F., William B. Bradbury, and Chauncey Marvin Cady. *Daniel, or the Captivity and Restoration*. Boston: Oliver Ditson, 1853.

Rosenblatt, Naomi. "Orientalism in American Popular Culture," *Penn History Review* 16, no. 2 (Spring 2009). https://repository.upenn.edu/entities/journalissue/39aa38d3-f4c8-4d65-a7ac-0eb6aa45fc0a.

Sanders, Charles W. "Music Books for Schools," *The School Reader, Fourth Book*. New York: Newman and Ivison, 1842, 312.

Sanders, Frank Knight. "Impressions of the Angola Jubilee," *Missionary Herald* 126, no. 9 (September 1930), 331–33.

Scrimsher, Lila Gravatt, ed., "The Diaries and Writings of George A. Maston, Black Citizen of Lincoln, Nebraska, 1901–1913," *Nebraska History* 52 (1971): 133–68.

Seager, R[ichard]. W[atson]. "A Correspondent's Opinion of 'Esther,'" *Daily Rocky Mountain News* (Denver, CO), April 9, 1874, 4.

Seager, R[ichard] W[atson]. "Letter No. 1," *Weekly Star* (Wilmington, NC), February 23, 1876, 4.

Seager, R[ichard] W[atson]. "Letter No. 2," *Weekly Star* (Wilmington, NC), February 23, 1876, 4.

Seager, R[ichard] W[atson]. Letter to the editor, *Boston Daily Globe* August 23, 1877, 2.
Seager, R[ichard] W[atson], ed. *Esther, the Beautiful Queen*. Boston: Oliver Ditson, 1874.
Sears, Robert. *Two Hundred Pictorial Illustrations of the Holy Bible*. New York: Robert Sears, 1841.
Seward, T[heodore] F[relinghuysen]. "Sketches of American Composers: William B. Bradbury," *New York Musical Gazette* 2, no. 2 (December 1867): 10–11.
Seward, T[heodore] F[relinghuysen]. "Sketches of American Composers: William B. Bradbury (concluded)," *New York Musical Gazette* 2, no. 8 (June 1868): 57–58.
Seward, T[heodore] F[relinghuysen]. "Sketches of American Composers: William B. Bradbury (continued)," *New York Musical Gazette* 2, no. 6 (April 1868): 41–42.
Seward, Theodore F., and B[enjamin] C[arl] Unseld. *Songs in Sol-Fa*. New York: Biglow and Main, 1882.
Shapiro, Anne Dhu. "Black Sacred Song and the Tune-Family Concept," in *New Perspectives on Music: Essays in Honor of Eileen Southern*, Josephine Wright, ed., with Samuel A. Floyd Jr. Warren, MI: Harmonie Park Press, 1992, 110–17.
Shaw, H. Watkins. "The Musical Teaching of John Curwen," *Proceedings of the Royal Musical Association* (1950–51): 17–26.
Sherlock, Frederick. *Ann Jane Carlile, a Temperance Pioneer*. London: Frederick Sherlock, 1897.
Shiman, Lillian Lewis. "The Band of Hope Movement: Respectable Recreation for Working-Class Children," *Victorian Studies* 17, no. 1 (September 1973): 49–74.
Shuey, A[lfred] M. "Veteran Musician Recalls City's Early Performance of Cantata," *Star Tribune* (Minneapolis), January 7, 1923, 25, 31.
Silver, Ariel Clark. "From the Palace of Shushan to Uncle Tom's Cabin: Esther as American Abolitionist," in Halpern, ed., 63–74.
Simcoe, H. Augustine. *Sullivan Vs. Critic; or Practice Vs. Theory: A Study in Press Phenomenon*. London: Simpkin, Marshall, Hamilton, Kent, and Co., Ltd., 1906.
Sinensky, Tzvi. "Vashti Comes to America," in Halpern, ed., 108–15.
Slonimsky, Nicolas. *Lectionary of Music*. New York: McGraw-Hill, 1989.
Small, Christopher. *Musicking: The Meanings of Performing and Listening*. Middletown, CT: Wesleyan University Press, 1998.
Small, Christopher. *Music of the Common Tongue: Survival and Celebration in African American Music*. Middletown, CT: Wesleyan University Press, 1987.
Smith, Mrs. Douglas [Allegra Doyle Smith]. Untitled article. *Missionary Herald* 126, no. 9 (September 1930), 333–34.
Smither, Howard E. *The Oratorio in the Nineteenth and Twentieth Centuries*, vol. 4 of *A History of the Oratorio*, 4 vols. Chapel Hill: University of North Carolina Press, 2000.
Smitherman, Geneva. *Talkin' and Testifyin': The Language of Black America*. New York: Houghton Mifflin, 1977.
Soloveichik, Meir Y. "Lincoln, Esther, and the Rav: A Study in Statesmanship," in Halpern, ed., 91–101.
Spencer, Jon Michael. *Sacred Symphony: The Chanted Sermon of the Black Preacher*. New York: Greenwood Press, 1987.
Spencer, Jon Michael. *Theological Music: Introduction to Theomusicology*. Westport, CT: Greenwood Press, 1991.
Spillane, Daniel. *History of the American Piano-forte; Its Technical Development, and the Trade* (1890). New York: Da Capo Press, 1969.

Staunton, Helen M. "Average Joe, Jane Satirized by Hill," *Editor and Publisher Magazine* 79, no. 52 (December 21, 1946): 16.

Steensma, David P., Carol A. Roede, and Robert A. Kyle. "Henry David Thoreau's Final Journey: Minnesota," *Mayo Clinic Proceedings*, July 2018. https://www.mayoclinicproceedings.org/article/S0025-6196(18)30401-4/fulltext.

Stevens, Robin S. "'Easy, Cheap and True': The Case for Promoting the Curwen Method of Teaching Choral Singing in Developing Countries," *Curriculum Innovation in Music: Proceedings of the 4th Asia Pacific Symposium on Music Education Research*. Hong Kong: Hong Kong Institute of Education, 2003, 343–48.

Stevens, Robin S. "A System Ahead of Its Time," *Music in Action* 6, no. 1 (Winter 2008): 8–13. https://music-ed.net/music-in-action/index_htm_files/MiA_2008_6-1.pdf.

Stevens, Robin S. "Tonic Sol-fa: An Exogenous Aspect of South African Musical Identity," in *Music and Identity: Transformation and Negotiation*, Eric Akrofi, Maria Smit, and Stig-Magnus Thorsén, eds. Stellenbosch, South Africa: African Sun Media, 2007, 37–51.

Stevens, Robin S. "Tonic Sol-fa in Asian Pacific Countries: The Missionary Legacy," *Asia Pacific Journal for Arts Education* 5, no. 1 (2007): 52–76.

Stevenson, Robert. "William Batchelder Bradbury in Europe, 1847–1849," *Inter-American Music Review* 2 (Fall 1979): 41–44.

Stopp, Jacklin Bolton. "James C. Johnson and the American Secular Cantata," *American Music* 28, no. 2 (Summer 2010): 228–50.

Stroebe, George G. "The Great Central China Flood of 1931," *Chinese Recorder and Missionary Journal* (Shanghai) 63, no. 11 (November 1932): 667–79.

Talbot, Edith Armstrong. *Samuel Chapman Armstrong: A Biographical Study*. New York: Doubleday, 1904.

Tawa, Nicholas E. "Serious Songs of the Early Nineteenth Century, Part 2: The Meaning of Early Song Melodies," *American Music* 13, no. 3 (Autumn 1995): 263–94.

Tawa, Nicholas E. *Sweet Songs for Gentle Americans: The Parlor Song in America, 1790–1860*. Bowling Green, OH: Bowling Green University Popular Press, 1980.

Taylor, Sarah E. "'Easy, Cheap and True': Tonic Sol-fa in Print and in the Concert Hall," *Brio* 40, no. 2 (2003): 8–23.

Tchen, John Kuo Wei. *New York before Chinatown: Orientalism and the Shaping of American Culture, 1776–1882*. Baltimore: Johns Hopkins University Press, 2001.

Teal, Mary D. "Letters of Thomas Hastings," *Notes: The Quarterly Journal of the Music Library Association* 34, no. 2 (December 1977): 308–18.

Thompson, Patricia D. *Foster's Richmond*. Richmond: Virginia Historical Society, 1991.

Thompson, Slason. *Life of Eugene Field, Poet of Childhood*. New York: D. Appleton, 1927.

Thomson, William McClure. *The Land and the Book: Biblical Illustrations Drawn from the Manners and Customs, the Scenes and Scenery of the Holy Land*. New York: Harper Brothers, 1858.

Tucker, John T. *Old Ways and New Days in Angola, Africa*. Toronto: Commission on Young People's Missionary Education, 1935.

Turczynowicz, Laura de Gozdawa. "La Jolla Woman's Club to Present Elaborate Pageant 'Esther, the Beautiful Queen,' with All the Gorgeous Trappings of 500 Years Ago," *San Diego Union and Daily Bee*, April 16, 1922, 8.

Turczynowicz, Laura de Gozdawa. *When the Russians Came to Poland: The Experiences of an American Woman during the Invasion*. New York: G.P. Putnam's Sons, 1916.

Van-Lennep, Henry J. *Bible Lands: Their Modern Customs and Manners Illustrative of the Scripture*. New York: Harper and Brothers, 1875.

Ward, Andrew. *Dark Midnight When I Rise: The Story of the Fisk Jubilee Singers*. New York: HarperCollins, 2000.
Ward, Susan Hayes. *The History of the Broadway Tabernacle Church*. New York: Broadway Tabernacle Church, 1901.
Warner, Charles Dudley. "Editor's Study," *Harper's New Monthly Magazine* 86 (April 1893): 800–3.
Warner, Charles Dudley. "Editor's Study," *Harper's New Monthly Magazine* 87 (April 1894): 800–3.
Warner, Charles Dudley. "The Education of the Negro," *Journal of Social Science* 38 (1900): 1–14.
Watson, Sue Ruple. "Local Historian Gives Story of the Beginning of Uintah County [UT] Library," *Vernal [UT] Express*, December 17, 1970, 8.
White, Sidnie Ann. "Esther: A Feminine Model for Jewish Diaspora," in Peggy L. Day, ed., *Gender and Difference in Ancient Israel*. Minneapolis: Augsburg Fortress, 1989, 161–78.
[Whitman, Walt]. "An Evening at a Children's Concert," *Brooklyn Evening Star*, February 20, 1846, 2.
Whittemore, Henry. *History of Montclair Township, New Jersey*. New York: Suburban Publishing, 1894.
Wilcox, Hazel Pearl (author listed as "Mrs. Lyle C. Wilcox"). "Malayan Union Seminary Presents Cantata," *Far Eastern Division Outlook* 37, no. 12 (December 1951): 6.
Wilson, Brian C. *Dr. John Kellogg and the Religion of Biologic Living*. Bloomington: Indiana University Press, 2014.
Wilson, Olly. "The Black American Composer," *The Black Perspective in Music* 1, no. 2 (1972): 33–36.
Wilson, Olly. "Black Music as an Art Form," *The Black Music Research Journal* 3 (1983): 1–22.
Wilson, Olly. "Composition from the Perspective of the African-American Tradition," *Black Music Research Journal* 16, no. 1 (1996): 43–51.
Wilson, Olly. "The Heterogeneous Sound Ideal in African-American Music," in *New Perspectives on Music: Essays in Honor of Eileen Southern*, Josephine Wright, ed., with Samuel A. Floyd Jr. Warren, MI: Harmonie Park Press, 1992, 327–40.
Wilson, Olly. "'It Don't Mean a Thing If It Ain't Got That Swing': The Relationship between African and African-American Music," in *African Roots / American Cultures: Africa in the Creation of the Americas*, Sheila S. Walker, ed. Lanham, MD: Rowman and Littlefield, 2001, 153–68.
Wilson, Olly. "The Significance of the Relationship between Afro-American Music and West African Music," *The Black Perspective in Music* 2, no. 1 (1974): 3–22.
Wingard, Alan Burl. *Life and Works of William Batchelder Bradbury, 1816–1868*, DMA diss., Southern Baptist Theological Seminary, Louisville, KY, 1973.
Wood, Eugene. "The Drama in Our Town," *McClure's Magazine* 28, no. 3 (January 1907): 265–74.
Wood, Eugene. *Our Town*. Boston: Gorham Press, 1913.
Woods, Donald Z. "Playhouse for Pioneers: The Story of the Pence Opera House," *Minnesota History* 33, no. 4 (Winter 1952): 169–78.
Yang, Fenggang. *Chinese Christians in America: Conversion, Assimilation, and Adhesive Identities*. University Park: Pennsylvania State University Press, 1999.
Yoshihara, Mari. *Embracing the East: White Women and American Orientalism*. New York: Oxford University Press, 2003.
Young, Kevin. *The Gray Album: On the Blackness of Blackness*. Minneapolis: Graywolf Press, 2012.

Zaeske, Susan. "Unveiling Esther as a Pragmatic Radical Rhetoric," *Philosophy and Rhetoric* 33, no. 3 (2000): 193–220.

Zeal, Tim. *Livingstone*. London: Heinemann, 1973.

Zerschling, Lynn. "A Royal Performance," *Sioux City* [IA] *Journal*, June 16, 2019, A9.

Zheng, Su. *Claiming Diaspora: Music, Transnationalism, and Cultural Politics in Asian / Chinese America*. New York: Oxford University Press, 2010.

Zucker, David J. "The Importance of Being Esther: Rabbis, Canonicity, Problems and Possibilities," *European Judaism: A Journal for the New Europe* 47, no. 1 (Spring 2014): 102–8.

INDEX

Abbott, Emma, 53, 112–13
Abbott, Seth, 53
Adams, H. S., 100–101
Agovi, Kofi E., 219
Allen, Calvin, 8
Armstrong, Edith, 187–88
Armstrong, Samuel Chapman, 184
Arp, Bill (Charles Henry Smith), 4, 233n6
Ashley, John Henry, 219

Balfe, Michael William, 53
Band of Hope, 210–11
Barkly, Henry, 219
Bartlett, Walter B., 194–95
Bassett, Ernest Knight, 146
Bassett, Lucille G., 146
Beal, Alonzo H., 130–36
Beecher, Henry Ward, 25, 237n65
Beethoven, Ludwig van, 75
Bellini, Vincenzo, 53
Benjamin, William T., 181–82
Bergson, Henri, 171–72
Birchell, Thomas E., 147–48
Bixler, A. G., 157–58
Blue, Debbie, 125
Böhme, Ferdinand, 18
Bond, Helen, 217–18
Borjes, John H., 253n44
Boston Academy of Music, 8, 44
Bowen, Henry Chandler, 237n65
Bradbury, Adra Esther Fessenden, 8
Bradbury, David, 7
Bradbury, Edward Grow, 22, 23
Bradbury, Sophia Chase, 7
Bradbury, William B.: early years, 7–8; in Europe, 16–19; *Flora's Festival*, 11–12, 20, 45, 56, 234n16; piano manufacturing, 22–24; as teacher, 8–12, 19–21, 45–49
Brantley, Paul, 193
Broadway Tabernacle, 9–12, 19–20, 234n11, 235n20
Buckley, Frederick, 77
Buckley's Serenaders, 244n17
Buell, Henry Clark, 88, 245n26
Bussie, Jacqueline, 172

Cadman, Delano, 94–95, 246n51
Cady, Chauncey Marvin, 33–35, 89, 124
Campanini, Italo, 67
Capiñala, Henrique, 222–23
Carbajal, Jovita dela Cruz, 197
Carbajal, Ulysses M., 196–97, 218
Carlile, Ann Jane, 210
Cary, Edward, 25, 237n65
Chalmers, Elizabeth Scattergood, 221–22
Cheney, Simeon Pease, 9, 30, 234n9
Christensen, Brigham Charles, 150
Christensen, Pearl J., 149–50
Christy Minstrels, 206
Chung, Mary, 196
Collier, Robert L., 107–8, 248n28
community music-making, 43, 48, 56, 66, 110, 128, 228–29
Conant, Frank S., 138–40
Corning, James Leonard, 237n65
Crawford, Richard, 43, 126
Cromwell, John Wesley, 179
Curwen, John, 203–5, 218–19, 227
Cuyler, Theodore Ledyard, 237n65

Daly, Augustin, 187–88
Davis, M. Alice, 140–41

277

Demorest, Charles H., 196
Dent, Patricia, 192
DeWitt, J. A., 93
Dickerson, Isaac P., 177
Diggett, James, 137
Dillman, Francis Fern, 149
Ditson, Oliver, 38, 67, 71
Donizetti, Gaetano, 78
Doré, Gustav, 123
Doremus, Philip Henry, 27
Douglass, Frederick, 197
Duhem Brothers Studio, 137–38, 252n19
Duniway, Abigail Scott, 113–14, 248n41
Dunn, Maud, 195
Dwight, John S., 31
Dwinell, Israel E., 108

Eaton, James Demarest "J. D.," 100, 109–10
Eliot, Thomas L., 113, 248n40
Emerson, Luther Orlando, 58, 68
Esther, the Beautiful Queen: African American performances, 169–92; Asian American performances, 192–96; biblical allegiance, 36, 113–14; as cantata, 33–34, 41, 91; horses in, 93–95; as instructional piece, 43–53; morality of, 45, 89–90, 95, 99–100, 103, 105–14; multiethnic/multiracial performances, 196–97; as opera, 84–86, 90–95; as oratorio, 89–95; recitative in, 41–43; revisions and editions, 36–66, 67–71, 203–9; sacred or secular, 71–89, 206; tonic sol-fa notation, 204–6
Evans, Edward W., 149
Evans, Greene, 177

Farwell, Arthur, 228–29, 261n8
Feeks, Charles W., 9
Ferguson, Philip James, 181–82
Field, Eugene, 121–22, 249n65
Fisher, Henry, 208–9
Fisk Jubilee Singers, 173–79
Fordham, Henry, 192
Foster, Stephen, 53
Foster, Walter Washington, 154–55, 253n45
Fränzl, Ignaz, 77
French, Justus C., 25, 237n65
Frothingham, Octavious Brooks, 237n65

Garrison, William Lloyd, 25, 187, 237n65
Gordon, Georgia, 177
Gordon, Margaret, 65
Gounod, Charles, 112
Grimké, Francis J., 170

Hackley, E. Azalia, 171
Halpern, Stuart W., 118, 123–24
Hampton Singers, 184–91
Handel, Georg Frideric, 17, 90
harmonium, 208–9, 259n28
Harmsen, Ludwig W., 129
Harmston, Hazel I., 150
Harvey, Lewis W., 158–59, 253n51
Hastings, Thomas, 15–16, 18–19, 30, 205, 236n43
Hauptmann, Moritz, 18
Haydn, Franz Joseph, 75
Hemenway, Henry Bixby "H. B.," 104
Hendrickson, John A., 158
Hewins, James M., 13
Hewitt, John Hill, 11
Higginbotham, Evelyn Brooks, 171
Hill, Edmund C., 64–65, 243n31
Hill, Sumner, 8
Hill, William Ely "W. E.," 161–66
Hipsher, Edward Ellsworth, 91–92, 228, 245n35
Hobbs, Lacassard Lazarus "L. L.," 101, 247n8
Holmes, Benjamin, 177
Howard, George Washington, 24
Howard, Oliver Otis, 25
Howes, George Leonard, 155–56
Hubbard, John P., 191
Hufty, Frank R., 153–54
Hullah, John Pyke, 16–17
Hume, C. Ross, 143–44
Huntington, Francis J., 24

improvisation, 38–39, 172–73, 178, 205
Irving, Washington, 117–18, 249n49
Iverson-Wood, Minnie, 217–18

Jackson, G. W., 93
Jackson, Jennie, 177
Johnson, Hazel, 151
Johnson, Jake, 96

Jones, Myrtle Gladys, 155–56
Josephus, Flavius, 36, 58, 143, 204

Keach, Leon, 67–72
Kellogg, John H., 160–61
Kent, Herbert, 200
Ketchum, Edgar, 237n65
Killinger, Alice Laura, 115
Killinger, Emanuel B., 115–16
King, Grace Adelaide, 142–44
King, Washington, 9
Knauff, Christopher W., 13
Knight, Reginald, 203

Law, Ann Celestia Southworth, 233n5
Law, Frederic S., 4, 233n5
Leavitt, Joshua, 237n65
Leipzig, Germany, 18–19
Leoncavallo, Ruggiero, 145
Levine, Lawrence W., 106
Levy, Shimon, 124
Lighte, Ferdinand C., 22–24
Livingstone, David, 222, 261n69
Locke, Ralph, 119–20
Low, Seth, 186
Lum, Lily, 196

Manwaring, David, 146–47
Marden, Henry W., 120–21
Marsh, Charles, 125
Martin, Sadie E., 53
Martini, Jean-Paul-Égide, 80–81
Mason, Lowell, 8–10, 15, 20–21, 205, 239n15
Massé, Victor, 112
Maston, George A., 104–5, 247n21
McDonald, George Freeman, 183
McGibney, James Benjamin "J. B.," 129, 251n9
McMahon, Henry, 216
melodeon, 33–34, 89, 208, 251n10, 259n28
Mendelssohn, Felix, 17–18, 58, 68, 75, 236n41
Mercer-Taylor, Peter, 75
Miller, Marjorie, 221
Monell, Elizabeth Crenshaw, 154–55
Moscheles, Ignaz, 18
Mozart, W. A., 75
Mueller, Christian F., 158–59, 253n52

Mullen, Bill, 197
musical conventions, 47–52
music education, 8–12, 19–20, 43–49
musicking, 229

Nance, Susan, 125
Newcomb, Alta, 148
Newton, Henry J., 22–24
Nichol, Mamie, 181–82
Nordica, Lillian, 67

Okihiro, Gary, 195
Orientalism, 5–6, 100, 116–25, 189–90, 200, 217, 249n49, 254n58
Orr, John William, 14

Patton, William Weston, 107, 248n27
Pence, John Wesley, 129
performed sermon, 172–73
Pferdner, Emil, 200
Pierre-Louis, Joni Mae, 191
Planquette, Robert, 112
Plummer, Clara M., 138
Poole, John Andrew, 154–55
Porter, Maggie L., 174–75, 177–78
Powell, Aaron Macy, 237n65
Powell, Maud, 67
Pratt, Sarah, 122
Putnam, Alfred Porter, 237n65
Putnam, Emily Smith, 187

Quashigah, Courage Emmanuel Kobla, 220

Raboteau, Albert J., 169, 172
Rainsford, William S., 186
Rathbun, Frederic G., 184
recitatives, 42, 90, 215
Reeder, Lawrence, 195
Richards, Isalyn, 203
Robinson, John, 148
Robinson, Martin E., 120
Root, Ebenezer Towner, 35
Root, George Frederick, 9, 15, 20–21, 35, 74, 92, 205
Rossini, Gioachino, 106
Rowels, James, 215
Rutling, Thomas, 175–77

Sanders, Charles W., 14–15
Sanders, Frank Knight, 220–21
Seager, Ella Knapp, 61, 65
Seager, Frank, 61
Seager, Mary Frances W., 61
Seager, Richard Watson "R. W.," 56–66, 68, 91, 93, 99, 103, 116, 179, 211, 241n3, 241n5, 242n21
Selika, Marie, 67
Serns, Mahon H., 160
Seward, Theodore Frelinghuysen "T. F.," 28–29, 30, 205, 227
Sheppard, Ella, 177–78
Shuey, Alfred M., 128, 251n4
Simcoe, H. Augustine, 203
Small, Christopher, 229
Smith, Allegra Doyle, 221
Smith, Charles Henry. *See* Arp, Bill
Smith, Freeborn Garrettson, 24, 28
Smith, Mrs. Douglas. *See* Smith, Allegra Doyle
Smitherman, Geneva, 173
Somerville, Tillie J., 181–82
Speer, William, 192–93
Spence, Adam Knight, 178
Steed, Joseph Arthur, 220–23
Stewart, Maria W., 171
Stoddard, Drusella, 4, 233n4
Strong, George Templeton, 88

TASB scoring, 38–39, 46–47, 239n12, 239n15
Tate, Minnie, 177
Tawa, Nicholas, 75
Taylor, George Sylvester, 101
Tchen, John, 118
Thoreau, Henry David, 238n78
Thorne, Leo C., 145–51
Thursby, Emma Cecilia, 67
Tilghman, Amelia L., 179–84
Tom, Lucy, 196
Tompkins, Richard W., 181–82
tonic sol-fa, 204–6
Truth, Sojourner, 171
Tucker, John T., 220
tunebooks, 12–16, 235n21, 240n32
tune family, 76–78, 244n13
Tunnicliff, Jabez, 210

Turczynowicz, Laura de, 94–95, 246n48
Turczynowicz, Wanda Jolanda de, 94, 246n50

Van-Lennep, Henry, 124, 250n76
Verdi, Giuseppe, 112
Villard, Fanny Garrison, 187
Villard, Henry, 187

Walker, Eliza, 177
Walker, M. Edith, 158
Warner, Charles Dudley, 116, 187–91, 248n44
Washington, Booker T., 186–88
Watson, Sue Ruple, 93–94
Webb, George James, 205
Weber, Carl Maria von, 75, 81–82
Wenzel, Ernst Ferdinand, 18
Whippy, Adeline, 216
Whippy, Louise, 216
White, George Leonard, 173–75, 177
White, Sidnie Ann, 171
Whitman, Walt, 11, 234n15
Wilcox, Hazel Pearl, 217–18
Wilson, Olly, 173
Wing, Tsw, 195
Wood, Alfred M., 237n65
Wood, Eugene, 3, 233n2
Woodbury, Isaac Baker, 205
Woodward, Don Carlos, 158
Workman, Jacob Reader, 151–52

Yankah, James Topp Nelson, 219–20
Young, Kevin, 171

Zerschling, Lynn, 3

ABOUT THE AUTHOR

Juanita Karpf played cello professionally, taught music in grades K-12 for many years, and has held faculty appointments at Case Western Reserve University, Middlebury College, Oberlin College, and the University of Georgia. Her previous publications include a critical edition of *Esther, the Beautiful Queen*, published by A-R Editions, and *Performing Racial Uplift: E. Azalia Hackley and African American Activism in the Postbellum to Pre-Harlem Era*, published by University Press of Mississippi. Now an independent scholar, she lives in a log cabin in the Vermont mountains with her husband and three adopted greyhounds.

www.ingramcontent.com/pod-product-compliance
Lightning Source LLC
Chambersburg PA
CBHW030610230426
43661CB00053B/1924